To Jean & Bill, good neighbors and friends

OUT OF
VIENNA

Ellie [signature]
11/26/2008

OUT OF
VIENNA

Eight Years of Flight
from the Nazis

By
Ernie Weiss

Library of Congress Control Number: 2007910239
ISBN: Hardcover   978-1-4363-1258-5
                 Softcover   978-1-4363-1257-8

This book was printed in the United States of America.

To order additional copies of this book, contact:
Xlibris Corporation
1-888-795-4274
www.Xlibris.com
Orders@Xlibris.com
45252

Acknowledgements

Many people have my gratitude for their help during the five years it took to research and write this book.

From the United States, they include the following: Ellen Bonnifield, Yampa, Colorado; Ann Bromberg and Dick Potter, Brookline, Massachusetts; Roger Craver, Chilmark, Massachusetts; Judith Herman, Brookline, Massachusetts; Captain Dennis Jason, Chilmark, Massachusetts; Polly McDowell, Vineyard Haven, Massachusetts; Hal and Ann Noyes, Steamboat Springs, Colorado; Nelson Potter, Chilmark, Massachusetts; the late Alex Redmountain (Saša Rosenberger), Scaly Mountain, North Carolina; Berl Schiff, Toronto, Canada; Clem Schoenebeck, Swampscott, Massachusetts; Lesley Schuldt, Steamboat Springs, Colorado; Louis "Slavko" Singer, Rochester, New York; and Frank Yeomans, Chilmark, Massachusetts.

Special thanks go to Deborah Edinburg of Marblehead, Massachusetts.

From Europe they are as follows: Bob Brüwer, Munich; Jeffrey Jerome, London; Maria-Grazia and Antonio Spinelli, Padova, Italy; Berenika Sterba and Vladimir Sterba, Vienna; and Jean Vizern, St. Maixent L'Ecole, France.

I also thank both the Howes House Writer's Group of West Tisbury, Massachusetts, and the Steamboat Springs Writer's Group of Steamboat Springs, Colorado.

Sources for this book include video interviews of my mother, Hedy Weiss, and my cousin, Hans Hacker, done by the Steven Spielberg Survivors of the Shoah Foundation; my cousin Jill Jerome's audio interview of her father, Gus Jellinek Jerome; my interviews with Heli Lampl Krouska and Alisa Amidror in Prague and Vienna, respectively.

Finally, I thank my wife, Leslie, a former newspaper editor, who read and reread the manuscript, and helped me finish the book so readers could understand what I wrote in the first place.

Can the Holocaust create values? Those who are unable to face their past are condemned to eternally repeat it—we know this saying of Santayana. The Holocaust is a value because it has led to immeasurable knowledge through immeasurable suffering, thus creating an immeasurable moral resource.

—Imre Kertész, *The Holocaust as Culture* (the periodical of the Federation to Maintain Jewish Culture in Hungary)

HITLER, ADOLF

Führer und Reichskanzler, leader and chancellor
of the German Empire (1889-1945)

Born in Austria, he settled in Germany in 1913. At the outbreak of World War I, Hitler enlisted in the German Army. He became a corporal and received the Iron Cross for bravery. Settling in Munich after the war, he joined the newly formed German Workers Party, soon reorganized it, and renamed it the National Socialist German Workers Party. In 1923, he unsuccessfully attempted to forcibly bring Germany under his nationalistic control. When his coup, known as the famous Beer-Hall Putsch, failed, Hitler was arrested and sentenced to five years in prison. It was at this time that he wrote *Mein Kampf* (My Battle). Serving only nine months of his sentence, Hitler reentered German politics and outpolled his political rivals in the national elections. In January 1933, German president Hindenburg appointed Hitler chancellor and head of a coalition cabinet. In 1934, the chancellorship and presidency were united in the person of the Führer, Adolf Hitler. He immediately set up a dictatorship. All other parties were outlawed, and opposition was brutally suppressed. By 1938, Hitler implemented his dream of a Greater Germany.

Preface

VIENNA: MARCH 22, 1938

It was 8:00 a.m., one month following the Anschluss, Austria's annexation to Germany. A few Jewish and mostly Christian boys sat in our second grade class waiting for our teacher, and for the school bell to ring.

The classroom door opened. The teacher, a tall woman carrying a leather briefcase in her left hand, entered the room and walked to the front of her desk. She faced us, quickly extended her right arm at a forty five degree angle and shouted, "Heil Hitler." It was the Hitler salute adopted by the Nazi Party as a sign of loyalty to its leader, Adolf Hitler.

We sprang to attention. We raised our right arms, imitating our teacher. We also shouted, "Heil Hitler." Then the school bell rang. Following the March 13 Anschluss, this is how we started each school day. As a Jew, did I know this was wrong? Are seven-year-old children aware of the politics that surround them?

I am the son of a Dachau Concentration Camp survivor.

My father died in 1984 and my mother in 1990. I never spoke with them about my school days in Vienna or his time in Dachau. Why didn't I ask? Was it because I wanted to forget the years we spent fleeing the Nazis?

It was after my mother's death that I became interested in my father's incarceration and our eight years of hectic flight through six countries. When we cleaned out her house, I took four large boxes of photographs taken by my father, an enthusiastic photographer. His collection spanned six decades and included family poses in our garden in Vienna, and action shots of us playing tennis and skiing. There were pictures of us climbing the Austrian Alps; spending time at beaches on Italy's Adriatic Coast; and vacationing in Venice, Milan, and Paris. My father developed, edited, cropped, and printed his photos in his own darkroom. When I was a baby, he bought a movie camera.

There were also photos of us during our long getaway through Yugoslavia, Italy, France, Spain, Portugal, and Cuba.

It took several years to organize my father's pictures. I created a scrapbook and then had the photos and silent movies put on DVDs. I have a movie of myself in a sandbox in 1932.

Then, starting in 2000, other things made me curious about our years of escape and the fate of other family members.

First my cousin, Jeffrey Jellinek Jerome of London, gave me a typewritten, single-spaced, twelve-page document. It had been written in German by my mother's aunt, Anna Weininger. It described in detail her life between 1938 and 1945. It was later translated into English by Jeffrey's father, my uncle Gus, one of my mother's two brothers. Tante (the German word for aunt) Anna was a Yugoslav partisan, a freedom fighter. She wrote her story after the war while living in a retirement home for war veterans in Zagreb.

In 2002, Mirta Ojito, a Cuban born reporter for the *New York Times*, wrote a compelling story about her experience in 1980. At age sixteen, she was one of one hundred twenty five thousand Cubans who fled Fidel Castro's communist regime to come to the United States. Mirta Ojito's story made me think about our five years in Cuba and how the Cubans saved our lives by letting us into their country when the United States would not.

Also in 2002, Mike Ditchfield, an acquaintance from Edgartown, Massachusetts, called and asked me if I knew his friend Alex Redmountain, who had just published a book of poems: *From Holocaust to Hiroshima, a Life Forged by War*. When I said I didn't know him, Mike told me Ernie Weiss was mentioned in one of the poems. He said Alex's name used to be Saša Rosenberger.

I searched through my scrapbook that day and found a photograph of my brother Peter, my friend Slavko Singer, Saša, and me. The picture was taken at La Concha Beach in Havana in 1944 or 1945. Looking at it took me back to my teenage years when I was learning Spanish, my third language.

I called Saša in North Carolina and in less than two weeks, via the Internet, found Slavko in Rochester, New York.

We hadn't spoken for fifty years, but the three of us met for dinner in New York City a few weeks later. It was an emotional reunion.

The third event that encouraged me to write my family's story happened in June of 2002 when my nine-year-old grandson, Matty Weiss, called to tell me he had participated in a Hebrew school class about immigration in the United States. Students played the roles of immigrants who arrived at Ellis Island, New York, the entry port for immigrants into the United States. The scene was an immigration office where U.S. officials, played by teachers,

Slavko, Ernie (in back), Peter and Saša at La Concha beach, Havana.

interviewed new arrivals from Europe, all refugees from Nazi persecution. The students played the refugees.

"My name is Ernest Weiss," Matty said when an immigration official asked for his name. For half an hour, my grandson pretended he was me.

That's when I decided to write this book.

Matty and his brother Alex and my grandchildren Danielle and Dylan, and my step-grandchildren Elizabeth and Robert, and my nieces and their children, and all my cousins' children, and all my relatives born after 1945, and anyone else who is interested should know what happened to twenty eight members of my family between 1938 and 1945.

This story is non-fiction. The dialogue and the physical descriptions of places and events are based on personal interviews, research and my recollections.

Introduction

A decade after immigrating to the United States, seven couples got into their cars and began their drive to Marblehead, Massachusetts, a seacoast town north of Boston. It was the middle of the afternoon, a Saturday. They came from several Boston middle-income suburbs. Their cars were modest, traditional, four-door sedans: the typical Dodge, Chevrolet, and Ford.

They were all European-born Jews. All were refugees from Nazi persecution. They were headed to a house overlooking the ocean, built around 1900 as a summer residence. There were five houses on the street in a seventy-five-yard area. Some were built on ledges at the edge of the sea. Others, including number 42, were across the street. The houses were not winterized.

The house at 42 Clifton Heights Lane was three stories high with a finished attic and a basement. It had four bedrooms, large living and dining rooms, and a large kitchen with a breakfast nook. In 1953, a family bought it as a summer residence. A year later, they winterized it and made it their permanent home. They moved there from the Boston suburb of Brookline.

They chose their new house because of its looks, its location and its spacious floor plan. It was typical summerhouse architecture, the "American Summer House," with projecting peaked gables, matching shed dormers, and second floor oriel bay windows. It had a wrap-around porch with lattice railings, canvas awnings and a wonderful color scheme. The outside walls were of traditional white cedar shingles. The new owners were not aware of its historical nature. Their attraction was based on the simple fact that it was beautiful. It was an American dream. It was the first house they purchased in America. It would become their home.

A thirty-foot flagpole, in the center of a flower and rock garden, flew the American flag daily, weather permitting. But it was the view from the third-floor attic window that made this house so special. The window was thirty feet above the ground, which was twenty feet above sea level. Thus, the window was fifty feet above the sea. At that height, one could see fifteen miles or more to the horizon. A house on the other side of the street stood between the home and the water, but the line of sight was over the roof of that house. The view on any day, sunny or cloudy, rainy or snowy, was simply breathtaking. No two days were ever the same. One could see lobster and fishing boats and all types of pleasure craft. There were freighters and tankers in the distance, heading for, or leaving, Boston Harbor. Sailboats racing out of Marblehead Harbor were fascinating to watch. When guests came, they were told to climb to the third floor to look at the view from the window. The attic was originally a storage area but in later years was converted into a bedroom. With a good set of binoculars, and a really good imagination, one could see Europe.

Hedy and Robert Weiss were the owners of the house.

Cars were arriving.

My parents and their friends had been getting together like this for several years. Food, coffee, drinks, and sheet music for the two baby grand Steinways had been prepared. The atmosphere was Viennese, and Viennese specialties were on the menu. The party was about to begin.

The guests walked in without knocking. This house was like home to them. Some brought their favorite home-baked goods. The night was to be filled with music and good times.

My parents and their friends arrived in the United States between 1938 and 1946. Most were born in Germany or Austria, some came from Hungary, and a few were American-born. All were Jewish. All the Austrians were Viennese. All spoke English although they had not given up their culture or language of birth. They were all United States citizens.

Fritz Kramer, a professional musician, was the guest of honor. He was born in Vienna and currently lived in New York City. Fritz was an accompanist to singers and a music arranger for concerts and musicals.

"Will someone please arrange the chairs in front of the pianos? Fritz and I will start the evening with many surprises," my mother announced. "We will start after we finish the goulash."

"Robert," my mother called to my father, "Robert, where are you?" There was no answer.

"Could someone please find Robert? He has to taste the chocolate cream for the cake."

"I haven't seen him since we arrived," someone said, stepping outside the house. "Robert, where are you?"

"Here I am. What you do want?" answered my father.

"Hedy wants you right away."

"Tell her I'm helping to park cars. I'll be right there."

My father came into the kitchen. He tasted the cream for my mother's Pischingertorte, a cake made with eight layers of very thin wafers. It was eight inches in diameter with milk chocolate cream between each layer and on top. He approved the cream.

The living room was now full of people. The women wore dresses, and the men wore coats and ties. The atmosphere was lively and filled with conversation. The chairs were arranged so everyone could sit comfortably while eating my mother's goulash. One by one the guests entered the kitchen, filled their bowls, found a chair, and began to eat and talk. The Szekeli goulash was very Hungarian with lots of paprika in the sauce. The German rye bread from Karl's Kitchen in Saugus was superb. It was a gourmet meal served on paper plates with plastic spoons. What could be better, they all thought.

The pianists, Fritz Kramer and my mother, approached the pianos. They sat at their pianos, facing each other. The baby grands were back-to-back. My father made sure everyone was comfortable. Then he turned to my mother and said,

"Hedy, do you think we can go through this night without any patzers (Viennese for a small mistake)?" Everyone laughed except my mother. Someone quickly came to her defense.

"Sit down, Robert. You're just jealous because you can't play the piano." Again, everyone laughed. They all knew of my father's love for music, which was possibly as great as my mother's. Throughout their lives together, they had shared the same feelings for classical music and opera. It was not unusual for my father to attend a Mahler symphony or Verdi opera in Vienna or Boston or Havana and at the end of a performance jump to his feet and yell "bravo, bravo," louder than anyone in the concert hall. My father also loved hosting these musical evenings in his home.

"Sit down, Mutsch (pronounced Mootch)," my mother said, using an endearing term my parents called one another at certain times, "and try not to talk too much."

Parties like these were created so that everyone had a good time. My mother, a learned musician, along with some of her piano playing friends and, on some occasions, singers and violinists were reason enough to get together as much as possible. Eight hands or four hands or two hands played the two baby grands often. These concerts were eagerly anticipated as a wonderful evening of entertainment. My mother, besides being able to improvise on the keyboard, was also able to hide a patzer on the keyboard and most listeners never knew it.

The performance was about to begin. My mother played a few chords to signal the start of the festivities. Fritz Kramer, in Marblehead just for this event, replied with his set of chords in tune with my mother's. It might have been the first few notes of Beethoven's Fifth Symphony. All took their seats. Without a word, without announcing what they were about to play, they began. The programs varied and often included Schubert and Mozart piano sonatas or Hungarian dances by Brahms. Wienerlieder (Vienna songs) were a must as were Johann Strauss's waltzes, and then there were the occasional George Gershwin or Rogers and Hammerstein tunes, American favorites.

My parents' friends always enjoyed every minute of the performances. Applause followed every piece with shouts of "Bravo, bravo." Pianists who play four- or eight-handed piano not only love to perform in front of an audience, they love to listen and enjoy the music they are creating.

The concert ended. The guests stood to applaud.

"Bravo, bravo, more, more." The guests applauded in unison, asking for an encore which, of course, they got.

It was almost 9:00 p.m., time for dessert and coffee. The chairs were removed. The guests stood at the dining room table and again served themselves. They entered the living room and finished the evening with Viennese pastries.

These refugees arrived in the United States in a variety of ways. One couple came by way of England, another through Belgium, and another from Berlin via China. Some came directly from Vienna. My family came through Cuba.

Chapter 1

VIENNA: SEPTEMBER 1936

Sabbath services for us at the Turnergasse Temple at Turnergasse 22 were a weekly event. The synagogue, founded in 1872, was a huge building in Italian Renaissance style. It was as large as five apartment buildings. It had a bell tower that could be seen from far away. The synagogue had been built by the Jewish community of Vienna.

Following services, a family luncheon was planned at our home. Three cars were on their way to Hietzing, one of Vienna's more glamorous suburbs.

My father, Robert Weiss, drove my mother, Hedwig (called Hedi), and me, along with my maternal grandparents, Jakob and Emma Jellinek.

Uncle Otto, my father's brother, drove his wife, Frieda; their daughter, my cousin Edith, age twelve; and my paternal grandparents, Marcus and Hermina Weiss.

Uncle Heinrich Hacker, my father's brother-in-law, drove Grete, my father's sister, and my cousins Hansi and Gerti, who were fifteen and ten. I was five years old at the time.

The three cars leaving the synagogue did not follow one another. They left, driving their own favorite routes.

When Uncle Otto was nearing the Mariahilferstrasse, Vienna's most famous shopping street, traffic suddenly came to a halt. There were ten or more cars in front of him. Hundreds of people were marching down the Mariahilferstrasse. The marchers held signs reading Juden Hinaus (Jews Get Out) and Saujude (Sow Jew). There were signs protesting politicians. Other signs read National Sozialismus Über Alles (National Socialism over Everything).

"Look at those signs," said Uncle Otto.

"This is a terrible disgrace," said Grandfather Marcus. (His grandchildren called him Grosspapá.) "Why aren't the police doing something about this?"

As soon as the marchers passed, the traffic started to move. The three cars of family members arrived at our house about the same time.

"Did you see the parade of Nazis?" asked Uncle Otto as they all walked into our apartment.

"No," said my father, "we didn't see anything."

"What happened?" asked Grandfather Jakob. (I called him Grossvater.)

Uncle Otto described the parade and the signs he'd just seen. No one was surprised. Incidents like these had occurred in Vienna before.

My family lived on the first floor of a grand three-story home. We had three bedrooms, a formal dining room, and a living room with a grand piano. The kitchen was big and equipped for serious Viennese cooking. There was a large foyer inside the front door. Facing the main entrance of the house, to the left, was a wrought iron fence that surrounded a garden. You could get inside the garden from the sidewalk through a gate next to the house, and from a hallway next to the kitchen. The garden had beautiful flower beds and apple trees and my sandbox. On the other side of the main entrance was a three-car underground garage. Our apartment also had sleeping rooms for Gretchen, our nanny and cook, and Katerina, our maid. The building belonged to my father's second cousin, Erich Zollschan. People unrelated to us lived on the second and third floors.

My mother greeted everyone at the door. She led our guests through the foyer and living room to the dining room, where the adults sat down at a large mahogany table. Katerina had taken their coats and hung them in a closet. We were all dressed in our best clothes for the Sabbath.

There were four chairs on each side of the table and one at each end. My mother's best linen, china, silverware, and crystal had been set out by Katerina. My father sat at one end and Grosspapá at the other. Wine was served. Two challahs, covered with a linen napkin, were in the center of the table on a silver platter. A challah is braided egg bread with a shiny crust. It is sweet and delicious.

Cousins Edith, Hansi, Gerti, and I, each stood behind our parents waiting for the Hamoitzi, the blessing of the bread. It is a Jewish tradition to start a meal, especially on the Sabbath and holidays, with the breaking of bread.

Following tradition, my father broke off a large piece of the challah. He tore small bites from his piece of bread and passed one to each of us. We held our pieces and waited for my father's next move. He raised his challah in his left hand and said, "Borukh atoh Adonoi Elohaynu melekh ha-olom ha-motzi lechem min ho-oretz. Omein (Blessed are You, Lord our God, King of the Universe, who brings forth bread from the earth. Amen)."

My father took a bite of his challah, and we ate ours. Edith, Gerti, Hansi, and I then went into the next room, a study that had been converted into our personal dining room.

The meal started with a simple beef consommé. It was followed by Tafelspitz (boiled beef), grated fried potatoes, and apple and horseradish sauce. Historians say Emperor Franz Josef of Austria ate this dish every day. Dessert was a Sacher torte.

My cousins and I ate heartily at our table, enjoying every bite, and each other's company. Twelve-year-old Edith took charge. Edith had curly blond hair and blue eyes. She was sincere and sweet, and her easy manner attracted the rest of us. We admired her. Hansi, the oldest, was nice to his younger sister and cousins and treated me like a play doll. Edith and Hansi led the conversation, mindful that a ten and a five-year-old were listening. It was all very simple. We were cousins, we were family.

After dinner, the five men went into the living room. The women remained in the dining room, talking.

Uncle Otto and Grossvater Jakob lit cigarettes, Uncle Heinrich a cigar. They got into a lively discussion about the Hakoah soccer club's upcoming match with Vienna's Rapid soccer club. Sport Club Hakoah Wien, founded in 1909, was the Viennese Jewish sports club that produced winning soccer teams year after year. Sportklub Rapid Wien was one of the best teams in European soccer. They talked a little about the weather and the arts, and they gossiped about their many relatives and friends in Vienna.

It didn't take long for the conversation to turn to politics. Adolf Hitler's takeover of Germany was reported daily in the Vienna press.

The discussion now centered on how Hitler had ascended to power in just three years and how few Austrians were paying attention. The Germans had been falling for the Nazi lies and propaganda since 1933. The fanatical speeches, the show of force by the Nazi political organization, and antisemitic acts like the one witnessed by Uncle Otto on this day were being ignored by the majority of nonpolitical Austrians.

Could what was happening in Germany, the creation of a Nazi government, be repeated in Austria? The Austrian economy was in a recession. Unemployment was a problem. Optimism, however, was still present.

"Hitler's ascent to power," said Grossvater "is the work of a small group of fanatics he recruited in Germany. For Hitler to remain in power for a long period of time is something the German people will not stand for. But on the other hand, I hear from my political sources that the Nazis in Vienna are holding secret meetings, and their numbers are increasing."

"Remember what happened just a few years ago," said Uncle Heinrich. "Engelbert Dolfuss, our late chancellor, attacked Social Democrats, killing hundreds of men, women, and children who were living in our city's housing complexes. His creation of the Wöllersdorf Concentration Camp proves he was a fascist, the ideology that considers the individual subordinate to state. He kept Austria from being a democracy. When he didn't like someone . . . Communists, Nazis, political opponents, or whoever . . . off they went to Wöllersdorf. It's a good thing he was killed. Now, Hitler's followers are encouraging Viennese hoodlums to organize in underground Nazi cells. And Schuschnigg, he hasn't been our chancellor for very long so he isn't able to help the situation much."

My father changed the subject. He wanted to talk about the shoe factory he owned with his father.

Uncle Heinrich was the production manager of the factory. Uncle Otto was the sales manager. Uncle Richard, my father's second brother, was the treasurer, and my mother's brother Gustl was the company's traveling salesman for all of Europe. My father wanted to know how production was.

"It's good, Robert," said Uncle Heinrich.

Grossvater, who owned two butcher shops, said, "The food business is also good, even with the slow economy."

Uncle Heinrich ignored the business talk and returned to politics.

"What really scares me is that Hitler is arresting people without cause. The Gestapo now has the power to place anyone into protective custody without a reason. The Nazis are passing laws no civilized nation would pass. Hitler is making illegality legal, and increased pogroms in Poland and Russia are being reported almost daily in the newspapers."

"What about the Nuremberg Laws Hitler passed depriving German Jews of their citizenship?" asked Uncle Otto. "This year, for the first time, German Jews are not allowed to vote."

My father responded with optimism. "Kurt Schuschnigg has been our chancellor for only a short time. He is doing his best to keep Hitler out of Austria. As long as his administration stays in power, Austria will be stable. Small incidents against Jews will continue, and radical groups will always be around. Antisemitism has been around for a thousand years."

"I heard that signs reading Juden Hinaus are appearing in German cities. What do you think?" asked Grosspapá. "Are the Viennese going to imitate the Germans? Have any of you heard of Dachau? The Germans are sending their opponents to this labor camp near Munich."

The discussion soon ended. The gathering was over. The men left the room, feeling confident their lives and businesses in Vienna would continue as in the past. Family gatherings, musical events, tennis, skiing, and leisure activities would not change. They walked into the dining room and called to the rest of us to go for a walk around the neighborhood. Strolling was a Viennese custom. It was a cool fall day, so the women put on their coats with fur collars, and the men wore their hats. The women walked arm in arm, and the men did too. The afternoon ended, and our guests went home.

My mother.

My father.

Number 52 Reichgasse, Hietzing; we occupied the first floor.

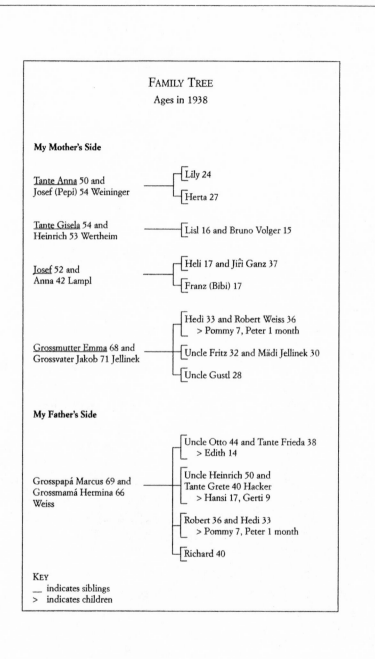

FAMILY TREE
Ages in 1938

My Mother's Side

Tante Anna 50 and
Josef (Pepi) 54 Weininger
— Lily 24
— Herta 27

Tante Gisela 54 and
Heinrich 53 Wertheim
— Lisl 16 and Bruno Volger 15

Josef 52 and
Anna 42 Lampl
— Heli 17 and Jiří Ganz 37
— Franz (Bibi) 17

Grossmutter Emma 68 and
Grossvater Jakob 71 Jellinek
— Hedi 33 and Robert Weiss 36
  > Pommy 7, Peter 1 month
— Uncle Fritz 32 and Mädi Jellinek 30
— Uncle Gustl 28

My Father's Side

Grosspapá Marcus 69 and
Grossmamá Hermina 66
Weiss
— Uncle Otto 44 and Tante Frieda 38
  > Edith 14
— Uncle Heinrich 50 and
  Tante Grete 40 Hacker
  > Hansi 17, Gerti 9
— Robert 36 and Hedi 33
  > Pommy 7, Peter 1 month
— Richard 40

KEY
__ indicates siblings
> indicates children

My family tree: included are only family members in this book.
There are many others I never got to know.

Chapter 2

SARAJEVO: JUNE 22, 1914

Twenty two years before our family luncheon in 1936, Archduke Franz Ferdinand, inspector of the Austro-Hungarian Army, and his wife, Sophie von Chotkovato, went to Sarajevo to watch his troops perform maneuvers. When Serbia's government announced the impending archduke's visit, a Serb rebel group known as the Black Hand made plans to assassinate him.

They did. And they were soon captured.

The next day, June 23, the Austro-Hungarian foreign minister, Leopold Anton Johann Sigismund Joseph Korsinus Ferdinand, better known as Count Von Berchtold, asked the minister of Serbia to hand over the captured assassins. The Serbian minister replied that to do so would be a violation of Serbia's constitution. The assassins were not handed over. An official Serbian apology for the assassination was unacceptable to the Austro-Hungarian Foreign Ministry, and five days later, the Austro-Hungarian imperial family declared war on Serbia. The war, World War One, eventually involved all the major nations of Europe as well as the United States. It ended in 1918 with the Austro-Hungarian Empire splitting into several independent nations, one of which was Austria. More than eight million military and civilians died during those four years. It was to be the war to end all wars.

Wien (German for Vienna) was the capital of the Austro-Hungarian Empire and the home of Kaiser Franz Josef of the Habsburgs. When the war ended, Vienna became the capital of Austria, whose history can be traced to 1278.

The city was and is famous for the Habsburg's palaces, museums and parks, exquisite literature, and opera and symphonic music. Viennese food, waltzes, and wine, women, and song, made this historic capital city different from the rest of Europe. Its Jews also made Vienna stand out. They were leaders in medicine, law, business, politics, and journalism. They were in the worlds of cabaret and coffeehouses. Among the gifted and well-known Jews who lived and studied in Vienna were Sigmund Freud, Franz Werfel, Gustav Mahler, Arthur Schnitzler, Franz Kafka, Martin Buber, Stefan Zweig, and Leon Trotsky. Vienna also was at times host to non-Jews such as Joseph Stalin, Vladimir Lenin, and Adolf Hitler.

During the late 1930s, the large percentage of successful Jews in their professions and businesses created envy and antisemitism among Austrians. Propaganda against Jews began appearing in newspaper articles, in parks, and on street corners. Restrictions were created in club memberships, and street demonstrations became common. Fifty-two percent of the Viennese dentists and doctors were Jewish. Twenty four percent of university professors were Jewish. Thirty five percent of shoe manufacturers, my father among them, were Jewish. In the advertising field, ninety-percent were Jews.

Also a product of the Viennese culture was Theodore Herzl, the founder of modern Zionism. He lived in Vienna until his death in 1904. Hungarian-born, he was a lawyer and journalist. While discovering closeted antisemitism in Vienna's professional associations, he also became aware of pogroms in Eastern Europe. He then began a movement to create a Jewish state in the British Mandate of Palestine.

My family lived no differently from non-Jews. We were assimilated Jews in Viennese society. Antisemitism did not affect our lives. We were Viennese and spoke Wienerisch, German with a Viennese accent.

A popular song depicting Vienna, as we knew it, could have been the city's anthem: Wien, Wien, nur du allein (Vienna, Vienna, only you alone).

> Vienna, Vienna, only you alone
> Should always be the city of my dreams!
> Where the old houses stand,
> Where the lovely girls walk!
> Vienna, Vienna, only you alone
> Should always be the city of my dreams!
> Here, where I am lucky and blessed
> It's Vienna. It's Vienna, my Vienna.

At the beginning of the 20th century, the Viennese Kaffeehaus (coffeehouse) became the center of intellectual life. Artists, writers, and politicians gathered in any one of dozens of cafés. They debated ideas and lingered over a newspaper and a kleiner schwarzer (small cups of black coffee).

The cafés in Vienna were frequented by many celebrities and world-renowned personalities, including Stalin, Hitler, Trotsky, and Freud. These men, and others, read, wrote, and held meaningful conversations in the coffeehouses. The buildings that housed the cafés are as distinguished as those who used them for meeting places. They have existed for more than one hundred years and can be found today on any tourist map.

My mother, born in Vienna in 1905, studied at the Vienna Conservatory of Music and became an accomplished pianist. Her youth revolved around her love of music. As a teenager she spent hours in lines, waiting for standing room tickets to her beloved musical performances. Then she stood for more hours through a Verdi or Wagner opera. Music was the passion of her life. She was able to identify most symphonies and operas by composer and title.

My father was born in Vienna in 1902. He studied at a vocational school and became a shoemaker and a prosperous businessman. Grosspapá and my father founded the Eldorado Schuhfabrik (Eldorado Shoe Manufacturing Company) makers of fashionable high-heeled shoes for women, and work shoes for men. Their factory was located in Vienna's Twelfth District, at Schönbrunnerstrasse 179. My father was the general manager, and Grosspapá was the elder statesman, the CEO. The company's letterhead read R and M Weiss for Robert and Marcus Weiss. The company employed more than two hundred twenty five workers.

My father first saw my mother in the summer of 1927 at a tennis club that boasted twelve red clay courts, a clubhouse, and an outdoor café. He had finished playing and was drinking beer with his doubles partners. Four women were playing a high-level tennis game. One stood out. She had dark wavy hair and was wearing a long white tennis skirt. Her nasty backhand slice caught my father's eye.

My parents on a motorcycle, with biwagon.

My mother in tennis dress.

What interested him most were her legs. He was well known among his friends as a "leg man." Without shapely legs and ankles, a woman never got a second look from him. My mother's were exceptional, he thought. When she finished her game, he invited her to a concert at the Vienna Philharmonic. Their first date was three days later. During their courtship, they played many hours of tennis at the club. My father was a lefty. He had a brutal reverse spin and played in the style of Bill Tilden, the world famous American who had once played an exhibition match at their club.

They married in 1928. A condition of their marriage was that my mother had to learn to drive a car. She did (and a motorcycle) and was one of the first women in Austria to get a driver's license. She liked to think she was the very first. It is possible.

Extended summer vacations were spent in Velden on the Wörthersee, a lake resort in the Austrian province of Kärnten. Vacations usually lasted three to four weeks. My father climbed the Alps, and both of my parents skied in the Alps. They traveled to Paris, Venice, Rome, and various resorts on the Adriatic. My mother once had an audience with the pope. She boasted about being a Jew who had met the pope. My parents had an active and wonderful life.

HIETZING: JANUARY 15, 1938

I called out, but no one answered. I called again, and again. Finally, Katerina came into my room and told me it was time for breakfast. I knew something was different. It was always my mother who came to me first in the morning. Besides, it was Saturday and my father was always home on Saturday. "Where is Mutti (mommy)?"

"Mutti will be back in a few days," said Katerina. "She has a present for you. Mutti will bring home the new baby."

"Where is Papa?" I asked.

"Papa went to visit Mutti and the new baby in the hospital."

I had been told there would be a new baby, but at six-and-a-half I didn't know when or how it would happen.

The next morning, I woke up with my father standing over me.

"Come, Pommy," he said, calling me by my nickname. "We are going to visit Mutti. You are going to meet your new brother."

An hour later, I saw Peter for the first time through a large window. I remember him laying in a crib in a big white room along side other babies.

He was born breach and had a big bump on the side of his head. A nurse came and picked him up, and my father took my hand and led me to where the nurse and Peter came through a doorway. We followed them down the hospital corridor to a room where my mother was lying in bed.

My father gave my mother a kiss, and she hugged and kissed me. We stayed for about thirty minutes and went home, leaving my mother and Peter alone in their room.

Peter and my mother stayed in the hospital for a week. When they came home a new nanny came to live with us, to take care of my brother.

The next day, a celebration was held for Peter's bris. This ceremony, a circumcision, identifies a boy as a member of the Jewish faith. It is held when the child is eight days old. The bris was in our home. My grandparents came for the event, as did the rest of the family, along with many friends who lived in the area. Uncle Otto, Peter's godfather, held him while the Mohel (circumciser) performed the ritual. Turnergasse Temple's rabbi and cantor honored us with a visit. A kosher meal, prepared by one of Grossvater's friends in the food business, was served. Adults drank wine, the children raspberry soda. Katerina served, and our nanny took care of Peter after his ordeal.

Ski vacations that winter were postponed because of Peter's arrival, but there was a possibility we would ski in the Alps in March. It depended on how my mother was feeling, how the nanny was performing, and how my brother was coming along. I remember wondering when Peter's bump would go away.

VIENNA: FEBRUARY 27, 1938

Austrian chancellor Schuschnigg was struggling to maintain good relations with Germany. His visits with Adolf Hitler kept Jews hoping that Germany would not invade Austria, but the Austrian Nazi party was gradually becoming openly active and gaining in popularity. Jews were beginning to realize that Germany's Nazi machine in Austria was now in full swing. Hitler's power in Germany was unquestionable. His desire to annex all lands containing German-speaking people was official. Chancellor Schuschnigg, in a last effort after several meetings with Hitler, announced he would hold a national confidence vote, plebiscite, on the independence of Austria. Hitler did not approve of this and threatened Schuschnigg with an armed invasion of Austria.

ZNOJMO: CZECHOSLOVAKIA, 1938

Znojmo, a small city near the Austrian border, was in the Sudetenland, the German-speaking area of Czechoslovakia. Famous for its pickles, Znojmo was the home of the Lampls, my only family members who lived outside

Austria. Czech was their native language. Dr. Josef Lampl was Grossmutter's brother, and my mother's uncle. His wife, Anna, was an active volunteer worker who organized many charity events for both Jewish and Christian children. Uncle Josef was a well-known veterinarian. His clinic was in their home, which was large enough for the Lampls and the animals he cared for to live together. Uncle Josef was an active member of Znojmo's B'nai B'rith, the worldwide Jewish philanthropic society. He had served as an officer in the Austro-Hungarian Army in World War I.

Their daughter, Heli, was born in 1921. As a teenager, she attended the English College in Prague and then enrolled in a German business school. She became fluent in English and German. Heli's brother, Frantisek, nicknamed Bibi, was a year younger. They were good friends, loved playing tennis together, and often travelled to Vienna to visit relatives. Heli especially loved my grandmother Emma.

VIENNA: MARCH 9, 1938

Arthur Seyss-Inquart, a member of both the Austrian Parliament and the new Austrian Nazi party, initiated parliamentary proceedings to replace Chancellor Schuschnigg with himself. Seyss-Inquart then formed a new government. The Nazis had taken legal power in Austria.

LINZ: MARCH 12, 1938

Troops of the German Wehrmacht (army) and the SS (Schutzstaffel-Protective Squadron), the black-shirted storm troopers who carried out Hitler's persecution of Jews and political opponents, crossed the Austrian border. There was no resistance. Not a shot was fired. The people in the town of Linz welcomed the Germans with a parade, and the soldiers were showered with flowers.

BERLIN: MARCH 13, 1938

Adolf Hitler announced the Anschluss (annexation of Austria). Austria was now part of the Third Reich. The border between Germany and Austria was eliminated. Austria became Ostmark with the Reichmark replacing the schilling as its currency. Austrian Nazis, thousands of them, appeared out of nowhere and terrorized Jews in their homes and businesses and on the streets. Hundreds of Nazi opponents were arrested. Laws were passed restricting

Jewish economic activity, and properties were taken from Jews. Antisemitism was rampant in Vienna.

VIENNA: MARCH 16, 1938

The skies were filled with German fighter planes dropping leaflets that said Deutsch Österreich Endlich Frei (German Austria Free at Last).

VIENNA: MARCH 22, 1938

Hitler's motorcade through Vienna was greeted by thousands of onlookers. He was on his way to the Heldenplatz (Heroes' Square) in the center of the city at the base of the Hofburg, the old Habsburg Imperial Palace. There, half a million people shouted "Sieg Heil, Sieg Heil, Sieg Heil (hail victory)" in tribute to Hitler. He was about to appear high on a balcony to address the admiring and hysterical mob.

Our nanny was at the rally. After Hitler's speech, she came home and packed her clothes. My mother asked her where she was going.

"I cannot say," she answered. We never saw her again.

VIENNA: SEVERAL DAYS AFTER THE ANSCHLUSS

Though the Nazis were constantly searching for Jews, my mother's cousin Lisl Wertheim, sixteen, and her boyfriend Bruno Vogler, who was fifteen, went on long walks together, being careful so they would not be accosted. Lisl lived with her parents, Heinrich and Gisela. With money their parents gave them for tram rides, the young couple instead bought sweets for themselves. As they walked, they stopped at grocery stores to buy small portions of butter to take home. Food was being rationed. Lisl and Bruno couldn't go to a movie or go dancing. But they were happy just being together, finding hideaways for their favorite pastime, kissing.

One day while walking, a patrol of soldiers appeared out of nowhere. They took Lisl and Bruno into custody and forced them onto a truck with other Jews. They were driven to the Stadt Tempel (City Synagogue). After unloading the group, an SS guard stood in front of them and yelled.

"Achtung (attention), line up in front of the main door, single file! Once you are inside this place you will start cleaning the floor, the benches, the walls and everything else."

The Jews went single file into the synagogue. Bruno and Lisl held hands. They were terrified. No one had ever forced them to do anything against their will. Lisl felt Bruno's hand tighten.

"Lisl," whispered Bruno, "look over there." He pointed to the far corner of the synagogue. "When I start pulling, we are going to run through that door. Do you see it?"

"Yes," said Lisl.

Seconds later, Bruno, holding Lisl's hand tightly, ran to the door. Bruno opened the door, and Lisl recognized the Seitenstettengasse. She knew the area, as did Bruno. They ran for a few minutes until they were away from the synagogue.

"What do we do now?" asked Lisl.

"We have to get home as soon as possible."

They walked to the Graben, a historic square in the old city of Vienna, and from there took their respective trams home.

Lisl and Bruno had another terrifying experience on the street a few days later when a Hitler Jugend (Hitler Youth) about their age, came up behind them and forced them to follow him to a police station.

"I have two Jews for you," the boy said to the policeman in charge. "I caught them after curfew in back of a building not far from here."

The policeman, who had a large mustache and was in his fifties, looked at the three and shook his head.

"All right," he said to the Hitler Youth. "I'll take over from here. Go home now. You did a good job bringing me the Jews."

"Heil Hitler," said the Hitler Youth, raising his right arm. The policeman responded with "Heil Hitler," and the boy left. Lisl and Bruno stood frozen with fear. This was their second encounter with Nazis. The policeman then turned to them and said, "Go home, children, as quickly as possible before somebody else finds you." Bruno and Lisl were surprised. Bruno looked at the policeman and said, "Thank you, sir, and thank you very much," and they quickly left the building.

"Lisl," Bruno said when they were outside. "We have to go home quickly, but do not run. You'll be home in five minutes. When you get there, call me. If I'm not home yet, talk to my mother until I get there. It will take me a little longer."

"Please be careful," said Lisl. She moved close to Bruno. With her left hand, she took his right hand; and with her right hand, she pulled Bruno close to her and kissed him good-bye. They turned and went in separate directions.

ZNOJMO: MARCH 1938

Heli's mother had died of cancer. Soon after, Uncle Josef went to Vienna to bring his mother, Sara Lampl, my great-grandmother, home with him to Znojmo. She had been living alone. Now that Austria was part of Germany, the Lampls were concerned for her safety in Vienna. Hitler had been making speeches about annexing the Sudetenland.

Chapter 3

VIENNA: MARCH 23, 1938

He was perspiring. The knot of his tie was pushed to one side, and the top button of his white shirt was open. Cousin Hansi was running as fast as he could to get home to 24 Dingelsant Gasse, in Vienna's Fifteenth District. He carried his school books in a leather backpack that looked like a briefcase, and it bounced up and down with every running step. As he reached the front door of his apartment house, he rang the doorbell several times. His mother heard the bell ring again and again and rushed to push the buzzer that would open the door lock.

"Mama," said Hansi, running up the stairs and short of breath. "Some boys chased me and called me a dirty Jew. I had a fight with one of them. It was that bully Tierer. But I ran fast and got away. Then I saw signs saying Juden Hinaus in store windows. I saw a bunch of hoodlums in those brown shirts with leather straps across their chests. They were the the SA (Strurmabteilung—Stormdivision, or Brown Shirts). Have you seen them?" he asked his mother as she examined his face for cuts and bruises.

"They smashed Herr Schwartz's store window," Hansi continued. The delicatessen was easily recognized as belonging to a Jew because it had a kosher sign in the window. "They smashed the window into a million pieces and went in and took what they could carry. Herr Schwartz was beaten and left on the floor. I saw him."

"Did anyone help Herr Schwartz?" asked Tante Grete.

"I saw some men go into the store and help Herr Schwartz get up. His face was bleeding, but he was standing when I left. I only stayed for a few minutes."

Jews had begun to leave Austria. The Nazis did not discourage it but made the process difficult. My parents, grandparents, uncles, aunts, and cousins also started to think about leaving, but none made a serious attempt. There was still disbelief about what was happening. It seemed impossible. The Israelitische Kultusgemeinde (IKG) or Jewish Community Vienna was forced to arrange for the departure of Austrian Jews under the auspices of the Nazis.

My parents' first opportunity to leave Vienna came through an offer from an uncle of my father, a banker living in Chicago who was a brother of Grandmother Weiss (her grandchildren called her Grossmamá). After the Anschluss, my father and his cousins wrote to him asking for affidavits to go to America. The uncle wrote back and told his nephews he was willing to give them the affidavits if they guaranteed never to call on him for financial help. My father was too proud to accept this condition, but the rest of the nephews did. They left Vienna in 1938 and went to America.

Though the Nazis were allowing Jews to leave Germany and Austria, most of them had nowhere to go. The United States, England, and France, among other countries, did not issue open visas to refugees from Germany and Austria. Only those with affidavits guaranteeing financial support received entry visas into the United States or England.

VIENNA: APRIL 5, 1938

It was an ordinary Tuesday morning, except that Vienna was inundated with Nazis. The sun was shining, a little snow remained on the side of the streets, and spring was not far away. My father awoke, got dressed, and went into our dining room where Katerina served him bread and coffee. With rationing, his usual breakfast of sausage, eggs, and rolls with butter and jam was no longer possible. When he finished, he said good-bye to my mother. My father left the house, got into his American made 1931 Erskine Studebaker sedan, and drove to his office. I was already at school, having been driven there by Johann, who was taking me there these days because it was safer. Johann worked full-time at my family's shoe factory as a driver. He was not Jewish and had a red-white-and-black swastika flag on the left front fender of his car.

As she watched my father leave for work, my mother thought about her plans for the day. It was her regular Tuesday lunch and bridge day at Marianne Vogl's. After the Anschluss, she and her friends stopped playing bridge and attending musical performances. However, my mother still planned to visit Marianne for coffee. Since Gretchen, the nanny, had left, she planned to take Peter with her.

It was 8:30. My ten-week-old brother had been up at 5:00 for a feeding and had gone back to sleep. My mother heard him gurgle in his crib and went to his room to nurse him.

Five minutes later, the doorbell rang, and my mother called to Katerina to answer the door.

Katerina looked through the security peephole.

"Yes, what do you want?" asked Katerina, looking out at several men dressed in black civilian coats and hats. They wore red armbands with a black swastika on a white background.

"Gestapo!" one of the men shouted. "We are looking for Robert Weiss. Open!"

"He isn't here."

"We're coming in. We are going to see for ourselves. Open the door."

When Katerina removed the security chain, one of the men pushed the door open and entered the house. Two others followed.

My mother overheard the conversation. She stopped nursing Peter, placed him in his crib, and went to the front door, where she was immediately confronted by the three men. Scared, she became pale and dizzy and held on to the doorframe. She recovered quickly, knowing she had to be strong to deal with these men.

"What do you want?" she asked.

"Is Robert Weiss your husband?"

"Yes," she replied.

"Where is he?"

"He left for work."

Two of the men began searching the apartment, room by room. Satisfied that my father was not there, they left, saying nothing to my mother. On the way out, one of the Gestapo turned to Katerina.

"Get out of here and stop working for these Sow Jews, or you'll end up with the rest of them," he said. "Start packing and get out!"

My mother sat down in the living room. Katerina said nothing. My mother telephoned my father. He had not yet arrived at his office.

"Please," said my mother to the receptionist, "have Herr Robert call me right away. It is very important." Then she cancelled her plans for the day.

She went back to Peter to continue nursing. But she couldn't. She made several attempts and realized she had no milk in her breasts. She carried Peter into the kitchen, took some milk out of the icebox, poured some into a baby bottle, placed it in a pot of water, and warmed it on the stove. She then gave Peter his first bottle.

Katerina came into the kitchen carrying a suitcase in each hand. She said an abrupt good-bye and left. My mother sat down in the living room with Peter on her lap. She telephoned my father a second time. He had still not arrived at his office.

By now, SS troops had marked all shops owned by Jews with signs saying Juden Hinaus. Non-Jews were forbidden to purchase anything from Jews, and if they were caught doing so, they were made to parade through the streets wearing a sign that read: "I, Aryan Swine, Have Bought in a Jewish Store."

Jews were being attacked in the streets. In the center of Vienna, Jewish men, women, and children were forced to scrub cobblestone streets on their hands and knees. Crowds mocked them. Jews were taken to the park and forced to eat grass. Thousand of Jewish businesses were seized.

The office staff, all women, greeted my father as they did each morning. He went to his office with Lutsi, his receptionist, following him.

"Frau Weiss called and said you should call her immediately."

Lutsi left, closing the door behind her, just as the front door opened, and three men walked in demanding to see Robert Weiss.

Lutsi knocked on my father's door and went back in.

"Herr Weiss, there are three men here. They want to see you."

"Who are they?" asked my father, who was about to call my mother. "I think they are Nazis," whispered Lutsi.

"Tell them I will be out in . . . ." Before my father could finish his sentence, the men who were at our home half an hour earlier walked into his office.

"Heil Hitler," said one of the men. "Are you Robert Weiss?"

"Yes, I am Robert Weiss," answered my father. He stood up. "What do you want?"

"We are Gestapo. We are taking you in for interrogation. You are a Jew, and all Jews are being questioned. You are now in protective custody."

My father looked at them in astonishment.

"What right do you have to come in here and demand I go with you?"

"We have every right. Come with us now!" The man's voice was stern, belligerent. He went behind my father's desk, grabbed his arm, and pulled him to the center of the room. My father was outraged. Never had anyone spoken to him in that tone of voice. No one had ever put a hand on him. No one had ever forced him to go anywhere. He also knew the Nazis were serious. He was sure they were armed. All Gestapo were armed, he thought. He began worrying about my mother, Peter, and me.

Several of the office workers stood outside the office listening to the confrontation. Some of the women covered their mouths with their hands, in disbelief. It couldn't be possible that these men were arresting Herr Robert.

As the Nazis took my father away, he told Lutsi to call my mother. He never did get to return her phone call.

A secretary began to cry. Others stood bewildered. With my father under arrest, the staff was in total confusion. Two women picked up their coats and purses and went home. Two others smiled, and went back to work. Lutsi picked up the phone to call my mother.

The Gestapo took my father down two sets of stairs to the street and led him to a black Mercedes. They shoved him into the rear seat and drove away.

The news of my father's arrest spread quickly through the factory. Many worried about where Herr Robert would be taken.

Lutsi then dialed my mother's phone number.

"Hello," said my mother, expecting my father to be on the other end of the line.

"Frau Weiss, this is Lutsi."

"Good morning, Lutsi," said my mother. She became frightened. In the four years Lutsi worked for my father, she had never called the house. My father always dialed his home number himself.

"Frau Weiss, some men came and took Herr Robert away. They were Gestapo."

My mother was silent for a minute. She realized my father had not learned of her phone call in time. "What happened?" she asked.

"They just took him away, Frau Weiss."

There was nothing more to say to Lutsi. She thanked her for calling and hung up, now thinking of me at school, not knowing what to do next. My mother then called her father, Grossvater Jakob.

At the same time, Lutsi paged Uncle Otto, sales manager of the business, who was in the factory inspecting new sample shoes. When he got to the office, she told him of his brother's arrest. Uncle Otto then paged my uncles Richard, Heinrich, and Gustl and told them to come to the factory showroom. It was too early for Grosspapá to be at work.

The showroom contained hundreds of sample shoes displayed on custom built shelves. A large mahogany conference table and chairs were in the center of the room. This room, where he entertained customers and presented his footwear collections each season, was Uncle Otto's pride and joy. My uncles were there in no time. The meeting was like no other Uncle Otto ever held.

"I can't believe what I have to tell you," he said. "Robert has been arrested. A few minutes ago, three Nazis walked into his office and took him away. Lutsi tells me they were Gestapo."

The men were stunned.

"We must leave at once," said Uncle Richard. "There is no reason they won't come back for the four of us. We must call Papá and tell him to stay home." They all knew they were in imminent danger.

Unable to reach my grandfather, Uncle Otto decided to stay. Grosspapá was on his way to work. Uncle Otto would wait for him. The factory's foremen could keep it running. But among the plant's two hundred and twenty five workers were twelve Jews. Uncle Otto called them to the showroom, explained the situation, and told them to go home.

Edlorado Schuhfabrik, Vienna.

Grandfather Marcus, in his office at Eldorado Schuhfabrik.

Chapter 4

GESTAPO HEADQUARTERS, VIENNA: APRIL 5, 1938

The room looked like a banquet hall in an elegant hotel. Standing in the room, guarded by four SS troopers, were more than two hundred men the Gestapo had arrested that morning. My father looked around, recognizing some of the men as casual acquaintances. His mind was alert. He tried to understand what was going on. It appeared the majority of the men were Jews. He identified the few non-Jews as local politicians and aristocrats. The men stood silent, shocked at their situation. They were all in business suits, still wearing their ties. All had been taken from their offices.

What did the Nazis want? What would happen next?

A large double door opened at the front of the hall. Over the door, etched into the wall, was a large M, the logo of the Metropol Hotel. An SS officer walked in dressed in the standard uniform: black jacket, black riding pants, black riding boots, and a black military visor cap. On his arm was the now familiar red-white-and-black swastika armband. Every eye in the room was focused on him.

"Achtung (Attention)!" he shouted.

"In half an hour, some of you will be taken to the Westbahnhof (West Railroad Station). You will board a train and be transported to Germany."

The officer said no more and stayed at the front of the room guarding the door.

"But I am a doctor," someone shouted. "I have patients who need me immediately. I must get back to my office." Other men made similar attempts, pleading or demanding to be let go. Their shouts were ignored. There would be no conversation, and no one could leave. They were in Nazi custody.

The windows were closed, and the room got warm. The men took off their ties, then their jackets. There were few chairs, so most sat on the floor. There was no food or water. The only comfort offered was the toilet. The prisoners were businessmen, doctors, and lawyers who were easy to locate. Jews working in trades or retail stores were more difficult to find.

This successful and prosperous group of Viennese men realized that for the first time in their lives they were helpless. They were humiliated. Several hours went by, and the big doors opened again. Four more SS guards marched in.

"Achtung!"

Reading from a sheet of paper, one of the SS called out names in alphabetical order, ordering the men to the front of the room as they were called. They did as they were told, slowly walking forward. Then the SS officer stopped calling names. There were twenty three men remaining. The men who had been called forward were told to follow two other SS guards outside the hall and out of the building. They were put on buses. The buses drove away.

Inside the hall, there was a second announcement.

"Achtung, the rest of you, leave the building. You will enter a bus parked outside. There will be no talking." My father, whose last name was at the end of the alphabet, had missed the first transport. He was among the group of twenty three.

The first buses took the larger group of men to the railway station, where they joined more than one thousand Jewish and non-Jewish prisoners who were put on a boxcar train headed for the Dachau concentration camp.

The bus with my father and his small group was driven to another destination.

Grosspapá Weiss came to work late that morning. My grandfather, as usual, stood erect and was impeccably dressed. Uncle Otto greeted him and gave him the news about my father. Grosspapá phoned Grossvater Jellinek and asked him to try to find out where my father was taken. My mother had already called her father, so Grossvater was ready with an answer.

"A policeman friend just told me that Robert was taken from his office to Gestapo headquarters in the Metropol Hotel," said Grossvater. "He told me all hotel guests were evicted. The staff was fired when the Nazis moved in. The cellar is now a prison. I also heard that many Jews were taken to Dachau yesterday afternoon. Many Austrian politicians who are against the Anschluss are now under arrest, and I think many more will soon be in custody."

Because he had two large butcher shops, Grossvater knew most of the local politicians, and had many friends who were policemen.

"I also heard that Heinrich Himmler, Hitler's man in charge of the SS, has arrived in Vienna to supervise the Gestapo takeover of the Metropol. Himmler is one of the most powerful men in Nazi Germany."

Grosspapá was silent.

"Thank you, Jakob. Give my regards to Emma." Grosspapá hung up the phone and called my mother.

My mother did not sleep that night. The next morning, with her life turned upside down, she didn't dare go outside. The Gestapo had invaded our home, her husband had been arrested, her domestic help had quit, her milk had dried up, and my baby brother was cranky and throwing up the bottled milk she was forced to feed him.

Fearful of Nazi teachers and parents, she kept me home from school. I was asking questions she could not answer. She did not cry, though she was close to panic. Her need to protect Peter and me was overwhelming. Her efforts to find my father had so far been fruitless. Although she had always been strong and determined, Hedi Weiss, a successful, educated, and capable woman, now felt helpless.

That night, Emil Zollschan, Grosspapá's nephew, who was the Vienna correspondent for the largest newspaper in Zagreb, a large city in Yugoslavia, heard about my father's arrest. He immediately telephoned Grosspapá.

"Marcus, you were born in Yugoslavia, weren't you?"

"Yes," replied my grandfather. "Why do you ask?"

"I think, Marcus, that if you retained your Yugoslav citizenship, you might be eligible for a Yugoslav passport."

"What do you mean, Emil?"

"If you could prove Yugoslav citizenship, you might be able to get passports for you and your children. I assume Mina is also Yugoslav-born."

"Yes, she is," said Grosspapá, realizing immediately that Emil's suggestion was probably the only way he was going to be able to get his family out of Austria.

"Marcus, I suggest you make inquiries at the Yugoslav Consulate right away. Let me know what you learn."

Grosspapá thanked Emil and hung up.

VIENNA: APRIL 7, 1938

Grosspapá Weiss phoned the Yugoslav Consulate and found out that he had dual Yugoslav-Austrian citizenship. Then he called his two sons, Otto and Richard; his son-in-law, Heinrich; and my mother's brother, Gustl. He told them they should meet him in the factory showroom at noon.

My uncle Richard stayed home, but the others arrived on time.

"I think what happened to Robert will happen to us," said Grosspapá to my uncles. "I believe the Nazis need us to operate the factory now, but when they have replacements for us, who knows what they will do?" My uncles listened.

"I just learned I still have Yugoslav citizenship and can get Yugoslav passports, not only for Mamá and me, but for all of my children and their spouses. Not you, Gustl, you are a Jellinek. I am sorry."

"I understand, Papá," said Uncle Gustl.

"Once we have the passports," continued Grosspapá, "we must leave Vienna at once and go to Koprivnica where I was born. I have many friends there and have been in contact with them over the years. We don't have much time. I am sure some kind of administrator will be assigned to run the factory. The Nazis are already running other Jewish businesses. It could be days or even a few weeks before this happens. The Nazis don't want to disrupt production, so they still need us to run the business."

"I agree," said Uncle Heinrich. "Our sales are just fewer than one million Reichsmark, the new German currency replacing the Austrian Schilling. We have more than two hundred employees. They do not want to fire that many people. Who can run it except us?"

"My guess is," said Grosspapá, "that this new administrator won't come before May or June. Even if he comes sooner, he will need time to learn how shoes are made and sold. But we must make our arrangements now."

Grosspapá turned to his two sons and his son-in-law. "I will start working on the passports tomorrow."

He turned to Uncle Gustl. "See what you can do to get out of Vienna as soon as possible. Do you still have your passport?"

"Yes," said Gustl. "I have some ideas about how to leave."

Uncle Gustl's mind was racing. His first thought was Paris. A boyhood friend had been living there for several years, and they had kept in touch. Also, Eldorado's sales agent in Paris, Jon Bojourjon, might be helpful. There were many pieces to put together in a short time.

Uncle Heinrich told the others he had plans to send his son Hansi to Switzerland with help from a German friend.

"Why doesn't your whole family go to Switzerland?" asked Grosspapá.

"I think it's best for him to go alone. Hansi is in more danger than we are because of his age. The Nazis are looking for young Jews. They want to eliminate anyone who can fight them. Hansi must leave Vienna as soon as possible. The rest of us can go to Yugoslavia together and decide what to do next."

"I understand." Grosspapá said. "Richard won't be coming with us. He has connections in the Uruguayan Embassy and plans to go to Uruguay as soon as possible. So it's done. We all have a plan. Let's get back to work."

"Papá, I will call Hedi and tell her about the plans with the new passports," said Uncle Gustl.

Uncle Gustl did not go back to work. He left the factory and got on a streetcar, and twenty minutes later he was at his parents' house. My grandparents Jellinek were happy to see him. He got a hug from his mother. She looked at him.

"What's wrong, Gustl?" asked my grandmother. "You look so serious."

"Mutti, the Nazis are looking for Jewish men, especially those under forty. I have decided to leave for Paris as soon as I can make arrangements."

His parents understood. His mother, however, was worried. She knew that if he left Austria there was a possibility she might never see Gustl again. Also, her older son Fritz and his wife Mädi were disagreeing about what they were going to do. Fritz wanted to go to England, and Mädi was determined to stay in Vienna.

Uncle Gustl called my mother. He told her about the meeting in the office and the plans to go to Yugoslavia and said that Grosspapá would call her and explain more.

"Grosspapá is sure you and Robert will get Yugoslav passports," he said.

"What good can a Yugoslav passport do for Robert if he is in a prison?" asked my mother.

"Hedi, the Nazis have diplomatic relations with Yugoslavia. We think they will honor Yugoslavian passports and visas. They don't want to stir up international problems; they are just out to eliminate all Austrian Jews."

My mother felt a surge of relief. This was the first good news in almost thirty hours. "That would be fantastic. But we still don't know where Robert is."

"No," said Uncle Gustl. "Vati (an endearing term for father) thinks he was sent away to Dachau, but we just don't know for sure. Hedi, I have to go. I have to begin making my own plans to leave. I'll call soon, and we'll talk more. I may be going to Paris."

Uncle Gustl said good-bye. He turned to his parents, kissed his mother, and gave his father a firm handshake. "I'll see you soon," he said with a smile. "Don't worry. I won't be going away for a while."

VIENNA: APRIL 8, 1938

"Hansi, we have to talk," said Uncle Heinrich Hacker as they started breakfast. "I have something to tell you before you leave for school." My cousin looked up at his father. He then turned to his mother, searching for a hint as to what was coming.

"Now that the Nazis have total power in Vienna, we aren't safe here anymore," Uncle Heinrich said quietly.

Hansi stared at his father. He already knew that.

"I think we will be evicted," Uncle Heinrich continued. "We might even be arrested. At sixteen, you are a prime target for the Nazis. Hansi, you've got to move out right away. You must go into hiding."

"Since your father is a wounded veteran from the first war, we think the Nazis will leave him alone," Tante Grete said to her son. "But we are very worried about you."

Hansi could not believe what he was hearing. First, there was the Jew-baiting in school, then the destruction of Herr Schwartz's delicatessen, and now he might be arrested.

"We want you to go to Switzerland as soon as possible," Uncle Heinrich said. "I have a friend I've known for many years who lives in Germany near the Swiss border. I have already spoken with him, and he will help you. You will go to Lörrach, a small town near the German border. It will be safe there. What do you think?"

Hansi said nothing. There was no alternative for him, and he knew it. He waited for his father to say more, to explain more. To Switzerland? Hansi was scared.

"It's urgent," said his father, "I received a phone call from another friend this morning. He told me you are on a list of young men who will probably be arrested. You must hide at once while we make plans for your trip to Switzerland."

Hansi packed two suitcases that Friday and moved to his paternal grandmother Etti Hacker's attic, where he lived for the next four months.

VIENNA: APRIL 11, 1938

The weekend had gone by, and there was still no word of my father. My mother was sleeping better. Her father's plan to go to Yugoslavia had lifted her spirits. But where were the Nazis keeping my father? She could think of nothing else.

Grossvater spoke again to Emil and learned that Gestapo headquarters in Berlin was the only place to obtain release papers for my father. It didn't seem to matter where he was being kept prisoner. If the Gestapo were willing to release him, it could be from any prison or concentration camp.

Grosspapá had begun his efforts at the Yugoslav Consulate. He applied for eight passports. He also needed twelve passport photos, eight for the adults and four for the children, whose pictures would appear on the passports of their mothers. My mother said she would provide the four photos for us.

Emil started making plans to travel to Berlin. He met my mother at a small café on the Kaunitzgasse near my grandparent's house. It was 3:00 p.m.

"Servus, Hedi, how are you?" said Emil, using an informal greeting.

"Emil, I am fine. Thanks so much for coming and thank you very much for suggesting we get Yugoslav passports."

Emil explained the Berlin situation to my mother.

"I must go there. Emil, will you travel with me?"

The waiter appeared and took their order for coffee.

"Yes," said Emil, "that was my plan. Hedi, I will help you get Robert back." As a newspaper correspondent, he had been to Berlin many times.

"Hedi," Emil said, "the situation is desperate. We should leave soon."

"Yes Emil, the sooner the better. I will go home and make arrangements for my children for the time I am gone."

"I think we should take a slow afternoon train to Berlin," said Emil. "The train will make many stops. With a lot of stops, fewer SS troops will be aboard. It could be the safest way. If we leave Vienna at midday, we get to Berlin twenty four hours later. It is a very long trip, but it's worth it to be safe."

"We have to do what we have to do," my mother said. "We must also be prepared to stay in Berlin for a while. My visit to the Gestapo will be unannounced. Who knows how long it will take me to get to see someone?"

"Fine," said Emil, "but let me make some phone calls to Berlin. I will find out exactly what to do when we get there, and where to stay."

"Look who's here," said Emil as Grosspapá approached the table. He got up from his chair.

"Hello Uncle Marcus."

They shook hands. My grandfather greeted his daughter-in-law with a kiss on her cheek. He squeezed her hand and told her to be strong. Emil had asked my grandfather to meet them at the coffee shop.

"Emil," said Grosspapá. "I want to thank you for your help." Emil smiled. He had always liked his uncle Marcus. Then Emil explained the Berlin plan to my grandfather. Grosspapá ordered coffee and listened.

"This sounds good to me, Emil, and again, I hope you understand what a wonderful thing you are doing. But I don't think you should leave until I have all the passports. I am going to the consulate again tomorrow. I will let you know when the passports are ready."

"Hedi," Grosspapá said, "I need your passport photos."

"You can have them today."

"Fine," said Grosspapá to my mother, "I would like to say hello to your parents. Emil, will you come with us?"

Emil agreed and paid for coffee. The three then walked to my grandparents' apartment. Peter and I were there waiting for my mother with Grossmutter and Grossvater.

"Servus, Marcus," said Grossvater, "how are you? I have not seen you in several weeks. Hello, Emil. I haven't seen you in a long time."

"Yes, Herr Jellinek. It's unfortunate that bad times have to bring people together."

They went into the living room where Grossmutter Emma was watching my brother and me. My mother picked up Peter, and my grandmother offered refreshments. Everyone declined, except me. Grossmutter went into the kitchen and brought me a cookie and a glass of apple juice.

It was not often that I saw Grosspapá Weiss and my grandparents Jellinek together. I thought it was great. I watched my mother go into the dining room with Peter. She opened the bottom drawer of her mother's sideboard and found what she was looking for. She took out a shoebox full of photos, came back into the living room, and asked her mother for scissors. She gave Peter back to her mother, cut three passport photos from two of the pictures, and gave them to Grosspapá.

"Here, Papá," she said. "What do you think?"

"This is perfect, very good. They are just the right size." my grandfather Weiss said. "But where is Peter's?"

"Just one minute please." My mother went into the foyer, opened her handbag, and took out a picture of Peter. It was taken by my father with his Leica when Peter was a week old. My father had developed and printed it in his darkroom. He had made several copies, but had not had a chance to give them to my grandparents.

Thirty minutes later, Grosspapá said he had to leave.

"Now that I have all the photos, I hope to get the passports tomorrow morning at the consulate."

Grosspapá kissed Peter and then came to me. First, we shook hands; and next, he hugged me. He went to my mother, took her hand, and kissed her. He said good-bye to Grossmutter and Grossvater, and Emil and headed for the streetcar.

At about the same time, my cousin Edith Weiss, now fourteen, came home from school. She had been called a Saujude several times that day. At the beginning of classes, she had been forced to stand, give the Hitler salute, and yell, "Heil Hitler." She was very aware that she was now openly identified as a Jew.

Walking home from school was very different from the past. Her relationships with her friends had changed. She was singled out. Jewish students were excluded by the others, and they had to stick together, feeling like outcasts, not sure what would come next.

That day, Tante Frieda told Edith she could not continue in school. Her cousin Hansi's parents had already taken him out of school and sent him to hide in his grandmother's attic. Edith was afraid for Hansi, yet sad for herself. An excellent student, she got top grades and excelled in English. She loved school.

Chapter 5

VIENNA: APRIL 19, 1938

Two weeks after my father's arrest, a notice appeared on the Eldorado office bulletin board. The same notice was posted at other locations throughout the factory. It read as follows:

> New laws of 13 April 1938 regarding the provisional administration and provisional supervisory personnel, Austrian law No. 80/1938, effective 3 July 1938, Kommisarischer Verwalter (Administrator) Eugen Loimann is ordered to appear as provisional administrator of The Eldorado Schufabrik, Wien XII, Schönbrunnerstrasse 179. Effective date is 25 July 1938.

VIENNA: APRIL 28, 1938

It was my father's thirty-sixth birthday. It was a difficult day for my mother. It had been more than three weeks since she had seen her husband, and she still had no idea where he was detained. She was consumed with worry.

That afternoon, Emil went to Grosspapá's home to discuss the trip he and my mother were taking to Berlin. My mother arrived a few minutes later. Grossmamá Hermina prepared coffee. The four of them sat in the living room. Emil had the train schedules to Berlin and back and his identification card as a journalist. With his credentials and my mother's Yugoslav passport, he felt confident they could travel safely. My mother also had my father's passport.

"When do we leave?" asked my mother.

"I don't know. It could be a few weeks. I have some work to finish for the newspaper. I don't want to create suspicion in my office. As I said before, we should take a local train that makes many stops so it will be less likely Nazis will be aboard. We will arrive in Berlin in the early afternoon. I think we should reserve a sleeper compartment so we can keep out of sight as much as possible. The departure from Vienna should be in the afternoon."

My mother and Grosspapá nodded in agreement.

"What are the plans once you are in Berlin?" asked Grosspapá.

"We should stay at the Hotel Adlon-Kempinski. It is not near Gestapo headquarters," said Emil. "We'll feel safer far away from that building. If we don't get Hedi's appointment right away, we will stay until we do."

As she listened, my mother was thinking about Peter and me. We would stay with my grandparents Jellinek while she was away. Peter was just three months old. How would he be without his mother for a week or even longer? I was not yet seven. I was not in school. What would I do all day with my grandmother?

"Since the passports were issued in Austria, they are not stamped with Austrian entry visas," said Grosspapá. "That should have been done in Yugoslavia. The Nazis will pick up on that. Hedi, you will need a letter from the Yugoslav Consulate, confirming that you and Robert are Yugoslav citizens and that your passports were issued in Vienna. I will get the letter tomorrow. It should take care of the problem."

"I think your plan will work," said my mother. "What I must do now is anticipate the Gestapo's questions and rehearse the exact words I will use when I get in to see them."

"You are right. Let me think about that," said Emil. "We should meet again after I purchase the train tickets."

Grossmamá offered more coffee. As she was pouring it, she cautioned her daughter-in-law. "Hedi, you realize how dangerous this trip is. I . . ."

"Mamá," interrupted my mother, "I have no choice. I must go to Berlin. We don't even know where Robert is being held. If I don't go and try to find out, we might never see him again." With tears in her eyes, she stood up, bent over, and kissed her mother-in-law on the forehead.

My grandparents and Emil were silent.

"I am not going to become another Ingrid Schnabel. I am strong," my mother said firmly. "Ingrid's husband is in Dachau, and last week, she went to the kitchen, turned off the pilot light, turned on the gas burners, and killed herself. There are hundreds of suicides in Vienna, but I won't give up. My children need their father back. I'm not afraid to go to Berlin with Emil."

My mother put her hands over her face and began to cry. It was the first time she had let herself weep. Grossmamá stood up and embraced her. When my mother stopped crying, she wiped her tears with her handkerchief and smiled.

"It's time to go home."

Emil stood up, and my mother put on her coat. My grandparents Weiss walked them to the door. Grosspapá shook hands with Emil and hugged my mother.

VIENNA: MAY 7, 1938

It was my seventh birthday.

Two days before, on May 5, my grandmother Emma had turned sixty eight. On that Thursday, with Vienna under Nazi control, the last thing on her mind was her birthday. Grossvater didn't forget. He gave her two yellow roses, her favorite flower.

At her age, she was still a beautiful woman. One of seven children, she was a loving, kind, and caring figure for everyone in the family. She always had time for anyone with a problem. She was also a great cook. Unlike her mother, my mother always had help and never had to cook.

On my birthday, our tightly knit family planned a small late afternoon party in my grandparents Jellinek's house for Grossmutter and me. My mother took me there the day before for an overnight visit. Tante Anna, my mother's aunt, and her husband Pepi had made the arrangements. Tante Anna, age fifty, and my grandmother Emma were sisters.

Tante Anna was the manager of Grossvater's downtown butcher shop. At noon that Saturday, as she was closing the Jellinek Yppengasse shop (it always closed at noon on Saturday), she saw a convoy of trucks loaded with Jewish men, women, and children pass by. Brown Shirts, the feared SA, drove and guarded the trucks. Tante Anna quickly closed the door and followed the trucks, which were driving slowly through the narrow streets toward the Ottakringerstrasse. When the trucks came to a stop, Tanta Anna yelled to one of the drivers and asked him where they were going. The Brown Shirt yelled "Michaelerplatz" naming the square that has one of the oldest churches in Vienna.

Curious, Tante Anna ran to the nearest streetcar stop, got on the next tram, and headed toward the Inner Stadt (city center) where the Michaelerplatz is located.

When she got there, people were on their hands and knees, scrubbing the street's cobblestones with toothbrushes and rags. She realized that these people were the ones she had seen on the trucks in front of her shop. She moved closer for a better look, and then she almost screamed out loud. She recognized my mother in the crowd with my brother in her arms.

"Hedi," Tante Anna whispered to herself. "Hedinko," she said again, using an endearing Czech name for my mother. My mother was not on her knees, just standing there holding Peter and talking to one of the SA men. Within seconds, my mother turned and disappeared into the crowd. Tante Anna followed but lost sight of her. She took the next streetcar to my grandparents' house. When she got there, my mother answered the door. Anna was crying.

"I saw you at the Michaelerplatz," said Tante Anna. "I was so worried." The women put their arms around each other with tears running down their cheeks. The doorbell rang again. It was my uncles Gustl and Fritz Jellinek.

"Is something wrong?" asked Uncle Fritz.

"Are you all right, Hedi? Did you hear from Robert?" asked Uncle Gustl.

Standing behind them, I was engrossed in the conversation. Uncle Gustl was one of my two favorite uncles; the other was Uncle Fritz.

"No, Gustl, there is no news about Robert. But I was taken downtown to wash the streets."

"What are you talking about?" said Uncle Gustl. "You washed streets?"

"Yes."

"I saw it," said Tante Anna.

"You saw it?" asked Uncle Fritz.

"Please listen," said my mother. She walked into the living room and sat down. Grossvater brought her a glass of water. The rest of us followed her. I stood next to Uncle Fritz.

"This afternoon, I walked out of the house with Peter to come to the party. I brought Pommy here last night. I was getting into my car when a truck with SA men in it stopped. The back of the truck was full of people, all Jews. Before I could get into my car, the SA hoodlums grabbed me by the arm and pulled me into the truck. Peter was in my arms, but they didn't care. It happened very fast. I knew some of the people on the truck. The SA drove us to St. Stephens Cathedral Square, made us get off, and marched us to the Michaelerplatz."

"I saw you," said Tante Anna. "I saw you talking to an SA. He let you go. What did you tell him?"

"He looked no more than nineteen. I spoke to him in my Viennese accent and asked him if he had a mother. Then I told him to imagine his mother holding him as a baby, going through what I was going through. He turned his face, and I walked away."

Uncle Gustl went to my mother and kissed her on the cheek. Then he gave me a big hug. Uncle Fritz pulled his chair near my mother and held his sister's hand.

No one was in a mood for a celebration. Uncle Gustl stood up, went to Tante Anna, and said, "Anna, come, we'll take you home."

Uncle Fritz got up and joined them. The three said good-bye, and then took several trams to get to Tante Anna's home. She lived in Währing, Vienna's Eighteenth District, far away from the Kaunitzgasse, which is in Mariahilf. Uncle Pepi, who never got to the party, greeted her. My uncles also went home.

VIENNA: MAY 10, 1938

It had been four weeks since my father was arrested. My mother got a call from Emil. He told her he had bought two open one-way tickets to Berlin. They would try to leave soon.

The Anschluss made the logistics of getting to Berlin less complicated. Borders between Germany and Austria had been eliminated. First, they would stop in Prague, then change trains in Dresden, a major railroad terminal, and eventually they'd arrive at Berlin's Anhalter Station. It would be easy for Emil to find the Adlon-Kempinski hotel. Through his contacts, he knew where Gestapo headquarters was located.

VIENNA: MAY 23, 1938

My mother and Emil had not yet left for Berlin.

Grossvater finally got the telephone call everyone was waiting for. He was told by one of his contacts inside the police department that my father had been in the Rossauer Lände Prison in Vienna since his arrest. Some time in the next few weeks, he would be moved to Dachau, the concentration camp near Munich. Though my father was still alive, this was not good news. Grossvater called my mother at once. They made plans to meet with Emil that afternoon at my grandparents' house.

Emil said he could leave the following Monday, May 30, and he told my mother to make her arrangements. She called my grandmother Emma.

"We will leave for Berlin next Monday," she said. "I will bring Peter and Pommy to you that morning. I hope it will not take long to get Robert released." She sounded confident.

VIENNA: MAY 26, 1938.

Two months before his official appointment, the administrator the Nazis assigned to my father's shoe factory walked through the front door. His name was Eugen Loimann and he had been unemployed for several months. He was anxious to begin his new job.

When Grosspapá arrived at work that morning, Lutsi immediately told him of Loimann's surprise arrival. Grosspapá went to my father's office assuming Loimann would be there. He was right. The office had been unoccupied since my father's arrest and a stranger was sitting in my father's chair. Grosspapá's bald head began to perspire. He took a handkerchief out of his breast pocket and wiped his head and forehead.

"Who, may I ask, are you?" asked Grosspapá.

"I am Ingenieur Eugen Loimann, you must be Marcus Weiss." Please sit down."

Grosspapá sat down, irate that a stranger was sitting in the chair that belonged to his son.

"Herr Weiss, I have been unemployed for more than six months. I welcome the opportunity to run this factory. Overnight, I have become responsible for the Eldorado Schuhfabrik and its many workers. I am a man without any experience in footwear manufacturing, but I am responsible to higher-ups in my government who assigned me to this position."

"Herr Weiss," Loimann continued. "Whatever help I can get from you and your family will be noted. I am not planning to exclude you from continuing to work here. The same goes for your sons and son-in-law, and Jellinek. I intend to work with all of you."

"The factory must continue to operate," he added, somewhat apologetically.

"Before I begin a work plan, I must insist that you and your family and all the other Jews working in the factory wear identification tags. They must be worn at all times. Do you understand?"

"Yes," answered Grosspapá. "Give me the tags, and I will distribute them." Agreeing to this first demand was insignificant to Grosspapá. He did not argue with the Nazi administrator. He would work with this intruder to the best of his ability and stay on his good side as long as possible. He did not want to cause any trouble, especially with my father on his way to Dachau.

Loimann appeared to be in his early forties. He told Grosspapá he was married with two children. He was friendly, and Grosspapá, who had years of experience working with more than two hundred employees, thought he could get along with this man as long as necessary.

The meeting was over. Grosspapá got up, said nothing, and left the office. He now had to speak with my uncles, who were due any minute. When they arrived, he called them into the conference room. They talked about Grosspapá's brief meeting with Loimann and the urgency of getting out of Austria. All their passports were in order.

Uncle Gustl, still planning to escape to France, told the others that when the time was right he hoped to persuade Loimann to send him to Paris under the pretense he would collect the five hundred thousand Reichsmark owed to Eldorado by French customers and try to sell several thousand pairs of shoes stored in a rented warehouse in Paris. Loimann would soon become aware of the outstanding money and the Paris inventory. Uncle Gustl thought he could convince Loimann that he was the only one who was able to do this.

BERLIN: JUNE 1, 1938

Emil and my mother had arrived in Berlin the day before. It was Wednesday morning. She tried, but was unable, to make contact by telephone with someone at Gestapo headquarters. That afternoon, she decided to just walk into the headquarters, and talk to anyone she could. My mother and Emil left the hotel and walked for thirty minutes toward Prinz Albrecht Strasse. They recognized the Gestapo building right away. A large flag displaying the swastika hung over its large double doors. They stopped on the opposite side of the street. My mother was smartly dressed in a long-sleeved, belted navy dress. Her shoulder-length brown hair was pinned neatly at the back of her neck. Her greenish brown eyes focused on the swastika. She took a cigarette and lighter from her handbag, lit the cigarette, took three puffs, and dropped it on the sidewalk. She stepped on it. Her heart was pounding.

Leaving Emil standing alone, she walked across the street, went into the building, and approached the reception desk. For more than a month, she had rehearsed in her mind what she would say to these monsters.

"What do you want?" asked the SS captain sitting behind the desk.

"I need to speak with a Gestapo officer."

"Why?" asked the SS officer.

"You are illegally holding my husband in a prison," answered my mother.

"Do you have identification papers?" he asked arrogantly.

As she handed him her Yugoslav passport, she hoped the SS officer was aware that Germany had diplomatic relations with Yugoslavia.

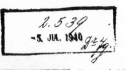

ELDORADO
SCHUHFABRIK R. und M. WEISS

WIEN, XII., SCHÖNBRUNNERSTRASSE 179
FERNSPRECHER: R-36-507, R-31-2-19
POSTSPARK.-KONTO: C-28.279
Der Treuhänder Otto Faltis

Wien, den 4.7.1940

An die
Staatliche Verwaltung des Reichsgaues Wien,
Abwicklungsstelle der Vermögensverkehrsstelle,
Abteilung III, zuhanden des Herrn
Reg.Rat Dr. J ä g e r ,

Wien I., Strauchgasse 1

Heute überreichte mir Pg Alfred Kepka den

beiliegenden Brief und kündigte mir für die nächsten

Tage die Vorlage eines Kaufvertrages an, den ich dann

ebenso an Sie weiterleiten werde.

Heil Hitler !

1 Beilage

Eldorado letterhead, April 1940, with R. and M. WEISS logo still
displayed.

ELDORADO
SCHUHFABRIK
BAUER/TEICHMÜLLER&CO./WIEN XII/82 SCHONBRUNNERSTRASSE 179

Herrn

OBERFINANZPRÄSIDENT - Wien

W i e n III./40

Vordere Zollamtsstrasse 5

| Ihr Zeichen: | Ihre Nachricht vom: | Unser Zeichen: Dir.T./Ho. |

Wien, den 29. Juni 194 2.

Eingang 29. JUL 1942
Anlagen

Betr.:Bezahlung des Restkaufpreises von RM 172.507.-
für Eldorado-Schuhfabrik,Bauer,Teichmüller & Co.,
Wien XII., Schönbrunnerstr. 179

Die unterzeichnete Firma hat laut Ihrem Bescheid vom 8.Oktober
1941 an die Vermögensverkehrsstelle in diesem Jahre 2 Kaufpreis-
raten, und zwar

am 30.Juni in Höhe von 30.000.-- und
am 31.Dezember   40.000.--

an Raten zu bezahlen. Infolge der im 3. Kriegsjahre neu aufgetre-
tenen Umstände, die wir im nachstehenden ausführen, bitten wir
Sie um eine Stundung dieser Zahlungen,nachdem die völlig verän-
derte Situation,infolge Rationalisierungsmaßnahmen, eine weit-
gehende Blockierung des Geldumlaufes mit sich bringt.

Durch die seitens der Reichsstellen angeordneten Rationalisierungsmaßnahmen,wurde auch im Sektor Schuhindustrie für unseren
Betrieb eine Umänderung der Produktion angeordnet und mit Wirkung
vom 1.VI.1942 die Erzeugung von Normalschuhwerk eingestellt.
Diese Maßnahme der Reichsstelle stellte unseren Betrieb urplötz-
lich vor eine ganz neue Situation, die uns daran hindert, unsere
Warenreserven flüssig zu machen,um so den Restkaufpreis verein-
barungsgemäß abdecken zu können.Nachdem die hier auf Lager befind-
lichen Waren infolge einer Verordnung der Reichsstellen gesperrt
wurden und ein Verkauf derselben nicht erfolgen darf, sind durch
diese Maßnahme unsere betriebsflüssigen Mittel derzeit äuserst
gebunden.Andererseits aber haben wir im Zuge dieser Maßnahmen
des Rüstungsministers, neue kriegsentscheidende Produktionsauf-
gaben in Arbeitsschuhwerk erhalten, die uns zwingen,die für diese
Produktion notwendigen Materialien neu einzukaufen und den Betrieb
darnach umzustellen.

Dieser Rohwareneinkauf für die neue Produktionsaufgabe erforderte
erhebliche Betriebsmittel, um das Produktionsprogramm der Reichs-

Eldorado letterhead one year later; displaying BAUER,
TECHMULLER & CO. as new owners.

Vollmacht

für

Name: Ing. Eugen L o i m a n n ,

Anschrift: d. A. Schuhfabrik Eldorado, Wien 12. Schönbrunnerstr. Nr.179.

Auf Grund des Gesetzes vom 13. April 1938 über die Bestellung von kommissarischen Verwaltern und kommissarischen überwachungspersonen, Gesetzblatt für das Land Österreich Nr. 80/1938 und der Anordnung des Reichsstatthalters vom 3. Juli 1938, bestelle ich Sie zum kommissarischen Verwalter der

Firma Schuhfabrik Eldorado, Wien 12. Schönbrunnerstr.179.

Sie haben Ihre Tätigkeit gemäß den gesetzlichen Bestimmungen und entsprechend der erlassenen Dienstanweisung auszuüben.

Wien, den 25. Juli 1938

Der Staatskommissar in der Privatwirtschaft

Zl. 6055 Dr. Rt.Wdr.

Ingenieur Eugen Loimann's certificate of appointment as Eldorado's general manager.

The Nazi told my mother to remain standing in front of the desk and left the room. He came back with a Gestapo officer in civilian clothes who had my mother's passport in his hand. He looked at it and turned to my mother.

"You are a Jewish hog," he said. "This document is false."

My mother was a handsome woman. The agent put his hand on her shoulder and asked her for sexual favors. He threatened her with jail if she did not comply. She stood silent, ignoring his advances, knowing that they were, for him, a way to humiliate and degrade her. Abruptly, he walked away, leaving my mother in front of the desk. She was uncertain of her next move.

The Gestapo officer came back a few minutes later and ordered my mother to follow him. They went into another office. Two more Gestapo officers sat behind desks. One of them looked at her passport.

"What are you doing here?"

"You have my husband in prison. He is a Yugoslav citizen and you cannot do that to him."

"This passport is not stamped with a visa into Austria. Why?"

My mother had anticipated the question and was prepared with her answer. "Because it was issued in Vienna: I have a letter from the Yugoslav Consulate verifying that." She handed the officer the letter.

My mother did not lose her composure. Hardened by the Nazis' injustices and incivilities, she was strong and stubborn and determined to bring her husband home. Once again she told the Nazis that her husband was illegally imprisoned.

Her passport and letter were handed back to her. As she put them in her handbag, my mother took out her wallet and offered to pay the men one thousand Reichsmark if they released her husband. They took the bribe. She was told to go into the waiting room.

Two hours later one of the Gestapo men came into the waiting room and told my mother that her husband would be freed. A letter would be sent to her in Vienna notifying her when and where my father would be released.

"When do you think that will be?" she asked.

"I have no idea," he said. "You have what you wanted. Get out now before we change our minds."

My mother left the building. Emil was still standing where she left him nearly three hours before. She crossed the street and lit a cigarette, and as they walked to a nearby café, my mother told Emil what had happened. Inside the café, she slumped into a chair, leaned back, and closed her eyes. She was exhausted. It had been more than forty eight hours since they left Vienna. Emil ordered two cognacs.

"Hedi, you did a superb job. I don't know if I could have done it," said Emil.

"I'm sure you would have done the same thing if the person in Dachau had been your Ilse."

They drank their cognac and returned to the Adlon-Kempinski Hotel to check out. Emil and my mother took the next fast train back to Vienna, where she collected Peter and me from my grandparents' house.

VIENNA: JUNE 2, 1938

More leaders of the Austrian opposition were arrested every day. Vienna was in turmoil. The two hundred fifty thousand Jews living in Vienna seemed doomed. Antisemitism in Germany had been common since 1933, but it wasn't until now that Germans and Austrians acknowledged to the world the depth of their hatred for Jews.

Grossvater realized more and more how little attention Austrian Jews had paid to Nazi sympathizers in their country. He was now totally convinced that Adolf Hitler's dream of a world ruled by Aryans, Hitler's definition of a pure white race, was shared by thousands of his fellow Viennese. It was terrible, he thought, that he and his family had not taken the Nazi rise to power in Germany seriously.

Uncle Fritz's problems with Mädi were getting worse. He wanted to leave Vienna as soon as possible. Mädi would not leave. She was not a Jew and felt she was better off alone than with a Jewish husband. Uncle Fritz went to my mother and told her about Mädi. He also said that he and Lilly, and her sister, Herta, (Tante Anna's two daughters) had planned their escape. They were making arrangements to go to London.

Chapter 6

VIENNA: JUNE 3, 1938

The first train carrying prisoners from Vienna to Dachau was called the Prominententransport (Celebrity Transport). The one hundred fifty prisoners selected for this transport were Christian Socialists, Monarchists, Social Democrats, Communists, all political opponents of the Nazis, and a few Jews. All aboard the celebrity transport were prominent Austrians.

VIENNA: JUNE 4, 1938

The second transport to Dachau carried six hundred Jews. Among them, many were well known. They included the actor Karl Bieder, author Emil Gabor, and the musician, Isaac Adler. Lawyers, scientists, and the psychiatrist Bruno Bettleheim were aboard. So was my father.

The head Gestapo officer had in his pocket the official entry log to Dachau concentration camp. It was known as KZ Dachau or Konzentrationslager Dachau. Near the end it read as follows:

> ROBERT WEISS
> Date of Birth: April 28, 1902
> Place of Birth: Vienna
> Nationality: Austria
> Last address: Reichgasse 52, Vienna XIII
> Profession: Manufacturer
> Family: Married, 2 children
> Religion: Jewish
> Prisoner Nr. 15212
> Category of imprisonment: Jew

Reason for detention: Protective Custody
Arrival Kz Dachau: June 3, 1938

Four thousand Viennese Jews were sent to Dachau in 1938. During those boxcar transports, SS staff humiliated and abused the prisoners. "Lazy Jew" and "priest-ridden coffeehouse riff-raff" were two of their favorite insults. Throughout the ride in the boxcar, my father was forced to stay on his knees, with his hands locked behind his head. When his arms got tired, an SS guard slapped him on the back of his head.

The first Austrian that year to die in Dachau was Hansi Kotanyi, a partner in the Austrian paprika mill of that same name. He committed suicide. There were some prisoners who were released because they got visas or had special connections that allowed them to leave the country.

A list from the IKG, under constant Nazi supervision, was used to identify Jews in Vienna by name and address. The list was used to find, and arrest, Jews at their homes and businesses. Ironically, at the same time, the IKG was allowed to issue exit documents which enabled thousands of Jews to leave Austria. The Nazis didn't care if the Jews left the country, or were arrested and sent to Dachau. They just wanted Austria to be Juden frei (free of Jews).

Bruno Heilig, author of *Men Crucified*, was sent to Dachau before my father. In his book, written years later, he wrote as follows:

> We were escorted by the police through a small door into the (railroad) station. We came to a siding. It was 9 p.m. A feeble light shone from a train. I saw dark figures in front of the train. A wild outcry greeted us, and the dark figures started moving. I got a blow in the back. Someone next to me fell down. We ran towards the train. I stumbled; it was the foot of one of those dark figures. The next moment I felt a blow in the neck; I fell, picked myself up again at once and was about to reach down for my hat and spectacles, which I had dropped in my fall, when I was seized under the shoulders and flung into the train. There, another one seized me and threw me into the corridor, and there stood yet another, who hurled me into the nearest compartment.

Richard Pollack, author of *The Creation of Dr. B.*, wrote in his book:

> Bruno Bettleheim, wrenched from the comfortable life that he had led for thirty five years, now found himself prisoner 15029,

with his thinning brown hair cropped short. Most inmates bore
a single-coded (yellow) triangle on the breast of their gray-striped
fatigues: pink for homosexuals; black for criminals, sex offenders,
and other so-called asocial prisoners; red for German politicals. Each
morning the targets of this degradation fell out for roll call onto
the Appellplatz (Assembly place), the camp's central square. From
there they marched off to labor details, which lasted from sunup
to sunset and sometimes longer. The prisoners were marched to
their barracks, issued striped inmates' uniforms and left alone for
several days. They were issued a blanket for their bed and a wooden
bowl for eating. They did not realize that the bowl was for more
purposes than food. The prisoners slept on the upper and lower
bunk beds on straw mattresses and pillows in a barrack holding
over seventy five men. The SS men wake up the camp prisoners in
the middle of the night. With horror they hear the words of the
SS commander, Baron von Malsen-Ponickau, who shouted: 'We
haven't come here to be friendly with these sons of a bitch. They
are not humans like we are; they're only second class people.' As
fast as possible, the SS increased their position of strength in the
camp. If the SS force consisted of approximately sixty men in the
beginning, it grows to one hundred ninety six by April 12, to two
hundred seventeen by April 20, and to two hundred thirty eight
by April 30.

Johannes Neuhäusler, auxiliary bishop of Munich, in an article titled "What
Was It Like in the Concentration Camp in Dachau?" wrote the following:

> At first, especially during the period before the war, an SS block
> leader was in charge of each block. Later, however, one man had
> to take charge of several barracks and blocks. In each block, one of
> the prisoners, called the "block senior," was put in charge. He was
> responsible to the SS. The "apartment senior," the block secretary,
> the barber and the manager of the canteen were in turn responsible
> to the "block senior."

Laurie Weiss Griffin, my daughter, recalls the following:

> One day, and I recall this only once, Opa (Grandfather) was telling
> me what it was like in Dachau. He said how horrible it was, how

awful it was. He said that he had one wooden bowl. That it was used both to eat from and go to the bathroom in. He said it was terrible but he seemed to not dwell on it at all, just said it like it was. He sounded sad about it but he wasn't crying or choked up. Rather like it was the fact. To me he seemed just plain grateful that he wasn't there anymore.

Dachau prisoners. File photo from Dachau archives.

Gestapo headquarters, Vienna; the former Metropol Hotel.

VIENNA: JUNE 6, 1938

It had been a little more than a week since the administrator, Loimann, had taken control of the shoe factory. He called my grandfather to meet with him for only the second time. The subject was the same. He needed as much help as possible to maintain production and to keep the employees satisfied that the business would not close.

Then Loimann told Grosspapá he had called my mother to meet with the two of them. Grosspapá could not imagine why Loimann wanted to meet with my mother. Loimann did not tell my grandfather that he had been ordered to prepare Eldorado for sale and that several Austrian and German Aryan businessmen were interested in buying it.

My mother walked through the door before my grandfather could ask why she was coming. It was 10:00 a.m. Lutsi took her into the office, and Loimann shook her hand.

My mother was wearing a dark gray suit, her skirt about six inches above her ankles, and a fashionable hat.

Grosspapá was also well dressed in a black suit and black tie. His shoes were polished to a high shine. My family always dressed well, even at home.

My mother looked around. My father's office seemed strange to her. Seeing Loimann behind her husband's desk bothered her terribly. This was her husband's office and not some disgusting Nazi's, she thought. Other than my father, the only thing missing were the dozen or more family photographs he kept on his desk and on the walls. He took great pride in his pictures. My mother wondered where they were.

Loimann asked Grosspapá and my mother to sit down.

"I asked you to this meeting so I can explain my function in this company, which I realize, belongs to you, Herr Weiss, and to your husband, Frau Weiss."

Grosspapá and my mother were silent.

"Frau Weiss, I want you to know that I have never been in a shoe factory before. I therefore need help from everyone in your family. It is my assignment to keep the business running. Richard has left the country, and I cannot afford to lose the others." He took a sip of water from his glass.

"What do you want from me, Herr Ingenieur?" asked my mother, addressing him formally.

"I want you to encourage your family members to continue working. If you do, I will transfer Reichsmark to your personal account every week. I understand your predicament regarding your husband."

Grosspapá sat motionless. He was thinking of a proper response and wondered what else Loimann was thinking. Was he being truthful, or was there a secret plan? Would he really give money to my mother in exchange for her family remaining at Eldorado?

Loimann needed my family to keep Eldorado profitable. He had been ordered by his superiors to prepare the business so it could be sold quickly. He wanted his superiors to be pleased with the financial status of the company.

My mother had heard about another meeting Loimann held the Friday before. It excluded my family and was for all factory supervisors and foremen. Loimann told them approximately the same thing he said to Grosspapá: he had no experience running a shoe factory, and he needed their help to run it. He also said he did not work for the Gestapo. He just wanted the business to succeed.

"I have specific requests," he said, looking at Grosspapá. "I need you to personally look after the manufacturing part of the business, and I need Herr Otto to continue managing sales. I intend to keep shipping shoes to customers in seven countries and keep our nine sales agents in those countries. I also expect Hacker to stay on as production manager and Jellinek to continue in sales."

Grosspapá did not like the fact that Loimann was not referring to my uncles without the customary title, Herr. He contained his anger. There was much too much at risk for him to object to any words spoken by this man.

"I have one request of you, Herr Loimann," he said. "If I am to come to work here in my business, I dare not walk the streets or take the streetcar. I will need to be picked up by a driver."

"It can be arranged. Speak to Johann, and he will do as you ask. By the way, Frau Weiss, you may also use the driver if you wish."

My mother said nothing. She wanted to harm Loimann, or even kill him, but she knew her family's safety depended a great deal on her relationship with this man. Der Schlag soll ihn treffen (Lightning should strike him), she thought to herself.

The meeting was over. Grosspapá and my mother got up and left the office. My mother looked at some of the women in the reception area and nodded her head. Lutsi stood up from behind her desk and said, "Auf Wiedersehn (Good-bye), Frau Weiss." My mother smiled. She said good-bye to Grosspapá and left. Grosspapá went back to work.

VIENNA: FOUR YEARS EARLIER, JUNE, 1934

Kaffehaus (coffeehouse) hopping was a favorite pastime of my Uncle Fritz. He and his friends would visit as many coffee-pastry shops as possible in an evening. They would order coffee and the shop's best dessert.

On this day in 1936, Uncle Fritz received a late-morning call from Josi, one of his buddies from school.

"Fritzerl, let's go Kaffehaus hopping tonight."

"Sure," answered my uncle, "I'll call the others."

"Good, let's start at the Landtmann on the Alser Strasse on the Ring."

"Wonderful," said Fritz. "We'll have everyone at the table guess which important historical person once drank coffee there. When should we start?"

"How about eight o'clock?" answered Josi.

Uncle Fritz called Hilda Zeltzer, Berthold Grun, and Harrietta Brenner, all friends since elementary school.

At seven, Uncle Fritz cleaned up, changed to his Saturday night clothes, and walked two blocks to the tram. It would take less than ten minutes to get to the coffee house. When he arrived at Landtmann, Josi was already there and had brought two more friends, Viktor Lüger and Josefa "Mädi" Fahringer.

"Servus, Mädi" said Uncle Fritz, "Wie geht's (How is everything)?"

"Fine, Fritzerl," answered Mädi.

My uncle thought Mädi was beautiful. She was five-foot-five. She had curly light brown hair and dark brown eyes, and she was always smiling. She worked as a chorus girl in a Viennese nightclub. She looked very attractive that night in a dark brown skirt that showed her ankles and a beige blouse with satin ribbon around the collar.

Mädi had a longtime crush on Uncle Fritz, and he knew it. She liked his neatly combed, shiny black hair and his fabulous full mustache. At thirty two, he was a year older, and Mädi had always thought she and Uncle Fritz would make a perfect couple. Until now, however, everyone knew that Uncle Fritz was not ready for a serious relationship.

The others arrived, and the seven longtime friends sat down at a table by the window at the front of the café.

The waiter arrived, dressed in a black suit and bow tie. He wrote down their orders in a little black book. A few minutes later, he came back with seven coffees and seven desserts.

"Does anyone know which very famous person drinks coffee here?" asked Josi.

"No, I haven't the slightest," said Hilda.

"Of course," said Berthold. "This is Freud's favorite coffee house. He sits in that corner over there." He pointed a finger to a dark corner far back in the room.

"How do you know that?" asked Josi.

"Everyone who knows about Freud knows it," said Berthold with a smile.

"Okay," said Josi. "Let's go next to the Café Central and play the game there."

Forty five minutes later, they paid the bill and walked for five minutes until they got to the Herrengasse. They walked into Café Central and sat down, again at a table by the window. Their café hopping was always the same. Order coffee, order the best dessert, and play the celebrity game. This time, the famous person was Leon Trotsky.

From Café Central, they walked to the Hotel Sacher and agreed that just about every Viennese celebrity had eaten there at some point. They all ordered the same thing, Sachertorte with Schlag (chocolate cake with whipped cream).

After three desserts, it was time to end the party. Uncle Fritz asked Mädi if he could walk her home. She was delighted. When they arrived, Uncle Fritz escorted Mädi up the three flights to her apartment. She invited him in. Uncle Fritz stayed the night.

In the morning, the sun was shining through the slats of the shutters outside the three large windows in her bedroom. Uncle Fritz was on the left side of the bed. He lifted his head and gazed at Mädi.

"How did I ever end up in bed with this beautiful woman?" he asked.

Mädi smiled. "And how did I end up in bed with this handsome man?"

Uncle Fritz put his right hand on Mädi's cheek and kissed her. They had been close friends for two years, but this was the first time they had shared a bed.

"Mädi, I want to marry you."

"Um Gottes willen (Oh, in God's will)!" she said. "Are you really asking me to marry you?"

"Yes, will you marry me?"

"I never thought you'd ask! Of course I will. Move a little closer."

Chapter 7

VIENNA: JUNE 13, 1938

By now, the men were on a first name basis.

"Eugen," Uncle Gustl said to Loimann. "We need the five hundred thousand Reichsmark from Jon. I should go to Paris and get that money myself." Uncle Gustl was referring to Jon Bojourjon, Eldorado's sales agent in Paris.

"The money is long overdue," he continued. "Robert is gone, and since you are running the factory, he is apt to keep the money. The only way to get it is to personally convince him of the consequences. We could sue him, you know. There is also a considerable inventory of shoes in a Paris warehouse that should be sold."

"Eugen, let me go to Paris to collect the money and sell those shoes."

To my uncle's surprise, Loimann agreed. Uncle Gustl was elated. His plan to escape Vienna was working.

"Gustl," said Loimann. "You go to Paris. I expect you back as soon as possible. But remember, your sister, parents, and all the Weisses are here. There could be consequences for them, should you not return," he warned.

Loimann sat down and wrote a letter of authorization so my uncle could get a French visa.

Uncle Gustl went to his office to collect Eldorado invoices made out to French customers. He planned to hide them in the linings of his suitcases so they would not be found and confiscated on his trip.

Applying for a visa at the French Consulate in Vienna was simple. He had a letter on Eldorado stationery with Heil Hitler next to Loimann's signature. Though hundreds of Jews were waiting in line on the sidewalk, Uncle Gustl was admitted immediately. In a few days, he would leave Austria.

VIENNA: JUNE 17, 1938

"Mutti, I've come to say good-bye," Uncle Gustl said to his mother. "I'm sorry Vati is at work. Tell him good-bye for me." He gave my grandmother Jellinek a long hug and left.

He was packed and ready to leave. He did not expect to return to Vienna, nor did anyone else expect him back. He had two small suitcases. He also carried an old leather briefcase his father had given him when he graduated from the Realschule (high school).

Vienna and Paris were both popular commercial and tourist centers, and trains between the two cities ran frequently. Uncle Gustl boarded at the Westbahnhof station with a second-class ticket. He carried sandwiches and two bottles of water he'd bought in the lobby. It was 9.00 a.m. The train was scheduled to leave at 9:15. He found an empty compartment. Five minutes later, three SS officers joined him.

"Heil Hitler," said one.

"Heil Hitler," my uncle responded.

This would not be a pleasant day, sitting in a small train compartment with three SS officers. It was the last thing any Jew would wish for.

To his advantage, he was an assimilated Jew. He looked and spoke the same as any other Viennese and could speak German with or without the typical Viennese accent. He was wearing a tweed business suit with a white shirt and tie. When he greeted the SS men with "Heil Hitler," he pronounced it "Heilitla" confident of his Viennese accent. He raised his right arm just slightly, trying to show that this gesture was ordinary. He was, however, very much afraid. Nazis did not need a reason to arrest or mistreat a Jew.

The train left on time. Uncle Gustl wondered how far the Nazis were going. They certainly were not going to Paris. The train's fourteen-hour route went through Munich and Stuttgart, but first it stopped in Salzburg, the city of music and birthplace of Mozart. Uncle Gustl remembered the good times he'd had in this wonderful city just two hours from Vienna.

There was no border control now that Germany and Austria had become one nation. In Munich though, during a short layover, Gestapo walked through the train inspecting the passengers. They paid no attention to Uncle Gustl, who appeared to be just another Aryan on business.

The German and French border towns of Kehl and Strasbourg were only a few hours away. In Kehl, there was a thirty-minute layover. German border guards and customs inspectors came aboard. The three SS men who had sat next to Uncle Gustl had gotten off in Munich. In their seats were two German businessmen and one businesswoman. Uncle Gustl kept conversation to a minimum. He was nervous. But the German border guards did not question him. France was only minutes away.

As the train approached Strasbourg, the German border control officers prepared to get off. The French inspectors, who had boarded the train in Kehl, began their passport inspections. When they stamped Uncle Gustl's passport 'Entry Approved,' he took a deep breath. He exhaled slowly. He was fully aware that he was now out of reach of the Nazis.

He thought of his parents, his sister and brother, and his many uncles, aunts, and cousins in Vienna. Next, he began to concentrate on Paris and what he would do next. He spoke a little French, what he'd learned in school. He would make up for his language deficiency with his personality and good looks. He was good looking, and he knew it. Tall, slim, outgoing, and full of fun, he was a ladies' man, and he was not bashful.

Gustl Jellinek got off the train and began his new life. He called his boyhood friend Paul Rosenzweig. The two men had been in touch, and Paul was expecting him. Paul had already called the Jewish Community Services in Paris for information about aid for his old friend. Uncle Gustl stayed at Paul's apartment on Paris' Left Bank for a few nights. Paul was married and had two children, a girl and a boy, ages eleven and fifteen. Uncle Gustl loved the bohemian atmosphere of the city and within a week, with the help of the Jewish agency, he found a small but comfortable furnished apartment, also on the Left Bank. It had its own toilet and bathtub, rare in France at that time. Eldorado had given Uncle Gustl enough money to sustain him for a few weeks.

VIENNA: JUNE 19, 1938

It was the middle of the morning. Blood poured out of my leg onto my socks and shoes and into the street. I was screaming, in pain, and scared. There was a deep cut inside my right thigh, four inches long.

Georg Brauer and I had been riding together on one bicycle. He was sitting on the seat pedaling, and I was standing over the fender on the rear axle. We crashed, and the fender sliced through my thigh. We were both lying in the street.

"Pommy, you have a bad cut," yelled Georg. "Look at all the blood. It looks awful. Stay where you are. I am going to get your mother." Georg ran the fifty feet to my house. He had only small scratches on his hands and elbow.

My mother came running with Georg and Grossvater Jellinek. It was Sunday, and his butcher shops were closed. They bent over me and looked at my leg. My mother was shocked when she saw the gash. It was an inch deep. My grandfather took off his tie and wrapped it around my thigh above the cut. He then used his handkerchief to cover the wound.

"I am going to get some towels to stop the bleeding," my mother said.

Georg and Grossvater tried to comfort me, telling me I would be fine. My mother returned with two white towels. They wrapped my thigh as tightly as they could and Grossvater carried me into our apartment, and into the living room. The towels were full of blood.

"I have to call Dr. Nagel," my mother told Grossvater. "We cannot take a chance on going to the hospital." My grandfather nodded. A visit to the hospital was impossible. No Jew, adult or child, could take that risk. It was a guarantee for disaster. My mother dialed Dr. Nagel's office. The phone rang several times, but there was no answer.

"Vati, I don't know what to do, Dr. Nagel's office does not answer. Do you think I should call him at home? He lives in Hietzing. He's Jewish, you know. He plays tennis at the club." My mother picked up a phone book and looked for Dr. Alfred Nagel. She found the number and dialed it. The doctor answered. He said he would come as fast as he could, though his practice had been closed, and he was no longer affiliated with the hospital.

Lying on the couch with my mother and grandfather standing by was comforting, but the pain was awful and I was crying. Dr. Nagel arrived. He was about sixty. He wore a suit and shirt with an open collar and that morning was unshaven. He was carrying his medical bag. My mother and grandfather held me down while the doctor stitched my wound. Dr. Nagel could not give me an anesthetic because he had none. When the suturing was over, the doctor gave me some pills for the pain.

Grossvater, who spent one day a week in a slaughterhouse, fainted to the floor.

PARIS: JUNE 21, 1938

His new Paris apartment had one bedroom, a living room, and small kitchen. Uncle Gustl was pleased. He decided to phone my mother and went to the nearest post office to place the call. The post office had ten telephone booths, all occupied.

"Bonjour, mademoiselle," said Uncle Gustl to one of the telephone attendants. "I would like to place a telephone call to Vienna," he said.

"Of course sir, please fill out this paper, and I will let you know what time your call will go through," she said, returning the smile Uncle Gustl always gave attractive young women.

"How long will it take to make the connection?" asked Uncle Gustl.

"Let me see," she answered, looking into her log book. "It will probably take one hour. Would you like me to book the call?"

Uncle Gustl was disappointed it would so long. "Yes, please book the call," he said.

The attendant continued smiling at Uncle Gustl and filled out a document while asking him for the number he wanted to call.

"Very good, Monsieur Jellinek, please return in one hour. I will make sure that you get through to Vienna."

Uncle Gustl thanked the woman and left the post office. With only an hour to spend, he didn't want to go back to his apartment, then back to the post office. He stopped at a local newsstand, bought a London newspaper, and began to read it with the English he had learned in school. He was surprised he could read the newspaper, and what he was reading disturbed him.

The Germans were threatening Poland. The British Prime Minister, Sir Neville Chamberlain, was trying to make peace with Hitler. An arrangement was about to be signed that would keep England out of the war. In exchange, Hitler's armies would end their aggressive threats against Poland and Czechoslovakia's Sudetenland, in areas where people speak German.

Uncle Gustl read as much as he could, slowly and deliberately. He wanted to understand it all. The more he read, the more troubled he became. He did not believe a single word of what Hitler promised Chamberlain. Uncle Gustl knew that France was rearming, but he worried that the German Army would be too strong for the French. The Maginot Line, the World War I fortification along the French-Belgian frontier, was supposed to be impregnable. It was meant to keep German invaders from crossing into France. But after World War I, the French did not extend that fortification west to the Atlantic, and they had not considered how superior the modern German tanks were to the French.

Uncle Gustl was even more concerned about what could happen to his family in Vienna. The hour passed quickly, and he went back to the post office. The attendant told him to enter booth number nine and wait for a ring. He liked the way the young woman looked at him, and he thought for a moment about flirting with her, but the telephone call to his sister erased that thought. He went into the phone booth and closed the door.

The telephone rang. He picked up the hand receiver, and the attendant told him the connection was made and not to hang up. Then he heard a ring he assumed was in Vienna. There was a second ring and then a third, and then he heard my mother's voice.

"Halo."

"Hedi, it's me, Gustl."

"Gustl, where are you? How are you? Are you well?" she shouted.

"Yes, Hedi, I am fine, I am in Paris."

"Oh, thank God," said my mother, "Tell me about your trip."

"Hedi the trip was fine. I am safe. I was staying with my friend Paul. Do you remember him? I have my own place now."

"I remember Paul," answered my mother.

"Hedi, tell me about Robert. Have you heard from him?"

"Yes, I have heard from him. I received his first letter just a few days ago. He is in Dachau. Did you know that?"

Uncle Gustl was silent for a moment. "No, I didn't know. What did he say?"

"He said that all is fine, and he is just trying to get adjusted. They have him working on some project, but I don't know what it is," she answered. "You know that I tried to get him released with the Yugoslav passports."

"I knew that." Uncle Gustl said. He paused again, almost losing his composure. "Are you getting along with Loimann?"

"Yes, I am," answered my mother. "He seems to try hard to keep the factory functioning. I think he is also trying to protect his job. Otto and Heinrich are still working there. He actually needs them. Papá comes in almost every day."

"I am afraid," continued Uncle Gustl, "that once he finds out that I am not returning to Vienna, he'll be angry."

"Don't worry. There is nothing anyone can do now," my mother continued. "We just have to wait and do the best we can."

"Hedi," Uncle Gustl said, "I know you will call Mutti and Vati and tell them I'm fine. Please tell them to make arrangements to get out of Austria. You must also get out of Austria."

"Gustl, listen to me," she continued. "Everyone knows the dangers, but I cannot leave Robert in prison. Robert will be released, I hope, but I don't know when. Call again soon please. Also, with all the connections and friends that Vati has, I think we will be safe for now. He and Mutti will follow us to Koprivnica after Robert is released."

"Hedinko," said Uncle Gustl, "I have to get off the phone now. My time is up. I will write to you. Give my best to everyone. I forgot to ask, how are the boys?"

"They are fine. Peter is now five months and he is a good baby. Pommy is not in school anymore. Edith and Hansi don't go either. Pommy had to say 'Heil Hitler' every morning. It bothered me more than it did him."

"All right, my dear sister," said Uncle Gustl, "I love you and send you kisses."

Uncle Gustl hung up the phone. He had tears in his eyes as he went to the attendant to pay for the call. "Merci beaucoup," he said, "I appreciate your help very much." The pretty attendant's eyes followed Uncle Gustl until he was outside the post office. He slowly walked home. The world has changed, he thought, it makes no sense at all.

When he arrived home, he lay down on his sofa. He closed his eyes and thought about his life in Vienna.

Uncle Gustl.

VIENNA: THREE YEARS EARLIER, MARCH 1935

At breakfast, my father said to my mother, "Hedi, Gustl called last night. He said there is new snow on the Schneeberg, and the skiing is terrific. They've got three feet of fresh powder."

"Oh, I know," my mother interrupted, "Gustl met a girl on the Schneeberg last year who lives in Puchberg, right on the mountain. She's a terrific skier. And you should go with him, right?"

My father laughed. He knew better; she was way ahead of him. She did not give him the chance to tell her, that, the day before, Uncle Gustl had called him and their friends, Hans Ehrlich and Walter König, who in turn called Franz Frölich, to plan the Schneeberg weekend. Puchberg is a valley town at the base of the Schneeberg region that includes the Rax, a popular mountain for summer climbing. It is the closest Alpine region to Vienna, a two-hour train ride away.

My mother began her weekend by chauffeuring Uncle Gustl and my father to the Südbahnhof (South Station). Walter, Hans, and Franz were waiting. They took the 6:54 a.m. train, already in their ski clothes. They didn't want to waste time changing when they got to Puchberg. They were dressed in identical lightweight beige pullover parkas, knickerbockers, and knee-high white knitted socks. Their hand-sewn leather boots were comfortable for walking. The five skiers each wore white flattop woolen caps with earmuffs folded inside.

They had second-class tickets because they would spend most of the trip eating breakfast in the dining car. By midmorning, they would be on the ski slopes.

Upon their arrival, a horse-pulled sled that served as a taxi took four of them to their hotel and Uncle Gustl went to the home of Helena Sterba, his lady friend. The men registered and thirty minutes later met Uncle Gustl and Fraulein Sterba at the Zahnradbahn (cog railway) terminal.

Built in 1897, the thirty-eight-year-old Zahnradbahn was already historic. The six skiers were anxious for deep powder skiing, high on the mountain. It took the train an hour and fifteen minutes to reach the top, stopping halfway to let some skiers off for shorter runs.

The Schneeberg at that time was one of the few mountains in Austria to offer uphill transportation. The cog railway went to the mountain peak, which was almost five thousand feet high. The terminal at the top, built that year, was called the Bahnhoff Hochschneeberg. At that altitude in the Alps, there are no trees, just snowfields with fresh powder.

My father and the other men were good skiers. They were surprised to find that Fräulein Sterba was even better. She was the one who lead the group downhill. It was thirty five degrees, a sunny day without a cloud in the sky. There was virgin snow in every direction, untracked powder as far as one could see. It was a skier's delight. The group made first turns with no ski tracks ahead of them. After a few good turns, high on adrenaline, they let out occasional bursts of yodeling.

There is a saying. "Skiing is not a matter of life or death. It's more important than that!" This was certainly true for the group on the Schneeberg on this beautiful day.

The skiers took three more trips up the mountain that Saturday with Fräulein Helena always leading the white-capped skiers to the bottom. She out skied them all. The group ate dinner and Uncle Gustl went home with his attractive friend. They met the following morning for breakfast. After three runs on Sunday the men took the 3:00 p.m. train back to Vienna.

My father, third from left, and friends skiing on the Schneeberg.

VIENNA: ONE YEAR BEFORE, JUNE, 1937

Lisl Wertheim, the daughter of Uncle Heinrich and Aunt Gisela, was a pretty fifteen-year-old, and one of my mother's many cousins. On this day, Lisl was watching a boy, standing alone, staring into space in a corner of the Makkabi Heim (Maccabi Center) a Viennese Zionist sports center. He was somewhat taller than she with brown hair parted on the right side. She felt sorry for him; he looked bored. So she approached him and began a conversation. Viennese girls, like the flirts in the operettas they all loved, were not bashful.

"Hello," said Lisl.

"Hello," he replied.

"My name is Lisl Wertheim," she said.

"My name is Bruno Vogler."

"I've never seen you before," Lisl continued. "Are you a member of the sports center?"

"No. I am just visiting for the evening. I was invited by a friend."

"Oh, how nice of him, or is it her? Do you live around here?" Lisl asked, hoping his friend was not a girl.

"I live just two streets away from here on the Landerstrasse. Where do you live?"

"I also live near here, but in the opposite direction," replied Lisl. She liked Bruno Vogler at once. He was easy to talk to, and she liked to talk. She found some boys awkward. Bruno was not, and he was very good-looking.

"Would you like me to buy you a glass of soda himbeer (raspberry soda)?" asked Bruno. He didn't know that was Lisl's favorite drink, soda water with raspberry syrup. Bruno left and moments later came back with two glasses of soda Himbeer, along with a small plate of sweet, buttery Viennese cookies. Lisl was overjoyed. She thought Bruno was nice. The young couple ate their cookies and drank their sodas, talking about their likes and dislikes. When they left, they agreed to meet again in a few days at the same place. On that day in June, it was love at first sight for Lisl and Bruno. She never did find out if Bruno had been at the sports center with a girl or a boy.

Chapter 8

VIENNA: JUNE 22, 1938

It was a great day for Adolf Hitler. The heavyweight boxing championship of the world between Max Schmeling, a German, and Joe Louis, a black American, was to take place. The two had fought once before, in 1936, with Schmeling the victor. Hitler followed that victory with many lectures about the racial superiority of Aryans. The fight today would be in New York City's Yankee Stadium.

In response to Hitler's bragging, Pres. Franklin Delano Roosevelt, wishing Louis luck in his fight, told him that the country needed muscles like his to beat Germany. Though the United States was not yet at war with Germany, newspapers and radio commentators were predicting that war was inevitable.

Just three months after the Anschluss, and at about the time that all nations were becoming aware of the dangers of Hitler's policies, Joe Louis became the hero of Jews throughout the world. In America, sixty million people would listen to the broadcast, and more than seventy thousand people were expected at Yankee Stadium. The match between Louis and Schmeling had worldwide implications. Could an American black man defeat a German white man? In America, no one cared more about this boxing match than did the Jews.

Uncle Otto invited my grandfathers to his house to listen to the fight on his Grundig shortwave radio. The fight was scheduled for 8:00 p.m. in New York, which was 4:00 a.m. in Vienna. My grandfathers declined, but Uncle Otto went to bed early and got up just before four. He'd heard that the fight was being broadcast in German as well as Spanish, Portuguese, English, and other languages. Uncle Otto made himself coffee and took some rolls, butter, and jam into the living room. He sat in his easy chair and turned on the radio. The broadcast was being carried by a Vienna radio station, so tuning into the shortwave band wasn't necessary. He listened to a German broadcaster while in the background he heard a few English language announcements to the crowd in Yankee Stadium.

Uncle Otto leaned closer to the radio. There was no static, and he could clearly hear the announcer in the ring and the cheers of the crowd in the stadium. He lit a cigarette.

"Ladies and gentlemen, the fight between the German and American champions is about to start. The referee has called the fighters to the center of the ring to shake hands. They have done so. The fighters are staring into each other's eyes. Now they are returning to their corners . . ."

My uncle heard the opening bell. "The fighters are coming out of their corners. Louis is quickly forcing Schmeling to the ropes," the announcer yelled. "A right to the body by Louis lifted Schmeling's left foot off the floor. Schmeling is holding on to the rope, trying to steady himself. Schmeling isn't moving. He has his left arm extended for protection only."

Uncle Otto yelled, "Hit him, hit him, hit him again."

"Louis is throwing a barrage of punches. They're landing against Schmeling's head. Schmeling is turning away from Louis."

"He's got him!" yelled my uncle. "Get him, get him! Come on, Louis."

"Schmeling looks like he is in trouble," yelled the announcer. "The last blow hit him hard. Schmeling is not moving. Schmeling is pinned to the ropes. Louis' right sends Schmeling to his knees. The referee is stepping between the fighters."

"Frieda, Frieda, wake up," yelled my uncle. "This is fantastic! The Nazi is getting killed." Tante Frieda did not hear him, and my uncle kept his ear next to his radio.

"One . . . two . . . three . . . wait, the referee is allowing the fight to continue. Schmeling is wobbling toward Louis. Louis hits him with a right hand. Schmeling is down. Schmeling is down. He crashed to the canvas. Schmeling is now getting up. Another left and right by Louis sends Schmeling down again."

Uncle Otto jumped from his chair. "He's down. Stay down, you Nazi son of a bitch. Stay down," Uncle Otto yelled again, this time waking his daughter. She got out of bed, put on her robe, and went into the living room.

"Papa, are you all right?"

"Yes, Edith, I'm fine. I am listening to a very important radio broadcast from New York."

"From New York?"

"Yes, from America. Shhhh, Edith. I want to listen."

"Good night, Papa," With that, Edith went back to bed. "It's very loud. You might wake Mama."

Uncle Otto did not hear her. The announcer's voice was now so loud that Otto's speakers crackled. "There's a towel, there's a towel. The fight is over! The fight is over! The Schmeling corner has thrown a towel into the ring. They have surrendered."

"We won!" yelled Uncle Otto. "Yes, we won."

"Ladies and gentlemen, the fight is over. Two minutes and four seconds into the first round, Joe Louis has knocked out Max Schmeling." Uncle Otto turned off his radio, finished his coffee and rolls, and went back to bed. Later that morning, he called my grandfathers and told them about "our" victory.

WASHINGTON DC: JULY 5, 1938

Pres. Franklin D. Roosevelt organized a conference regarding the problem of Jews trying to leave Germany and Austria. It was held in Evian-les-Bains on the shore of the French side of Lake Geneva. It was called the Evian Conference. Thirty-two countries participated: Australia, Argentina, Belgium, Bolivia, Brazil, Canada, Chile, Colombia, Costa Rica, Cuba, Denmark, Dominican Republic, Ecuador, England, France, Guatemala, Haiti, Honduras, Ireland, Mexico, the Netherlands, New Zealand, Nicaragua, Norway, Panama, Paraguay, Peru, Sweden, Switzerland, the United States, Uruguay, and Venezuela.

The United States did not send a high-level official. Myron C. Taylor, a businessman and close friend of President Roosevelt represented the United States. During the nine-day meeting, delegate after delegate stood up to express sympathy for the Jews, who were now referred to as refugees. But the United States and Britain, along with most other countries, offered no excuse for not admitting Jews to their lands.

The Nazis then claimed that the lack of a decision by so many countries to open their doors to Jewish refugees made it a hypocrisy to criticize Germany for its treatment of Jews.

"Nobody wants them," claimed the German newspaper *Völkischer Beobachter*. "It is a shameful spectacle to see how the whole democratic world is oozing sympathy for the poor tormented Jewish people, but remains hard-hearted and obdurate when it comes to helping them . . ."

In the meantime, the *New York Times* and the Columbia Broadcasting System were filing numerous reports of long lines of Jews standing in front of the United States Consulate in Vienna, unable to apply for entry visas to the United States. They also reported that the atrocities the Nazis carried out in the streets of Vienna led to thousands of suicides by Viennese Jews.

VIENNA: JULY 8, 1938

We had still not heard from my father.

The money my mother was getting from Eldorado was not enough to pay all the expenses for our apartment, so she planned a move to her parent's house.

The Kaunitzgasse apartment was my mother's birthplace. My family was very close, and we did not need permission to move there. The uncertainty of life in Vienna made most formalities obsolete. She started packing some personal things. I was playing with a puzzle and Peter was lying on a blanket on the floor.

"Mutti, why are you packing?" I asked.

"We have to move. We cannot stay here any longer. Because we are Jewish, people don't like us. That is why you are not in school anymore."

"Is that why I didn't go to the hospital when I cut my leg?"

"Yes, that is why."

My mother stopped packing and picked up Peter. She sat down with him on her lap and pulled me on to the sofa, beside her.

"Pommy, this is what we are going to do. Papa hasn't been here for several months, but we will see him again very soon. In the meantime, we are going to move in with Grossvater and Grossmutter. We have to be careful that the Nazis don't . . . we have to be careful that the Nazis, you know, those new soldiers in Vienna who are everywhere, don't bother us. We will be safe with Grossvater. He was in the army, and he will protect us. Everything will be fine, Pommy."

"What army was Grossvater in?"

"He was in the Austrian Cavalry in World War I. He rode a horse." She got up, placed Peter back on the floor and went back to packing. "Please play with Peter while I finish," she said.

My grandfather sent a moving company to help us pack. My mother asked for three medium-size wooden crates that could be safely stored or shipped somewhere. She did not care about leaving furniture behind, and her piano would not fit into my grandparents' apartment.

The following day, a truck moved the crates to a public warehouse owned by a family friend. They had hinges and locks on the covers and were small enough to be carried by two men. My mother was hopeful that after my father's release from Dachau, the crates could be shipped to Koprivnica, where we planned to live. In the three boxes were my mother's sheet music, my parents' tennis racquets, my father's 35mm Leica camera, and his 9mm Eumig movie camera and projector. There was also clothing, books, bed linens, a few small pieces of art, my electric train, and our ski boots.

My mother had asked the movers to build a false wall inside one of the crates. She then had them nail a tightly wrapped package, smaller than a shoebox, to the inside of that wall. In the package was my mother's jewelry, including a diamond her mother had given her.

Johann drove us in the Erskine to the Kaunitzgasse. We took five suitcases with us. When we got there, she told my grandfather about the hidden jewelry.

"I am not going to stand in line to sell my jewelry to anyone," she said. "I can't get much money for it that way, and it's all I have left that's valuable. I'm going to keep it with us."

Living with my grandparents was fine. I had lots of family around me, but it was not like being home in Hietzing. I soon realized we would never see our Hietzing house again. That first evening, Uncle Fritz and Lilly stopped by. I was told Uncle Gustl had moved to Paris.

There was little to do during the day. We were discouraged from being on the streets. But from time to time, my mother and grandmother took Peter and me to a nearby park so I could play with other children. Peter was now almost six months old. We were in a neighborhood with few SS troops or Nazi sympathizers roaming the streets, but one couldn't really tell who was a Nazi and who wasn't.

Grossvater and Uncle Fritz kept busy running the butcher shops, but they knew it was just a matter of time before they would have to close, or the shops would be taken over by some Aryan. All businesses owned by Jews would eventually be "aryanized", and Jews would not be employed by the new owners. Aryan was now a key word in my seven-year-old vocabulary. I knew that if you were Aryan, according to Nazi ideology, you were part of a pure and superior German race. If you were not Aryan, you were considered to be inferior.

PARIS: JULY 11, 1938

Newspapers and radios reported daily on the Chamberlain-Hitler conferences. Uncle Gustl became more fearful of Hitler. The British prime minister had been negotiating with the German Führer since 1933. Hitler now admitted that he wanted to conquer all of Europe. Chamberlain did not seem to take Hitler seriously.

Uncle Gustl frequently reminisced about the last five years in Vienna. He had never thought Austria might become part of Germany. The assassination of Dolfuss and the conferences between Schuschnigg and Hitler had not worried him or the rest of the Viennese Jews. Yet overnight, Uncle Gustl thought, Austria had become Germany.

The Jewish agency in Paris found Uncle Gustl a job repairing shoes. His original plan in Paris, to collect Eldorado's outstanding debts and keep the money for himself, did not materialize, but he kept lying to Loimann by letter that his attempts would soon pay off. He had to keep Loimann on his good side to protect my mother's income and that of the others who were working at Eldorado.

In one letter he sent to Loimann, Uncle Gustl wrote, "Dear Eugen, I went to see our agent, Jon Bojourjon. He offered to give us the stock of shoes in exchange for the invoices. However, Bojourjon is very clever. A friend of mine informed me that Bojourjon has denounced me at the German Embassy. He told someone there that I have the invoices and that he would tell them where the shoe inventory was located."

Uncle Gustl felt confident Loimann would believe him and understand why he could not go to the German Embassy. He continued to report to Loimann in this manner as long as Loimann believed him.

Uncle Gustl's pay at his shoe repair job was barely enough to survive financially. It was his only income, along with the few francs he received weekly from the Jewish agency. He had to earn more money, so he decided to start working for himself. He rented a small storefront near his apartment, and began repairing shoes for other refugees. As his customer base increased, so did his income.

VIENNA: JULY 12, 1938

My mother called Grosspapá. She had just received a letter from my father, saying he'd been in Dachau for more than a month.

"Papá," my mother said. "I have something important to tell you," she said. "I finally heard from Robert. He tells me he is fine." Grosspapá listened. "He says the food is fine," my mother continued. "He sleeps well. He feels well. And at the end of the letter, he writes, 'Und alles ist laf' (and everything is laf). Papá, 'laf' is a word Robert and I use when we tell each other that something is . . . ."

"Hedi, I know what 'laf' means," Grosspapá interrupted. It was a family code word to tell one another that something was bad, or a lie. No, not everything in Dachau was good; it was bad. But at least my father was alive.

VIENNA: AUGUST 8, 1938

Eugen Loimann received a letter from the Nationalsozialistische Deutsche Arbeiterpartei (National Socialist Workers Party), directing him to aryanize the Eldorado Schuhfabrik immediately. He put notices on the factory's bulletin boards that said all Jews were dismissed, effective immediately, and to leave their identification badges in the main office. There was no mention of salary compensation. Grosspapá called my mother to tell her the news. She sat down and wrote to Uncle Gustl to tell him he was free of any obligation to Loimann; all of their family members had been dismissed. The Eldorado Schuhfabrik was Judenfrei (free of Jews).

VIENNA: AUGUST 15, 1938

Grosspapá and Grossmamá were packed and ready to leave their Turnergasse home. By now all Jews in Vienna, whether they left voluntarily (as did my grandparents) or by eviction, left their furniture behind. My grandparents packed only four suitcases. Johann picked them up and drove them to the Südbahnhof. Grosspapá was relieved that he was able to obtain Yugoslav passports for his children and their families.

VIENNA: AUGUST 18, 1938

Hansi left his hideaway in his grandmother's attic and went home for the first time in four months. During his stay with his grandmother, his parents made frequent visits. They finally told him they had contacted their friends, the Loewis, whose son, Karli, was Hansi's age. The two boys were good friends. The Loewis and the Hackers agreed that Karli and Hansi should escape together to Switzerland and would leave at once.

Hansi packed a small suitcase and his backpack. His father had asked his neighbor, a Christian, to drive them to the Westbahnhof. The Loewis were to meet the Hackers at the train station. Hansi's father bought tickets for the boys, destination Lörrach, in Germany.

On the train platform, Hansi asked, "Papa, how did you plan all of this?"

"It was not difficult," said his father. "First, to get your passport, I had to pay our taxes. But more important, I know someone in the immigration office who accepted a gift. I was also able to get Karli's passport."

A few minutes later, Karl Loewi and his parents arrived. They greeted each other somberly. Uncle Heinrich gave Karli his train ticket. Departure time was noon, thirty minutes later.

Hansi and Karli, the night before, had memorized their itinerary. They were told not to write anything down on paper. Uncle Heinrich had given the boys detailed instructions. They had to get to Lörrach, a small German town near the Swiss border. There would be two train changes and finally a bus ride. The trip would take twenty eight hours. In Lörrach, they had to look for Alfred Zeinberger, Uncle Heinrich's friend. He was the general manager of the regional electric company. Zeinberger, however, would only instruct them how to get across the Rhine into Switzerland. Once in Switzerland, they would have to find a train to Zurich, where they would look for the Jewish refugee agency.

The boys were dressed for hiking. Both wore knickerbockers, knitted socks, and climbing boots. Karli's knickerbockers were leather. They wore jackets over their sweaters. Hansi wore a Tyrolean hat with a feather stuck in it and Karli had a tweed cap with a brim. They looked like serious hikers, not like Jewish boys from the city.

Uncle Heinrich put his arm around his son and told him to be careful. Tante Grete hugged Hansi and kissed him. She started to cry and took a handkerchief out of her handbag. Gerti approached her brother and hugged him. Hansi put his right hand over his face, trying to hide his emotions. He knew his trip could be dangerous. But he was more worried about his parents and sister. Would they be arrested and taken to a concentration camp? He thought they should all be leaving together. Karli said good-bye to his parents and his older brother.

Uncle Heinrich reached for Hansi's arm. He pulled him away from the others. "Hansi, I have something to tell you. Listen, it is important.

"When you need to use the toilet or stand at a urinal, make sure no one watches you. Make sure no one knows you are circumcised. German and Austrian Christians are not. Being circumcised will identify you as a Jew. Do you understand?"

"Yes, Papa," Hansi said. "Boys in school have been teasing me for a long time. I know."

"Einsteigen (all aboard)," the red-capped stationmaster shouted. The boys got on the train. Uncle Heinrich worried as he watched many SS troopers also board the train. Tante Grete and Gerti were watching the car Hansi was in, when he opened a window and stuck his head out. He waved, and his family waved back. Tante Grete was still crying. Uncle Heinrich put his arm around her shoulders, and Gerti held her mother's hand. The train moved slowly out of the station. Soon the last car passed by. The Hackers and the Loewis stood there, motionless.

"It is time to leave," said Uncle Heinrich. It was noon. The Hackers and Loewis left the platform. The Hackers' Christian friend was waiting on a side street to drive them all home. It was a silent ride.

Hansi and Karli's trip to Switzerland included a long and indirect route to Lörrach. It would have been easier to go from Vienna through Salzburg, Innsbruck, and Feldkirch, crossing the border at Buchs. But that route was too dangerous. The Germans closely guarded that border crossing. The safest way for them to get to Switzerland was through Munich, then on to Reutlingen and Freiburg. The last part of the trip would be on a local bus to Lörrach.

The first leg, through Salzburg, to Munich made a lot of stops but went smoothly. Their compartment was half full, with only one Wehrmacht soldier sitting with them. He was young and slept the whole time.

The boys arrived in Munich at 7:00 p.m. They had until 5:00 a.m. to make their next connection, a ten hour wait. The huge Munich train station was spotless. Signs giving passengers directions and train schedules were clear and visible. The train platforms and passenger waiting areas were well lit. In the morning, they would leave for Reutlingen.

"What are we going to do for ten hours?" asked Karli.

"Maybe we can go to a movie. We're too young to go to a bar," answered Hansi.

"You're right," said Karli. "Let's get out of here and see what's going on in town."

They found a baggage room and checked their two suitcases. When they left the station, they found themselves in the center of the city. They were hungry. They bought franks and raspberry sodas at a kiosk and walked the streets, looking in store windows. They listened to beggars playing their instruments. They saw SS and SA troops and many Wehrmacht soldiers. They noticed that not as many civilians wore lapel pins with a swastika as they did in Vienna. Nazism was new at home, and the pins were fashionable with Hitler's new followers.

As they walked through the city, they found themselves in Munich's red-light district with its many bars, low-class restaurants, and cheap hotels. They looked but kept going. Occasionally, they were approached by prostitutes.

Two blocks later they, found themselves in a heavily trafficked area called the Stachus. They crossed the main street to the Karlstor (Karl's Gate) and entered the Altstadt (old town) which led to a Munich landmark, the Frauenkirche (Woman's Church) with its two towering steeples. All the buildings had Nazi flags hanging from the roof.

By midnight, the streets were empty. Hansi and Karli went back to the train station and fell asleep on benches. The sound of a train whistle woke them. It was 3:30 a.m. They washed in the WC (public restroom), found a small restaurant, and ate a breakfast of fresh rolls, butter, hardboiled eggs, and coffee. At 4:50 a.m. they had retrieved their luggage and were aboard the train to Reutlingen.

LÖRRACH: AUGUST 19, 1938

My cousin and his friend had their second uneventful train ride. It stopped frequently and civilians and Nazi military men got on and off at almost every stop. Hansi and Karli got off at one stop and bought sandwiches and drinks. Three hours later, they got off the train in Freiburg. At 10:00 a.m. they got on the PostBus (Germany's bus service) and at 4:00 p.m. they arrived in Lörrach. Like the trains, the bus made many stops. By now, Karli and Hansi had been traveling for twenty eight hours.

The Lörrach station was small. Hansi and Karli were among only five who got off the bus. They looked around, trying to figure out what to do next. The bus station and the railroad station were combined and in the center of the town. The railroad tracks ran parallel to the main street. Their instructions were to find a tavern called the Goldener Hirsch (Golden Buck) and look for Alfred Zeinberger. The small town was busy with pedestrians. They started to walk down the Haupstrasse (Main Street).

"Karli," Hansi whispered to his friend, "there are two guys following us. They look like Gestapo. Look at the leather coats they are wearing, and their hats."

Hansi's warning was barely out of his mouth when the two men caught up with them.

"Who are you, and where are you going? Let me see your papers," demanded one of them. My young cousin and his friend produced their passports. The men read them and looked at the boys. The passports looked okay, and the boys looked like local kids.

"We are going to visit friends," Karli answered. He was not going to divulge Herr Zeinberger's name.

The Gestapo let them go. Hansi and Karli looked at each other in amazement and walked away. "Karli," said Hansi, "there's the Goldener Hirsch. Let's go in!"

The tavern was full of late afternoon beer drinkers. Hansi and Karli were looking around for someone who might be Herr Zeinberger when a short balding man in his mid forties quietly approached them.

"Are you new in town?" he asked

"Are you Alfred Zeinberger?" asked Karli, almost whispering.

"Yes, I am Zeinberger," answered the man with a smile. "I am glad to see you. I have been waiting for you. I assume you had no trouble getting here."

"No, we had no trouble," said Hansi. "It just took a long time. Out on the Haupstrasse, two men asked to see our passports, but they let us go."

"Good. How is your father?"

"My father is fine, thank you," said Hansi.

Zeinberger asked them to sit down and offered them food and drinks. They refused. They felt uncomfortable in a tavern full of Germans.

"Boys, you have a long night ahead of you," began Zeinberger. "I want you to stay out of sight, so come home with me and sleep for a few hours. You will leave at midnight. I will give you exact instructions."

Five minutes later, they were in Herr Zeinberger's home. He asked them again if they were hungry or thirsty, and before they could answer, Zeinberger opened the icebox and took out a plate of assorted sausages and cheeses and a huge loaf of peasant bread. He put a slab of butter on the table and two glasses of water. The boys eagerly ate almost everything on the table.

Then Zeinberger took them to their room. It had two beds and a washbasin. When they asked about a toilet, Zeinberger pointed through the window to an outdoor shed to the left of the house. During years of hiking with their parents and Hakoah excursions into the mountains, they had used sheds like this before. It was now 6:30 p.m. Zeinberger told them to go to bed and get as much sleep as possible. He would wake them in a few hours.

Just before midnight, Zeinberger woke my cousin and his friend. Hansi and Karli dressed quickly and went into the kitchen. They drank the coffee that was ready for them while their host gave them their instructions.

"Here is the map you need to get to Switzerland. You have to follow it exactly."

The boys looked at the paper in astonishment. They had never seen a map like this one.

"Once we are outside, I will point out a light in the distance. It is about two and a half miles from here. Walk toward the light. It is on top of a utility pole with electric and telephone wires. When you get to the pole, look at the metal marker nailed to it. The marker is about three feet from the ground and has a number on it. It says H58. The next pole will be number H59 and so on. The poles are about two hundred feet apart."

"I understand," said Karli. "You want us to follow the poles by number."

"Exactly," said Herr Zeinberger.

"How many poles do we follow?" asked Hansi.

"Look at the map. There are three sets of lines: the H line, the C line, and the Y line. You are going to follow all three lines, one after the other. It is like a road map, except you follow utility poles. You start at pole H58, and when you get to pole H90 in Inzingen, you turn left and follow the line of poles that start with C108 until you get to C198, which is in Degenfelden. From there, you take the Y route, beginning at pole Y5 until you get to the River Rhine."

"It looks easy," said Hansi, "but it's the middle of the night. How can we see the pole numbers?"

Zeinberger gave them a small flashlight. "Use it carefully," he said. "Cover the light with your hands so you are not discovered. Do you have any questions?"

'No," said Karli. Hansi was silent.

"Remember, at pole Y5, you head directly to the Swiss border. From Y5, it is about five miles to the Rhine, which is the end of your utility pole route. At that point, look through the woods, and you will see a six-foot wire fence. You must climb over it to the other side, where you will see border markers. They are steel posts painted blue and yellow and are next to the river. You need to cross the Rhine before you are in Switzerland."

Herr Zeinberger gave them each a bottle of water, half a loaf of bread, and a chunk of cheese large enough for several meals. Realizing they had a river to cross, Hansi and Karli decided to leave their suitcases behind, but they stuffed their backpacks with the clothes they thought they could not do without. They left the house and walked to a side street where they saw their first pole.

"Good luck, boys," said Zeinberger, shaking their hands. "Good-bye." He turned and went home.

LÖRRACH: AUGUST 20, 1938

Hansi and Karli followed the poles through the woods toward the light, but it didn't get any closer. It was farther away than when they began. They were lost and on a dirt road with no poles in sight. They walked until they reached a small village where the only sound was barking dogs. They circled the town twice, trying to avoid the dogs, searching through the trees for the lost utility poles, but to no avail. Having no choice, they decided to stay on the road. They walked six hours until daybreak and stopped to rest. They ate some bread and cheese and were refilling their water bottles from a stream when Karli screamed.

"Hansi, look, there is a utility pole in the woods!"

They ran to the pole and read the number on the marker. It was C153. Karli took out the map and found C153.

"This is where we are. I think we are near Degenfelden. We're not lost anymore. Oh, oh, look at that man over there," he whispered.

The man walked toward them.

"Guten Tag (Good morning)," said Karli, trying hard to speak in the German spoken by Berliners.

"Heil Hitler," replied the man and kept walking.

"Hansi," Karli whispered, "that man is a Nazi. What do we do now?"

"We must keep going," said Hansi. "We are going the right way. Somehow we bypassed all the other poles. Now we must follow these poles until we get to C198. It's only about a mile away. Then we will be at the Y route."

Twenty minutes later, they were at C198, which was in the intersection of two one-lane roads. They sat down, exhausted. They'd been walking for almost seven hours, but they were sure they were headed in the right direction. The C route went one way, and the Y poles went the other. They were five miles from the Swiss border.

Wearily, Karli and Hansi located Y5 and kept going. About two hours later, they saw the six-foot wire fence Herr Zeinberger had described when he gave them their map.

"Karli," Hansi said with excitement, "we are near Switzerland. There's the fence. We have to climb to the other side. The boys looked at the top of the fence and saw that barbed wire ran along the top. They would have to find another place to climb over. They followed the fence along the Rhine for half an hour, but there was still barbed wire. Eventually they came upon a small barn with three walls. The August sun was high in the sky, and it was hot.

"Karli," said Hansi. "It's empty. Let's go in and get out of the sun. We have to rest."

The floor was covered with straw, and there was a large barrel full of water in a corner. Using their backpacks as pillows, the boys promptly fell asleep on the warm straw floor. It was almost noon.

"Grüezi (Hello)." The boys woke up with a start to find a tall man with a bicycle standing in front of their shelter. They had been sleeping for three hours.

"Karli," said Hans. "I think he is speaking Schweizerdeutsch (Swiss German)."

"Why are you sleeping in a goat feeding station?" asked the man. He was smiling.

"A goat feeding station?" said Hansi. "We didn't see any goats." Hansi was worried. He had not disguised his Viennese accent. It would surely give them away as Jews.

Then he recognized that the blue and gold shield on the man's bicycle were the colors of the Swiss province of Zurich. He had skied many times in the Swiss Alps with his parents.

The man put his bicycle on its side. "What are you fellows doing here?" he asked.

"We want to go to Switzerland," said Hansi. "Are you a Swiss policeman?"

"No. I am a Swiss border guard. You are still in Germany. I patrol both sides of the border." he said. He looked at the boys sympathetically. "This is what you have to do. Follow the fence for half a mile. It ends there at the river edge."

"Is the river narrow enough for us to swim across?" asked Hansi. He couldn't believe their good luck in finding this friendly man. The man surely knew they were Jews.

"It depends on where you cross. At some points, it is eight hundred feet wide, and at others it is less. You will have to look for a narrow place if you are going to swim across.

"But you might not have to," he said. "When you get to the riverbank, you will see small docks tied to the shore. These docks belong to local people who fish off them. Some have small boats tied up to them. I'm not sure they have oars, but you may be able to float across the river. You will have to use your heads to find a way to get across. It may not be easy, and remember to keep your passports dry."

"Thank you very much," said Karli, extending his hand. Hansi did the same. They said good-bye and picked up their belongings and started to walk along the fence. When they got to the river, it looked as wide as a football field. Karli put his hand in the water.

"It's not too cold," he said. "I'm sure we can get across."

There were docks on both sides of them, and on the other side of the river, but there were no boats.

"Karli," said Hansi, "those docks are floating. They are tied up with ropes."

Hansi went to the smallest dock, which was about six feet long and four feet across, and knelt down to examine how it was tied to the shore. Within a few seconds, he had untied a rope. There were four ropes, one on each corner. Karli immediately untied the second and third ropes. To keep the dock from floating away, they left the fourth for last; they had created a raft.

"Good," said Hansi. "Let's take off our boots. We have to keep them dry, so let's put them in the backpacks with our passports. You have to take off your leather pants. If they get wet it will take them forever to dry and they will be stiff as wood." Karli took off his pants and put them into his backpack. They placed both packs in the middle of their raft.

"You look pretty funny standing there in your underpants," laughed Hansi.

They were ready. Hansi tied a rope around his body on the diagonal, from his left shoulder to the right side of his waist. He was going to pull the raft. Karli would swim behind and push it. The years they swam competitively at Hakoah were about to pay off.

They got into the water and untied the last rope. In the front of the raft, Hansi swam a breaststroke. In back, Karli used a scissors kick. Hansi was pulling and Karli was pushing. In fifteen minutes, they had crossed the river Rhine into Switzerland. It was 4:00 p.m.

There were cows grazing in a large meadow. Nearby, close to the riverbank, a dozen teenage boys and girls were playing soccer. One of them kicked the ball toward the river.

"Kurt," yelled one of the girls, "get the ball, it's going to roll into the water."

Kurt chased the ball but suddenly stopped.

"Hey!" he yelled to his friends. "Come here. Hurry up. There are two guys with a raft."

The kids got to the river just as Karli and Hansi were pulling the raft onto the bank. The boys gave them a hand while the girls giggled at the sight of Karli in his underpants.

"Are you escaping from Germany?" asked one of the boys. "Are you Jews?"

"Yes, no . . . yes, we are," Hansi stuttered, not sure what he should tell them.

"Are we in Switzerland?" asked Karli. He had quickly found his knickerbockers and pulled them up over his wet underwear.

"Yes," answered one of the girls. "You are just outside Augst."

Hansi and Karli put on their boots, unsure of what to do next.

"Come with us," said Kurt. "We'll take you to our farm, and you can meet my parents."

"Karli," said Hansi. "Welcome to Switzerland!"

"Thank you, Hans Hacker. And you too, welcome to Switzerland."

They shook hands and the two friends put on their backpacks and followed the Swiss boys and girls. Ten minutes later, they were at Kurt's family's farm. Kurt's father greeted them, and Kurt told him what had just happened. His mother came out of the house.

"I am Wolfgang Schwender," said Kurt's father, "and this is my wife, Frau Schwender. Are you boys Jews?"

"Yes," said Hansi.

"Don't worry. We are glad to see you. Come in the house. Are you hungry?"

Hansi and Karli nodded, "Yes, we are, thank you."

"Come along, boys," said Frau Schwender. By now, six farmhands had joined the young soccer players. "The rest of you go along."

The soccer players said good-bye and left. The farmhands returned to their chores.

The Schwenders took Hansi and Karli into the house, and Frau Schwender hung their wet clothes to dry. It was dinnertime. Hansi and Karli sat down with the family at the kitchen table, and Frau Schwender fed them a delicious venison stew with black bread.

"Herr Schwender," Hansi said, looking serious. "There are two things I must tell you. First, we have to get to Zurich. Is this possible?"

"Yes," said Herr Schwender. "I will take you to the train station in the morning."

"And second, will you get into trouble if someone finds the raft on your property?"

"Maybe so," answered Herr Schwender. "I will have Kurt and his friends return the raft tomorrow."

"Thank you very much," said Hansi.

After dinner, Kurt took them to a small room with two beds and told them to go to sleep. His mother would wake them in the morning and feed them breakfast. Then Herr Schwender would drive them to the train station. The train left for Zurich at 8:30 a.m.

The next day, after breakfast, Hansi and Karli said good-bye and were driven to the station in Herr Schwender's truck for the one-hour ride to Zurich.

"Where do we go when we get off the train?" asked Karli as the train left the station

"We have to look for the Jewish agency. I don't have an address," Hansi answered.

It wasn't long before the boys realized they were in the outskirts of Zurich. When they got to the Hauptbahnhof, Zurich's central train station, Hansi and Karli picked up their backpacks and got off. The first thing they noticed was that they were the only ones wearing hiking clothes. They were nervous. They stood out in the crowd.

Within seconds, two men in civilian clothes approached them.

"Ihr seids Wiener (Are you Viennese)?" asked one of the men. "We need to see your papers." The men had heard Hansi and Karli's Viennese accent. "We are Fremden Polizei (Federal Police for Foreigners)," said the other, showing his identification card.

Hansi looked at Karli, who was sweating. They opened their packs and gave the men their passports. They looked at each other, trying not to show their fear.

"What are you boys doing here?" asked one of the policemen. "You are from Vienna. Are you Jews?"

"Yes," answered my cousin. "We are looking for the Jewish refugee agency."

"We have to take you to the police station so you can register as refugees. Then we will call the Jewish refugee agency for you."

Hansi and Karli were astonished. They looked at each other with relief. They got in the back seat of the police car, went to the police station, and within minutes had filled out forms registering them as refugees. Then, as they said they would, the police called the Jewish Social Services Refugee Agency. In twenty minutes, a social service worker arrived at the station to pick up the boys.

"Merci vilmal (Thanks a lot)," said Hansi in Schweizerdeutsch, as they said good-bye to the two policemen.

When they got to the Jewish agency, Hansi immediately asked an employee if he could place a telephone call to his parents in Vienna, which he did.

Chapter 9

VIENNA: AUGUST 21, 1938

Uncle Fritz and his cousins Lilly and Herta (Tante Anna and Uncle Pepi's daughters), who were twenty four and twenty seven, were making arrangements to escape to London. They came to my grandparents' house that Sunday to tell us about their plans for leaving Vienna. Uncle Fritz also told us he was still having problems with Mädi. He wanted to leave Vienna as soon as possible, but Mädi refused to go. Since she wasn't Jewish, she felt there was no danger for her in Vienna. With a Jewish husband, wherever she went, she would be considered a Jew sympathizer.

That same morning, Uncle Otto told Tante Frieda and Edith he had something important to talk about. Their home on the Margaretenstrasse, in Vienna's Fifth District, was his pride and joy. His family occupied the second floor. The apartment was large and comfortably furnished. Uncle Otto sat in the living room in his favorite tapestry easy chair. On his right was his mahogany cigarette stand, and on his left was his treasured Grundig radio and record player. As usual, he held his cigarette between the middle and ring fingers of his left hand. He removed his thin-rimmed metal eyeglasses. He looked worried.

"Kinder," began my uncle using a word of affection he used for all the people he loved, "it is time to leave our home. We are lucky to have been here this long."

"I think Robert could be released from Dachau soon. When that happens, he will take Hedi and the boys to Koprivnica at once. Papá is already there and still has many friends there from his childhood. The Hackers will probably follow us. We can't stay in Vienna any longer, always fearing what tomorrow will bring."

"Otto, we are ready to go. Edith and I have talked about it, and we will do whatever is necessary," said Tante Frieda. "We'll take a few suitcases and leave everything else. We should leave tomorrow. I just heard that Trude Friedman's husband was arrested, and they are just two houses away from us. What do you think?"

"Papa, let's go," said Edith. "We should be with Grosspapá and Grossmamá. We'll learn Croatian quickly. There is a Yugoslav boy in my class, and I've heard him say a few words. I already know how to say Dobre-Dan, which means good day, and Dovidjenja, which is good-bye. Yugoslavia's Croatian province has its own form of the Yugoslav language. In Serbia, another Yugoslav province, the language is Serbian. In the province of Slovenia, they speak Slovenian." Edith loved learning languages and already had learned Italian and English in school.

Edith's encouragement was good for her father. He seemed relieved and said they would pack and leave in a day or two.

VIENNA: AUGUST 30, 1938

The Jellinek shops were still operating. Though they were run by Jews, meat markets were a necessity. It was unlikely the Nazis could find experienced licensed butchers like my grandfather, Uncle Fritz, and Tante Anna.

When Uncle Fritz went home that evening, he found Mädi sitting in the living room, dressed up, with silk stockings and high-heeled shoes, ready to go to work at her nightclub. She was waiting for him.

"Fritz," Mädi said, "I want you to move out as soon as possible. I cannot continue living with you. Besides your being a Jew, I have no feelings for you anymore."

"Mädi, what are you saying? I love you. Don't you love me anymore? You know it is imperative that I leave Vienna. I want you to go with me. We'll go to England, or anywhere you want to go," said Uncle Fritz.

"I am not leaving Vienna. There is nothing more to be said," replied Mädi. "Please pack your things and leave. I have contacted my lawyer. He has already started divorce proceedings.

"Fritz, I am afraid of what the Nazis will do to us, you and me, if they find out that I am married to a Jew. My lawyer told me that in Germany, there is a law that prevents sexual relationships between Aryans and Jews. He said the law even includes kissing. And a Jewish man is forbidden to stare at an Aryan woman. People have gone to prison for breaking that law."

Uncle Fritz was beside himself. He sat down and stared out the window. He sat for several minutes in silence. His droopy eyes, under his heavy eyebrows, had tears in them. He twirled his mustache with a finger. Mädi got up off her chair, went into their bedroom, and closed the door behind her.

A few minutes later, she came out, and Uncle Fritz was gone. He went straight to his parents' home.

Grossmutter Emma.

Uncle Fritz, my mother, and Grandfather Jakob.

Ernie, center, going to school in Vienna with friends.

VIENNA: SEPTEMBER 16, 1938

The Hackers, Uncle Heinrich, Tante Grete, and cousin Gerti left Vienna for Koprivnica with their Yugoslav passports, carrying just a few suitcases.

DACHAU: SEPTEMBER 17, 1938

A bugle sounded through the loudspeakers mounted on the roofs of the barracks. It was Saturday, 4:00 a.m. The workday had begun for the thousands of prisoners. Following the blare of the bugle, the prisoners heard an announcement.

"Achtung, the following prisoners report to the Appelplatz (Assembly Square) in your civilian clothing. Bring all your personal belongings."

Only two names were called. One was my father's.

MUNICH: OCTOBER 1, 1938

Hitler announced his intention to annex the Sudetenland to Germany. British Prime Minister Neville Chamberlain responded by declaring that Czechoslovakia was not one of the "great issues," which justified war, but simply "a quarrel in a far-away country between people of whom we know nothing about." France then said it agreed the German-speaking part of Czechoslovakia, the Sudetenland, should be given to Germany.

"I believe it is peace for our time," Chamberlain said to a cheering crowd in England.

Representatives of Great Britain, France, Italy, and Germany determined the location of the new borders between Czechoslovakia and Germany and said the Czechs were free to fight if they wished but would get no support from any of their nations.

Hitler then announced his one-thousand-year plan to change the German Reich into a superpower. He promised Chamberlain that this was the "last problem to be solved," and Chamberlain responded by saying Hitler was "a man who can be relied upon." Then Chamberlain persuaded the Czechoslovak government to relinquish the Sudetenland freely. The Nazis marched into the Sudetenland unopposed.

Mass arrests of non-German-speaking Czechs and political opponents began. Many escaped from the Sudetenland. Znojmo, home of the Lampls, was in the Sudetenland. The Lampls talked about leaving Znojmo but didn't because Grandmother Sara was now nearly eighty.

VIENNA: OCTOBER 1, 1938

Just short of six months from the day my father was arrested, my mother got a letter saying he had been released from Dachau on September 17 and would arrive at the Gestapo headquarters in Vienna that day, October 1. He could be picked up after noon. She was shocked. She showed my grandparents the letter and told me my father was coming home.

Then she sat down in an attempt to relax. Could this really be true? Was my father really in Vienna? Her heart was pounding but she quickly regained her composure and called Johann at his home.

"Herr Robert is in Vienna. He is free," she said to Johann. "Can you take me to the Gestapo building to pick him up?"

Ten minutes later, Johann picked her up in the Erskine and drove her to Gestapo headquarters, the same place my father was taken on April 5. It was 3:00 p.m. Hanging from what was the old Metropol Hotel, was a huge swastika flag. Two uniformed guards were stationed at the entrance. Johann parked the car on the Salztorgasse at the rear of the hotel, near the door my father had entered as a prisoner.

My mother got out of the car, walked to the front, and went in the main door. She presented her letter to an SS guard seated at a desk in the lobby. She was told to wait in the reception room. She sat down, her mind racing with excitement. Was Robert really here?

Thirty minutes went by before the door opened. My father walked in, took two steps, and stopped. He looked at my mother, and then walked across the room. My mother stood up.

My father was wearing the same clothes he had on the day he was taken from his office, but he had no belt or tie. They had been taken from him when he was arrested. His shirt was open at the collar.

"Servus, Mutsch," my mother whispered.

"Servus, Mutsch," said my father.

They put their arms around each other and stood quiet for a few minutes. Then, my mother, placing her hands on his shoulders, turned my father toward the door.

"We must go," she said softly. She took his arm and led him out of the room into the lobby.

As they approached the SS officer at the desk, he looked up at them. "You are lucky to be getting out of here. You Jews should all be locked up for good." My parents said nothing. The Nazi gave my mother a sealed envelope. It was addressed to Hedwig Weiss. She took it and put it in her handbag without opening it, anxious to leave the building.

They walked out and went around the corner where Johann was standing next to the Erskine. He opened the rear door, and my mother got in first, followed by my father. Johann closed the door and got behind the wheel.

"Where are we going?" my father asked quietly.

"We are going to the Kaunitzgasse," my mother replied. "Vater and Mutter are waiting for us. Pommy and Peter are there. We are going to celebrate and have a good meal." She was holding his hand tightly.

My father looked healthy, though he had lost weight and his head was bald. He had been nearly bald for many years and the little hair he had left was always combed neatly over his bald spot. Those hairs were gone, cut off by a concentration camp barber.

Johann drove slower than usual. He wanted to avoid any traffic violations. My parents held tightly to each other. My father was free, thanks to my mother. Looking around the car he suddenly realized they were in his Erskine. It occurred to him that he had never sat in the back seat of his car, and no one else ever drove his car. He wondered if it was still his. The American made Erskine was the best automobile he had ever owned. It had given him immense pleasure, driving through Vienna and on vacations over the winding Alpine mountain roads. The car was a momentary distraction for my father on his first day of freedom after months in Dachau.

"Hedi, why is Johann driving my car?"

"It was confiscated along with the factory," said my mother. "It is a factory car now. Johann is taking care of it very well, as you can see."

Twenty minutes later, they were at my grandparents' house. My mother opened her door, which was next to the sidewalk. Johann got out, opened my father's door and offered to help him.

"Thank you, Johann, I can get out myself. Thank you for everything. How are you and your family?" he asked, stepping on to the street.

"Fine, Herr Weiss, all is in order at home. I bring you regards from some people at the factory," Johann replied, as he shook my father's hand. "Good bye, Herr Weiss. Best wishes."

Johann drove away. My parents went inside, walked up to the second floor to my grandparents' apartment, and rang the doorbell. Grossmutter Emma opened the door. Without a word, she embraced my father, kissing him on the cheek. Grossvater Jakob was behind her. He held out his hand, and when my father took it, he shook it firmly and wouldn't let go. I was standing behind my grandparents. My father picked me up and gave me a kiss.

"Servus, Pommy," he said.

We walked into the bedroom I shared with Peter and my mother. Peter was standing in his crib, holding on to the railing. My father put me down and picked up Peter, who was now eight months old. He hugged and kissed him, and at that point, began to cry. My mother gently took Peter from him.

It had been almost six months since I had seen my father, and I never really knew where he was or why he was away. Now, it didn't matter. I was just very happy to see him.

When my father regained his composure, we all went into the living room and sat down. Peter was on my mother's lap; I sat next to my father. Then Grossmutter made an announcement.

"I have the best Wienerschnitzel ready, with cucumber salad and roasted potatoes. Vater has his favorite Gumpolkskirchner wine on ice. The table is ready, so let's sit down and celebrate."

Although most food was rationed in Vienna, my grandfather, through his butcher shop, had many connections at the central market place and could still purchase food others could not. This would be a feast for my father. His meals for months had been enough to keep him in healthy, but every day was the same, potato soup, black coffee, and stale bread. About once a week, he got vegetable soup with bits of meat in it.

We sat down in the dining room, with me between my parents, and Peter in a high chair on the other side of my father. Grossmutter first served a Viennese specialty Leberknödelsuppe (liver dumpling soup). We picked up our spoons and for a minute, no one spoke. It was strange to have my father back at our dinner table.

"Robert," Grossvater broke the silence, "we're so happy to see you and have you home with us. Here's to you."

He raised his wine glass, but he was too emotional to continue. I raised my water glass, and the adults raised their glasses and drank their wine. The conversation that followed was mostly about the food. Before the schnitzel was served, my mother excused herself, remembering the envelope the SS guard had given her several hours before. She went into the foyer and quickly read it, then returned to the table.

"Robert," she said, "we must leave tomorrow."

We were all surprised. She told us about the letter she had just read. The Gestapo had ordered us to leave within twenty-four hours. She passed the letter around the table.

"I almost forgot about it. I opened it when I left the table. The letter says we can each take only ten Reichsmark with us. We will go tomorrow to Koprivnica to join Papá."

My father was not surprised. In her letters he received in Dachau, she told him his parents were already in Koprivnica, and that we had Yugoslav passports.

"We can pack tonight. We must call Johann and ask him for a ride to the train station. It's good it's a Sunday. He will not be at the factory. There is a midmorning train to Koprivnica."

She waited for a response, but my father sat motionless and said nothing. In the past, he was in control of his business, our travel arrangements, our finances, and most everything else. Now my mother was taking charge, arranging everything. At this moment, he was drained of emotion, trying to digest how his world had changed. Where were we going with our lives?

My grandfather broke the silence. "What was it like in Dachau?" he asked. My father didn't answer.

"Don't you want to tell us about it?" asked my mother.

Again, my father didn't answer. He shook his head no.

The schnitzels were crisp on the outside and tender inside. They were larger than the plates they were served on. For dessert, Grossmutter served Palatschinken, a crepe with chocolate sauce, and whipped cream, and nuts on top. My father relished every bite. The table conversation was still mostly about the food. It was awkward for all of us.

After dinner, my mother changed Peter's diaper and put him to bed. I sat with my father for a while, and then they sent me to bed. I started the night in the bed I had shared with my mother since we moved into my grandparents' house. When my parents were ready for bed, they carried me into the living room to the sofa. I fell back to sleep but vaguely remember hearing strange sounds coming from my parents' room.

Chapter 10

VIENNA: OCTOBER 2, 1938

I woke up to the smell of coffee. My mother told me to get dressed. We had breakfast, and then the doorbell rang. It was Johann. My parents had ready three suitcases and Peter's stroller. They had our passports, stamped with exit visas, and the letter from the Gestapo ordering us out of Austria. They carried the exact amount of money allowed in the letter, ten Reichsmark per person.

My grandparents went with us to the car. There was not enough room for them to go to the train station, so we kissed and hugged and said good-bye on the sidewalk. My grandparents wished us good luck.

"Vater, please take care of the three crates," said my mother.

"We need them sent to Koprivnica. We will need our winter clothes and I will have to sell my jewelry. We will need the money to live on."

"Hedi, I will take care of it," said my grandfather.

Johann put our suitcases and Peter's stroller in the trunk. We got in the car and drove off. My father made small talk with Johann about the factory, but all the time he was looking at the Nazi flags on most buildings, and the civilians walking the streets wearing swastika armbands. He seemed more relaxed than the night before. I was glad he was finally talking.

Vienna was not the same. My father thought back to Christmas, when every year he drove through the Inner Stadt with me in the back seat, handing out cigarette packages to traffic policemen. "Guten Abend, Herr Weiss (Good evening, Mr. Weiss)," they would say. "Danke Schön (thank you)," my father would say, and then he would drive to the next intersection and give out more cigarettes. Those days were gone forever, and life for us would be very different.

"Johann," he said, "I want to thank you for what you did for Frau Hedi and my children while I was gone. I know you drove them to many places, and that was dangerous for you."

"Herr Robert, we do not all agree with the Nazis," said Johann, looking in the rearview mirror to the back seat. "Though we live in dangerous times, you must know that I will always be loyal to you and your father. I appreciate everything you have done for me. You are a good man and were always kind to your workers. Everyone in your factory liked working for you. I hope someday to see you again."

My father sat quietly for the rest of the ride. He was thinking about the last six months of his life. Johann, and all the others he saw on the streets that day, had no idea how he'd been humiliated. Jews, men like himself, had been beaten, insulted, and made to sleep on straw mattresses. He'd been forced to do hard labor, eighteen hours a day. Did any of them know how many were killed in Dachau, or how many committed suicide?

Johann found a parking space at the Südbahnhoff, and we got out of the car. We said good-bye, and my father watched Johann drive off in his Erskine. He had tears in his eyes. We were standing in front of the railroad station, where we had begun many vacations. Now, we were being evicted from our own country. We were like strangers in a foreign land. Our only belongings were three suitcases and a stroller.

Train 45A through Hungary to Zagreb, Yugoslavia, via Koprivnica, was scheduled to depart at 11:00 a.m. from track 12.

My mother pushed the stroller. I carried the smallest suitcase, and my father carried the other two. We looked like everyone else at the station, my father in a suit and tie, and my mother in a long brown skirt and silk blouse. I had on short pants with knee socks, and a coat and a cap, and Peter was dressed in a blue one-piece outfit, knitted by our grandmother. Once we had our tickets we went directly to track 12, where there was a control station with two SS officers inspecting identification papers and passports.

My mother quickly took Peter out of his stroller and took the lead. I followed her, pushing the stroller which now carried my small suitcase. My father was behind me. An SS officer asked for documents. My mother gave him the letter she was given at Gestapo headquarters, and showed him our passports.

We were told to proceed. The car next to us was second-class seating. We immediately got aboard, found an empty compartment, and sat down. Soon, we were joined by a civilian couple and one German soldier. They paid no attention to us.

Grossmutter Emma had prepared ham sandwiches for us, just as she had for Uncle Gustl when he left Vienna for Paris. Once the train left the station, we began to relax. The conductor took our tickets and a vendor came through the train with a cart. My father purchased drinks and pastries to have with our sandwiches. The trip to Koprivnica would take four hours, with several stops along the way.

Leaving Vienna was difficult for both my parents. They loved the city they'd grown up in. But even harder for them was what Adolf Hitler had done to us and the rest of the Jews in Austria and Germany. That so many Jews were suffering was impossible to comprehend.

Our train took us through the border town of Eisenstadt into Hungary, where our passports were again examined by Nazi guards. My parents were apprehensive because we did not speak Croatian and we were carrying Yugoslav passports. But the border guards said nothing, and we continued through Hungary into Yugoslavia. When we crossed that border, my father took my mother's hand, and mine, and held tight. Peter was on my mother's lap. Yugoslavia had no affiliation with Austria or Germany and we were free of Nazis. We expected Grosspapá and Grossmamá to be waiting for us at the railroad station in Koprivnica.

The train was on time; it was the middle of the afternoon. I was sitting next to the window. As we came to a stop, I saw Grosspapá and Grossmamá, who was waving a white handkerchief, on the platform. I lowered the window and waved back with my handkerchief.

"Papa, there are Grosspapá and Grossmamá."

My father stuck his head out the window and waved to his parents. He had not seen them since April. We kept waving until my mother told us to stop. It was time to get off the train.

My father and I picked up our suitcases, and my mother put Peter in his stroller. The conductor helped her get off. My grandparents greeted us with hugs. My grandfather put his arm around my father.

"Robert, it's so good to see you. You look well."

Grossmamá approached my father. "Robert," she said as she held my father's hands in hers, "how are you?"

"I'm fine, Mamá. I am feeling good. I'll tell you about everything soon."

"Papá, you also are looking well," said my father. He was holding back tears. "You saved our lives. Without the Yugoslav passports, we would never have been able to escape, and I would still be in Dachau."

My grandfather looked into my father's eyes.

"Our family has always taken care of each other. We will continue to do that here. We had a wonderful life in Vienna, and I hope these times will end soon, and we can all go home."

My mother hugged and kissed my grandparents, and they hugged and kissed Peter and me. Then my grandfather held my mother's hand and said, "Hedi, your courage made it possible for your husband and children to be here safe with us. You have been strong and very brave."

To my surprise, Grosspapá had arranged for a horse-drawn carriage to take us from the train station. The six of us sat on the benches, and our luggage was stowed under the seats. I had ridden in a horse-drawn carriage on a few special occasions in Vienna. Called Fiakers, they were a fashionable alternative to a taxi or tram and had leather-upholstered benches facing one another. The carriage we were riding in now was not as grand.

My grandparents' home was a small apartment on Koprivnica's Florijanska Ulica (street) on the opposite side of Koprivnica from the train station. They told us they had arranged for us to live with a family on a farm about a half mile out of town for a small amount of room and board. The weather was sunny and warm for an October afternoon. We rode through the middle of the town on paved streets, but once we got to the other side there was only a dirt road with moats on both sides. Small bridges, built with four foot culverts, crossed the moats so people could get to their houses or farm buildings.

The trip took about forty five minutes, and during that time, I saw no Nazis, anywhere. That was a relief I thought . . . we were safe now.

My grandparents arrived in this small farming town of about twelve hundred people a month before. Koprivnica is near the Hungarian border in northern Croatia, which was then a province of Yugoslavia. Its history goes back to the year 1356. It was well known for growing fruits and vegetables, and its livestock.

Eventually, the two horses pulled our carriage over a culvert and onto a narrow driveway that led us to a large house. The owners, Jan and Maria Jasovic and their daughters, Paula, twelve, and Ency, sixteen, were waiting to greet us. Grosspapá got off first, said hello to the Jasovic family, and then introduced us. Grosspapá spoke Croatian. He thanked them for letting us live with them and said good-bye. My grandparents hugged us good-bye and left to go to their apartment.

As the carriage went down the driveway, I looked around in amazement. Tall trees and lots of grass surrounded a very big house. In the distance, I saw huge fields, cows grazing, sheep and goats inside a fence, and hundreds of chickens. There was a barn a few hundred feet from the house. It was bigger than any barn I had ever seen.

The Jasovics invited us in. Their living room was different from ours in Vienna. The floor and the walls were dark wood. The ceiling had wooden beams and wooden boards. Nothing was painted. There were a few scatter rugs on the floor. The doors had very large keyholes and black iron hinges. The wooden tables and chairs were the same color as the walls, floor, and ceiling. There were dim light bulbs hanging on wires from the ceilings. It was very dark.

"Mutti, I need to go," I said after a few minutes.

"Frau Jasovic," my mother said in German, "could you show my son the toilet?"

"Ja natürlich (Yes of course)," said Frau Jasovic, also in German. She took my hand and took me out through the door we had just entered. Once outside, she let go of my hand, and I followed her. We walked to the back of the house, and she opened the door to a small shack. She motioned for me to go in and went back to the house. I closed the door and looked around. I was in my first outhouse. A small window let in some light and allowed the air to circulate, but it didn't smell very good. I did what I had to do, using pieces of newspaper, which were hanging on a nail next to me. I went outside and looked around for water to wash my hands, but there wasn't any.

As I headed back to the house, I saw a stone wall in the shape of a circle, about six feet in diameter and three feet high. It had a wooden arch and a pulley with a thick rope attached to it. A pail was attached to the rope. I looked over and saw a deep hole with water at the bottom. I had never seen a well before either. This was our new water supply for washing and cooking. Next to the well was a log about six feet long, carved into a trough and full of water. I assumed it was for washing, so I rinsed my hands and dried them with my handkerchief.

I went back to the house. Frau Jasovic took us to our rooms, which were on the second floor. My parents' room had two single beds, separated by a night table, and a crib for my brother. I had my own very small room. Each bedroom had a basin of water and a large pitcher with drinking glasses. There were towels hanging on wooden racks. The beds had straw mattresses, rough tan-colored sheets, and woolen blankets. There was a pot underneath my bed. My mother told me what it was for, and to use it in the night if I had to.

We unpacked and went downstairs to the living room. In the next room, the dining table was set for dinner. It was 5:30 p.m. It had been a long day, and we were hungry.

We sat down with the four Jasovics. Frau Jasovic had brought her children's high chair down from the attic for Peter. I sat between my parents. Ency, the oldest daughter, brought a pot of soup to the table, and Frau Jasovic filled a bowl for everyone. There was an enormous loaf of bread on a wooden board, along with a large bread knife. Another plate held a massive piece of butter. There were two pitchers of red wine and another of milk. But there were no wine glasses. We all drank out of milk glasses.

We waited for Frau Jasovic to begin eating. The vegetable soup was thick and tasty. My mother mashed up Peter's soup and filled his bottle with some of the milk. The main course was roast lamb, and for dessert Frau Jasovic had made a rice pudding with raisins. After dinner, my mother and I helped the Jasovics with the dishes. Then we went into the living room, and Herr Jasovic turned his radio to a classical music station. There was little conversation because only Frau Jasovic spoke German, and we soon went to bed.

Roosters woke us early in the morning. It was about 6:00 a.m., and the sun was starting to come up. I got out of bed and looked out my window. The house was surrounded by acres of cornfields, as far as I could see. Some of the fields had full corn stalks, and others had stalks that had been cut down to about four inches.

I put on the clothes I'd worn the day before and brushed my teeth in the basin. I didn't know what to do with the dirty water, so I left it there and went downstairs to the kitchen. My parents and Peter were still sleeping.

"Good morning, Pommy," said Frau Jasovic. "Did you sleep well?"

"Yes, thank you, but I have to go outside. I'll be right back." I went straight to the outhouse. Then I washed my hands and looked into the pig pen, and at the cows in the field next to them. When I got back to the house, my mother was in the kitchen, and the dining table was set for breakfast. Frau Jasovic was frying bacon and making scrambled eggs. My mother was taking bread and butter, marmalade, and an assortment of cheeses and cold cuts to the table.

VIENNA: OCTOBER 6, 1938

Uncle Fritz had been living in his old room at his parents' house for six weeks. Just a few days after we left for Koprivnica, Mädi had served him with divorce papers. In the papers, she claimed she had had not known of the difference in race between Uncle Fritz and her. She said Uncle Fritz had not told her he was Jewish; therefore, she deserved an immediate divorce.

KOPRIVNICA: OCTOBER 29, 1938

My cousin Edith, Uncle Otto and Tante Frieda, who had moved to Koprivnica two months earlier, lived near us on another farm. So did my uncle Heinrich, Tante Grete, and my cousin Gerti. That day, Edith and Gerti rode their bikes to play with me. Even though Edith was fourteen, Gerti was ten, and I was seven, we were good friends. We saw each other more now than we ever had in Vienna. We did not play with the local children because none of us spoke Croatian, and none of them spoke German, so we often spent afternoons together playing cards or hiking around the farms. We loved petting the goats and sheep since none of us had pets in Vienna.

That afternoon, a huge hog had been slaughtered. We discovered it hanging over a tree branch, upside down with its hind legs tied with a thick rope. The hog had been cut open from neck to tail and its organs were exposed. Blood was seeping out and it had a terrible odor. We stood nearly paralyzed by the sight, and the stench. The hog was going to provide all of us in the Jasovic house with bacon, ham, and sausages for a long time. The farm also produced almost all the Jasovics' milk, cheese, vegetables, wheat for bread, and the hay for their livestock.

VIENNA: OCTOBER 14, 1938

Bruno, Lisl's boyfriend, received a phone call from the Betar headquarters, a Zionist youth movement founded in 1923, which arranged for groups of young Jews to move to Palestine. Bruno, a member of Betar, had applied to go to Palestine with one of the groups. He was told he and nine other teenagers had been accepted and would leave for Palestine as soon as arrangements could be made.

PARIS: NOVEMBER 9, 1938

Uncle Gustl had been in Paris almost five months. His shoe repair business was doing well, and he was becoming fluent in French. He usually had his radio on to keep him company. On this Wednesday morning, his music was interrupted with a news bulletin that said a Jew in Paris had assassinated a German Embassy official.

The newscaster reported that Herschel Grynszpan, age seventeen, who was living with an uncle, had received news that his family had been expelled from Germany. Grynszpan was so upset by the news that he went to the German

Embassy in Paris to assassinate the ambassador. The ambassador was not in the embassy, so he shot another official instead. Uncle Gustl thought this had to be the first attack on a Nazi by a Jew.

He left his shop and went to a local bar to listen to what the Parisians had to say. It was before lunchtime, the bar had no radio, and it seemed no one there had heard about the assassination. But the story of the assassination was in the afternoon newspapers, and soon was all over Germany and Austria.

On that day and the next, rampaging mobs throughout Germany and Austria attacked Jews in the streets and threw rocks through their windows. More than ninety Jews were killed and hundreds more injured. At least a thousand synagogues were burned, and almost seventy five hundred Jewish businesses were destroyed. Jewish cemeteries and schools were vandalized. Thirty thousand Jews were arrested.

The assassination in Paris had given the Nazis the excuse they needed to launch a pogrom, a killing spree, and claimed Grynszpan's attack was a conspiracy by the International Jewry against Germany. The pogrom was called Kristallnacht (the Night of Broken Glass).

Nazi officials said Kristallnacht was a spontaneous attack carried out by furious German citizens. Hitler said future outbursts would not be organized by the Nazi Party, but spontaneous pogroms would not be discouraged.

VIENNA: NOVEMBER 10, 1938

Uncle Heinrich was at work that Thursday morning in his butcher shop, which was downstairs from his apartment. He closed the shop for an hour to go upstairs for lunch. He sat down and told Tante Gisela and Lisl about Kristallnacht. Everyone who'd come into the shop that morning was talking about it.

At that moment, they heard the screech of tires on the street below, the Schönbrunnerstrasse. They left the table and through the window saw six German soldiers and an officer, wearing helmets and carrying weapons, jump out of a truck and run toward the butcher shop. The entrance to the apartment building was next door to the shop. Seconds later there was a loud knock on their door.

"Aufmachen (Open), Wertheim?" yelled a soldier.

"Yes," answered Uncle Heinrich.

"Open the door! I have papers here for your arrest. You are being placed in protective custody. Open the door."

Uncle Heinrich opened the door, and soldiers burst in. Without another word, they grabbed each of the Wertheims by the arm and forced them down the stairs. Uncle Heinrich, Tante Gisela, and sixteen-year-old Lisl were loaded onto the truck and told to sit on the wooden benches. They were driven to a small neighborhood police station, which was used for misdemeanors and traffic violations, and led inside. They were among dozens of Jews who had been taken from homes and businesses in their neighborhood that morning.

All were asked just one question: "Are you a Jew?" If the answer was yes, they were arrested.

These men, women, and children had no idea what was to become of them, just as my father did not know his fate when he was taken to Gestapo headquarters in April.

Later that night, women and children, including Tante Gisela and Lisl, were released without explanation. Uncle Heinrich remained in jail.

KOPRIVNICA: NOVEMBER 11, 1938

It was my parents' tenth wedding anniversary, the first anniversary they did not celebrate.

BERLIN: NOVEMBER 11, 1938

The Nazi minister of the interior in Berlin issued regulations against Jews possessing weapons. The new law prohibited Jews from "acquiring, possessing, and carrying firearms and ammunition, as well as truncheons or stabbing weapons." Jews owning weapons and ammunition were to turn them over to the local police.

BERLIN: NOVEMBER 12, 1938

A meeting of the top Nazi leadership was held to assess the damage done during Kristallnacht. It was decided that German and Austrian Jews were responsible for the events of the last three days and that new laws were needed to remove Jews from the German economy.

After the meeting, Adolf Hitler reported the following:

> Since the problem is mainly an economic one, it is from the economic angle that it will have to be tackled. I am the final authority for coordinating the German economy. If a Jewish shop is destroyed, if goods are thrown into the street, the insurance

companies will pay for damages. We will confiscate that money.
Future attacks will be directed so as not to hurt us economically.

He said German and Austrian Jews would be fined a billion Reichsmark for the slaying of the embassy official; and the six million Reichsmark the insurance companies were paying to Jews for broken windows would be turned over to the state treasury.

Kristallnacht was a crucial turning point in the Nazi policy regarding Jews. Many more antisemitic laws were passed with the intention of aryanizing the entire German population. And during the next several months, Jews were required to turn over all precious metals to the government; pensions for Jews in civil service jobs were reduced; and Jewish-owned bonds, stocks, jewelry, and artworks had to be willed only to the Reich. Jews were forbidden ownership of carrier pigeons; drivers' licenses were suspended; and their radios were confiscated. A curfew was imposed to keep Jews off the streets between 9:00 p.m. and 5:00 a.m. during the summer, and 8:00 p.m. 6:00 a.m. in the winter. Laws that had previously protected tenants were made non-applicable to those who were Jewish.

KOPRIVNICA: NOVEMBER 12, 1938

Five weeks on a farm was too long for my parents. My father was bored. He had no work, and there wasn't anything about farm life that interested him. He had never spent so much time doing nothing. He also wanted me to be in school.

He asked Grosspapá to lend him money so we could move into a hotel in Koprivnica and we moved into its only hotel. We had two rooms with a door between them, a toilet, and running water. Pulling a chain to flush the toilet was a luxury after using an outhouse for five weeks. Two weeks later, I started second grade. Not knowing the Croatian language turned out to be an advantage. My teacher, a woman, had sympathy for me because I was a refugee, and since I didn't understand a single word she said, she left me alone. I sat through all her classes, daydreaming. When other students didn't know the answers to her questions, or misbehaved, my teacher called them to the front of the class and told them to hold out their hands, palms up. Then she whacked them with a stick. I was never punished by her, but I was often teased, and chased, by other boys on the way home from school.

Cousins Edith and Gerti were happy we had moved into town. They loved coming to visit and did so frequently on their bicycles. My cousins and I got friendly with the carriage driver who took us from the train station the day we arrived in Koprivnica. The driver sometimes took us with him to pick up passengers on incoming trains. One morning, just Gerti and I rode to the station with our new friend. When we got there, he said we could walk around for a while, and he would look for us when he was ready to return to town.

The train arrived, made its stop, and after five minutes left. No one got off, so it was only Gerti and me going back to town with the driver. On the way back, I needed a toilet but was too shy to ask the driver to stop. I wet my Lederhosen. The leather pants already had stains from previous accidents. I hoped I didn't stain the seats of the carriage. My mother knew about the accidents but told me not to worry about it. She told me we had been under a lot of stress and it would stop. Eventually it did.

Koprivnica was a haven for the Weiss and Hacker families as well as other Jewish refugees. It had a longtime small Jewish community, and its members helped refugees who came there from Austria find housing and food. But there was no work available, so most refugees spent long days walking around the streets talking with other refugees.

We often went to Grosspapá's apartment where the conversation among the adults was usually about European politics and leaving Koprivnica. We had only a minimal amount of money from Grosspapá, and my mother started to think about the box containing her jewelry, which was still in Vienna. She had to get the crates sent to Koprivnica, but Grossvater had told her in his letters he could not go to the warehouse because it had been seized by the Nazis.

In spite of the Nazi annexation of Austria, the mail was getting through as always, and Uncle Heinrich received his first letter from his son in Switzerland. Hansi told him about the Red Cross Kindertransport (Children's Transports) of thousands of Jewish children from Austria and Germany to England. Hansi urged his parents to find a way to get Gerti on one of those transports. He thought maybe it could be arranged through the Jewish agency in Zagreb.

VIENNA: NOVEMBER 17, 1938

Uncle Heinrich Wertheim, Lisl's father, was released from prison after only a week. No explanation was given. He went home to Tante Gisela and Lisl.

VIENNA: DECEMBER 3, 1938

Uncle Fritz received the following document in the mail:

IN THE NAME OF THE PROVINCIAL COURT

The Provincial Court of Vienna has given the following Judgment in the proceedings by Josefa Jellinek, Soubrette, of 20 Alser Strasse, Vienna IX, Petitioner, versus Fritz Jellinek, Master Butcher, of 16 Kaunitzgasse, Vienna VI, Respondent, in the matter of Divorce:

The civil marriage between Fritz Jellinek and Josefa nee Fahringer, which took place on the 10th AUGUST 1935 before the Registrar in Vienna (Marriage Register: Volume 46, page 162, Registration No. 325, is annulled.

The marriage is dissolved when the present Judgment becomes final.

The Grounds of the Decision:

On the basis of the credible statements by both parties, the Court considers it to have been proved that at the time of the marriage the Petitioner actually had no knowledge of the essence of the difference in race. She was brought up in a fifty percent non-German family, when she joined a theatrical company as a Soubrette, was only in Germany until 1930, and afterwards worked in Italy and Austria. It is quite credible that in that way, and especially in view of the fact that the employer was non-Aryan, no one ever drew her attention to the implications of the difference in race.

Accordingly, even disregarding the fundamental conceptions of the law for the protection of German blood and German honor, this would appear to be an exceptional case, such as that which the Supreme Court had in mind in the decision first cited above.

The annulment of the marriage therefore stands. No claim has been made for costs.

The Provincial Court for Civil Matters, Section 13.

Dr. Klamfi, The Chief Registrar, The Provisional Court for Civil Matters, Vienna, 3rd December 1938

VIENNA: DECEMBER 9, 1938

Grossvater got a phone call from his friend, a policeman, telling him Uncle Heinrich had again been arrested. Grossmutter immediately telephoned a friend who had political influence. To gain Uncle Heinrich's release, my grandfather made a deal to give up the Wertheim's large and beautiful apartment to a high-ranking SS officer who had arrested him. After a week in the Rossauer Lände Prison, Uncle Heinrich was again released. He went home by streetcar and surprised Tante Gisela and Lisl. The Wertheims immediately moved out of their apartment and moved in with friends in the same building, leaving all their belongings behind.

The Wertheims began to search for a way to get out of Vienna. They found out that the IKG was issuing exit permits to China, which was the only country in the world that would take European refugees. Uncle Heinrich bought three tickets for passage on a ship that would take them to Shanghai from either Genoa or Naples, Italy.

Lisl refused to go. She wanted no part of China. She was in love with Bruno and was determined to follow him to Palestine. She and her parents argued for days about this, until Grossvater offered to mediate the family dispute. He asked Lisl's parents to come to his home to talk about it. They talked for three hours. The Wertheims were adamant that they would not leave Vienna without their sixteen-year-old daughter and they would not agree to let her undertake an illegal, risky, and lengthy trip to Palestine. Grossvater then proposed that Lisl move in with my grandparents when her parents left for China.

"You must leave," he said. "Your daughter is stubborn and in love. Let her stay with us until we find her a safe trip to Palestine."

The Wertheims agreed, reluctantly. So did Lisl, happily.

Chapter 11

BERLIN: JANUARY 1, 1939

German and Austrian Jews were ordered to take Jewish middle names if their first names were Aryan. They were told they had to use either Israel or Sara. My grandfather remained Jakob Jellinek, and my grandmother became Emma Sara Jellinek. Jakob was a recognized Jewish name; Emma was not.

VIENNA: TUESDAY, FEBRUARY 7, 1939

Tante Gisela answered the telephone. It was the IKG saying their travel documents to Shanghai were ready. Within half an hour, Uncle Heinrich picked up exit visas for Austria, entry visas for Italy, and tickets to board the *SS Conte Biancomano* in Genoa. Their Austrian passports were valid. The ship would depart on February 17. They had only ten days to get to Genoa.

Reality set in. The Wertheims were on their way to China. They sat in their friends' living room, and talked about Lisl. She still refused to go to China, and her boyfriend, Bruno, had not left for Palestine.

They talked about what to pack. They decided they would take as many valuables as possible; jewelry, lace, small crystal items, and anything else that could eventually be sold. That afternoon, Uncle Heinrich went to the Südbahnhof to buy two train tickets to Genoa for the next day. It would take them two full days and nights to get to there, and then they would spend five nights in Genoa before boarding the ship. Then it would be four weeks by sea to Shanghai. Since Lisl was not coming with them, their last evening was spent packing, saying good-bye, and wondering what they would do when they got to China. The next morning, Lisl saw her parents off at the Südbahnhof. After they boarded the train, Lisl went to live with my grandparents.

The train ride took them through the Brenner Pass into Italy to Milan and then to Genoa. The *SS Conte Biancomano* was tied up in Genoa ready to leave for Shanghai. Tante Gisela and Uncle Heinrich spent their last days in Europe shopping for incidentals they would need during the next four weeks.

Shanghai was virtually on the other side world. In 1938, it was unheard of for a European to travel to the Orient. A year before, in 1937, the Japanese had won the Sino-Japanese War, a war between China and Japan. Shanghai, known as The International Foreign Settlement, became a city divided into sectors. The British, French, and Japanese each administered one of three sections in the settlement.

Jewish refugees made their homes in Hongkou, the Japanese sector. Hongkou was a ghetto, the poorest and most crowded area of the city, an area of approximately one square mile. About twenty thousand Jewish refugees moved there during World War II, having fled from Nazi Germany, Austria, Poland, and Lithuania. Chinese and Russian refugees also lived in the ghetto. The Wertheims knew all this before they boarded the *SS Conte Biancomano*.

Four weeks later, with many rough days on the sea, they were greeted by Japanese immigration officials and processed as new refugees. The Wertheims then met with other Austrians, who were already settled, and told how to go about selling valuables so they could pay for an apartment. Uncle Heinrich rented a butcher shop in Shanghai's central market. He set up shop, with Tante Gisela working alongside him as she had in Vienna. They met other Jews at the Ohel Moishe Synagogue, which had been in existence for many years before the new refugees arrived.

The climate in Shanghai was a new experience for the Europeans. The winters were very cold and damp, with lots of rain. The summers had oppressive humidity with temperatures of more than one hundred degrees in the shade. People stayed inside between noon and 2:00 p.m. Sanitary conditions were also different from Vienna. Water had to boil for five minutes before it was drinkable. Fruits and vegetables, when they could get them, had to be cooked thoroughly. At least three times a year, Tante Gisela and Uncle Heinrich had to be inoculated against tropical diseases they'd never heard of. Their new life in China was strange and their future unpredictable. They missed Lisl and worried about her constantly.

VIENNA: FEBRUARY 11, 1939

Lisl had been with my grandparents only four days, and Bruno was leaving for Palestine that afternoon. She said good-bye to him at the Südbahnhoff.

KOPRIVNICA: FEBRUARY 25, 1939

My mother and her parents exchanged letters frequently, and she called them when she could. She kept insisting they leave Vienna. She also needed her three crates shipped to Koprivnica. She went to the post office and placed a call.

"Vati, Servus," she said. "How are you?"

"We're fine, Hedi, and you?"

"We are fine, thank you. Vati, please listen to me. You and Mutti, and Anna and Pepi, are the only ones left in Vienna. Please, all of you must pack and leave the city."

"Hedi, many of our friends are still here. Remember, I am seventy two years old and it isn't so easy," my grandfather replied. "Also, the Nazis seem more relaxed than before. Maybe the novelty of chasing Jews has worn off."

"No, Vati, it is a mistake to think like that," said my mother. "Listen, I am coming to Vienna. With my Yugoslav passport, I will not be bothered. I will buy a train ticket and come next week. I will call when I know what time my train arrives."

"Hedi, are you sure you want to do this? It is dangerous," said Grossvater, though he knew my mother would not change her mind.

"Vati, I have made up my mind. I will let you know in a few days. Someone is waiting for the telephone. Please give Mutti a kiss for me."

"Give my love to everybody, Hedi. I look forward to seeing you soon."

THE TRAIN TO VIENNA: MARCH 4, 1939

My mother had no trouble leaving Yugoslavia, or crossing the Hungarian border into Austria. She spent most of the four-hour trip in the dining car, something she had always enjoyed. She watched the scenery from the moving train and enjoyed a nice lunch with a glass of wine. She had Apfelstrudel for dessert, an indulgence after five months of a provincial life in Koprivnica.

Grossvater Jakob was at the Südbahnhof a few minutes before my mother's train arrived. He was walking toward the end of the track to avoid soldiers and SS on the platform when he saw the train approach. When it stopped, and passengers started to get off, he went back, looking for my mother.

He smiled when he saw her: she was as beautiful as ever. She walked with confidence, shoulders high, looking straight ahead. She was wearing a tailored grey suit and a white blouse with a matching hat sitting slightly slanted on her head. Grossvater had the urge to hurry to greet her, but restrained himself. My mother smiled when she saw her father, but she too did not run. Neither of them wanted to attract attention. Her father was tall and handsome, and he looked distinguished in his black overcoat and hat. She realized how much she had missed her parents.

When my grandfather caught up with her, they kept silent. My grandfather took her small suitcase in one hand and her arm in the other, and they walked to the exit. When they left the station, my mother kissed him on the cheek, and they took a streetcar to the Kaunitzgasse.

"Hedi," my grandfather said, "do you know that Anna, Pepi and Lisl are all staying with us?"

"No, I didn't, since when?"

"Anna and Pepi were evicted. They've been with us for about three weeks. Gisela and Heinrich left for China a month ago, and that's when Lisl moved in with us."

"Things have changed for everyone, haven't they," she said thoughtfully.

My grandfather did not respond.

When they arrived at the Kaunitzgasse apartment, my grandmother was at the door with Tante Anna and Uncle Pepi. It was late afternoon, and Lisl wasn't home.

They had an early supper, talking about my mother's mission in Vienna: to move her parents and her three crates to Koprivnica. But they decided not to make actual plans until the next morning. Then my mother went to bed in the same room that was hers as a child. It had been used by Lisl since her parents left for China. Tante Anna and Uncle Pepi were using her brothers' old room. When Lisl got home later that night, she slept on the sofa.

VIENNA: MARCH 15, 1939

My mother always slept late on Sunday mornings. For her, it was a luxury, a habit she started as a teenager. She woke up at 9:30, took a bath, got dressed, and went into the kitchen. My grandmother was making breakfast, and my grandfather, Uncle Pepi, and Tante Anna were setting the dining room table. Lisl greeted my mother with a big kiss.

"None of us are working anymore, Hedi," said my grandfather, after they were all seated. "My butcher shops are closed. I heard someone one else will reopen them soon."

"When did this happen?" asked my mother.

Tante Anna answered. "Some hooligans came to the Yppengasse shop about fifteen days ago and told everybody to get out, including your father and me."

"When we went to the shop in the marketplace, we found a similar situation. They made Fritz leave," said my grandfather. "There was nothing we could do. We had to do what they said."

"And then we were evicted," said Tante Anna. "Our landlord came to the apartment and told us two SS men wanted our apartment in two days."

"So we packed up and came here," said Uncle Pepi. We had to leave almost everything behind."

"Did they close Gisela and Heinrich's shop also?" asked my mother.

"Yes, that happened last month," said my grandfather.

"Lisl," said my mother, "you didn't go to China with your parents. Does that mean you will go to Palestine? Do you love Bruno that much? You are young, you know."

"Lisl will be on her way soon, we hope," said Tante Anna.

My mother was reluctant to talk about her crates. They didn't seem important right now. The first thing was to get her parents out of Vienna, but what would happen to Tante Anna and Uncle Pepi? Fritz, Lilly, and Herta would be leaving for London soon. There would be no other relatives left in Vienna. And she had to go back to Koprivnica the following day.

"Vati," said my mother, "Papá knows a man at the Yugoslav Consulate quite well. His name is Alexander Stojka. I have his home telephone number. If we can arrange a meeting with him, maybe he can provide visas for you to go to Yugoslavia."

"Hedi, make the phone call. Let's at least find out what he has to say."

Then she brought up the subject of her crates. "Vater, how can I get my crates to Koprivnica?"

"I've been working on that," said my grandfather. "A few weeks after you went to Yugoslavia, my friend, the one who owned the storage facility, was arrested, and the Nazis took it over. Just recently it was bought by a local businessman I've known for many years. He is Aryan but is still a good friend. When I knew you were coming here, I called him and begged him to help us. He said he will."

"When do you think this will happen?"

"I'm not sure," said my grandfather, "but I trust my friend, and I am sure the crates will get to you as soon as possible."

The following day, my grandparents had an appointment at the Yugoslav Consulate, and my mother returned to Koprivnica, hoping her parents would follow her soon. Before she left Vienna, she borrowed money from her father and bought a Hohner accordion and a few other things she could not get in Koprivnica. The Hohner, made in Germany, is considered the best in the world. My mother missed her piano and thought it would be a good substitute, though she'd never played one before.

KOPRIVNICA: APRIL 5, 1939

"Hedi," said my father as we were eating breakfast, "we cannot stay here any longer. We have to move to Zagreb so I can earn some money. I have to get a job, and there is nothing I can do in Koprivnica. We are almost out of funds, and besides, I cannot stand doing nothing all day long."

"What can you do in Zagreb?" asked my mother.

"There are quite a few women's shoe factories there. I can try to reopen my contacts in Italy and buy some shoe models to sell to the Zagreb factories."

"Do you think Sergio is still in Milan?" asked my mother, referring to an old friend, and supplier of shoe models to Eldorado.

"Yes. I already wrote to him to ask if he can help me."

"Fine," said my mother. "Let's go. We only have a few things to pack. I can be ready tomorrow."

"I will call Herman Frankl in Zagreb," said my father, "and ask him to look for an apartment for us." Frankl was a family friend who had moved to Zagreb ten years before. "I'm also going to talk to Papá and Mamá and ask them to come with us."

"I'm not sure how Papá will feel about that," said my mother. "What do you think?"

"I don't know. I'll go see him after breakfast."

Koprivnica was never meant to be a permanent home for us, but my grandparents felt differently. Born there, Grosspapá was at home and felt safe. At seventy, he was not interested in moving to a big city again. The Hackers also had no plans to leave. Gerti was in school. Hansi was safe in Switzerland. Uncle Otto and Tante Frieda had not mentioned any plans to leave.

"Papá," said my father.

"What is it, Robert?"

"Papá, Hedi and I and the boys cannot stay in Koprivnica any longer."

"I understand, Robert. Mamá and I are also concerned about your future, and bringing up children in Koprivnica is not the best thing for them. What is on your mind?"

"Papá, we are going to leave for Zagreb as soon as possible. I have some connections in Zagreb and Milan. I think I can sell Italian shoe models to some of the factories in Zagreb. What do you think?"

"I'm sure you can. Do you remember Adrian Zokovic? He has a factory in Zagreb. I know he will help you," said my grandfather.

"I remember him. I will look him up when we get there."

"Mamá," my father said, turning to my grandmother, "please come with us. We can settle in Zagreb together. Maybe Otto and Grete will come too."

My grandmother turned to Grosspapá and said, "What do you think, Marcus? Should we go to Zagreb too?"

"I'm not sure, Mina. I like it here. We are very comfortable here."

"Robert, why don't you and Hedi go first and see how things go? I will talk to Otto and Grete and tell them what we have discussed."

It was settled. We made plans to take a train to Zagreb, the capital of Yugoslavia's province of Croatia, which had a large Jewish population. Zagreb was the industrial center of Croatia and had many manufacturing industries, including heavy machinery; electrical and metal products; cement; textiles and footwear; and chemicals and pharmaceuticals. The city had main roads and train lines leading to and from Western and Central Europe.

The following morning we began to pack. I was sad to leave Edith and Gerti, but I was also getting used to packing and moving. My father was looking forward to getting back into the shoe business.

ZAGREB: APRIL 17, 1939

Two weeks later, Herman Frankl met us at the Zagreb train station. He drove us to our new home, at Gajdekova Ulica 30, in a suburb of Zagreb. He had arranged for us a furnished apartment on the first floor of a small apartment building. A kitchen door in the rear opened to a small ground-level porch. From the porch, four steps led to a dirt field. I stepped outside.

A dozen boys were kicking a soccer ball. I watched them, imagining an instant group of friends.

"Can I go over there?" I asked my mother. She told me it was okay.

The field was about a hundred feet long. The boys had set up goals on each end, using their jackets as goal posts. As I watched them, one of the boys waved and invited me to join in. This was the first group of kids I had played with since leaving Vienna. In Koprivnica, my only friends were my cousins, and they were girls. By now, I had learned enough Croatian to play soccer with my new friends. Maybe I could score a goal!

I started school a few days later. It was the third time I was in the second grade. My teacher spoke German. I was now a month away from my eighth birthday and happier than I'd been in months.

That same week, my father took a train to Milan, where he'd gone many times on business trips. Sergio Iadicicco welcomed him at his office and sold him two dozen shoe models. A shoe model is a simulated shoe designed to illustrate what a finished shoe will look like. My father went back to Zagreb the next day, expecting the models from Italy would be smart enough for the shoe manufacturers in Zagreb to want them. They turned out to be better than he thought. He sold them in large quantities and quickly became successful. A month later, he traveled to Trieste, Florence, Bologna, and Milan to buy more.

Meanwhile, my mother sent her father our new address in Zagreb and asked him to ship her crates there.

They finally arrived, and we opened them immediately. In the first box, we found my mother's sheet music, our bed linens and clothes, and some dishes, flatware, and kitchen utensils. Next, we unpacked my electric train, the tennis racquets, the film projector, fourteen reels of home movies, and a movie projection screen.

The jewelry box was nailed to the wall of the third crate, and in that crate were more odds and ends and some of Peter's toys. What did not get packed was my mother's collection of German-language classics: Shakespeare, Shaw, Goethe, and others. She told herself it was okay. She had no use for them anymore.

Selling her jewelry was easy. She kept a few items for sentimental reasons. One was a diamond necklace her mother had given her on her twenty-first birthday. The things she sold included gold and precious gems for which she was paid large sums of money. With that money and my father's new income, we were again financially secure.

My mother felt even more secure about family. Her parents were going to leave Vienna. Alexander Stojka at the Yugoslav Consulate in Vienna had provided visas for my grandparents. Our apartment had three bedrooms and could accommodate us all.

Chapter 12

VIENNA: APRIL 17, 1939

The *Neues Wiener Tagblatt* (New Vienna Daily), a morning newspaper, had a story on the front page that particularly interested Tante Anna. It said that Jewish men from Vienna were to be moved to Poland. The newspaper reported that the IKG was facilitating the transport.

The men would be moved to a Judenreservat (Jewish Reservation) in cities and towns, which included Nisko, Opole, Kielca, Modliborzyce, Lagow, Minsk, Riga, and Isbica. The purpose of the move, according to the paper, was to provide a new life for Viennese Jews. The project was called Poland Transport.

Tante Anna called her husband. Uncle Pepi, an accountant in a bank, was one of few Jews in Vienna still working. She told him about the Poland Transport and he hung up and called Grossvater, who then called his friend, the police sergeant.

"Jakob," said the sergeant, "I have not heard about this. I will make a few phone calls and let you know."

KOPRIVNICA: APRIL 18, 1939

Grosspapá asked his daughter, Grete, to come to his house to talk. Uncle Heinrich and cousin Gerti stayed home.

"Grete, please listen to me," began Grosspapá. "Otto tells me he plans to go to Zagreb to join Hedi and Robert. Your mother and I plan to stay here. We're too old to move and all our friends are here. But you, my dear daughter, must go too. There is nothing in Koprivnica for the three of you."

"Why Papá?" she asked. "We like it here. We feel safe here. Koprivnica is a small town, and there will never be a war here."

"I hope you are right, but please think about it," said Grosspapá.

"I will, Papá. I will tell Heinrich what you said." Then she began to cry. "I miss Hansi," she said. "We get letters from him, and he tells us he is fine. But, Papá, he is only seventeen, and he lives alone in a small room. He sees Karli now and then, but he has only a few friends in Zurich. I am terribly worried. I wish he was here so I could take care of him."

"Grete, go home and talk to Heinrich. Maybe we can find a way to bring Hansi to Yugoslavia too. Then we would all be together."

ZAGREB: APRIL 19, 1939

Our new telephone rang.

"Hedi," said Grossvater, "your mother and I are ready to leave, but I'm not sure when. Herr Stojka was expensive. We had to pay him a lot of money for our visas, and I need to sell a few things so I have enough money to leave. Also, we feel responsible for Anna and Pepi. We don't know what will happen to them."

My mother was upset. She wanted her parents to leave at once. She said she was going back to Vienna to get them. Grossvater said no, Vienna was now more dangerous than before.

"I promise we will leave soon," he said. "But you must not come here again."

VIENNA: APRIL 22, 1939

Uncle Pepi received a notice from the IKG. The Nazis had ordered the IKG to provide them with a list of names for the Poland Transport. Uncle Pepi's name was on it, having been selected in a random drawing. The notice told him he would receive another letter giving him more details and the date he was to appear at the Aspangbahnhof (Aspang train station) a small railroad station located in Vienna's Third District. A new life was to begin for him, he was told. Wives and family were to follow later.

ZNOJMO: APRIL 24, 1939

Heli's father received a letter ordering him to Gestapo headquarters. He was interrogated and kept there for three weeks. The Gestapo confiscated his car. With Uncle Josef in a Nazi prison, the remaining Lampls decided to leave Znojmo. They packed a few things and walked sixteen miles to

Moravské Budějovice, a small town outside the Sudetenland. When Uncle Josef was set free, friends took him to Moravské Budějovice. He then took Heli, Bibi, and Grandmother Sara back to Znojmo. He wanted to continue his veterinary practice.

VIENNA: MAY 5, 1939

It was my grandmother's birthday, but no party was planned. Few relatives were left in Vienna. After breakfast, my grandfather got up, walked toward the window, and stood in silence. They had lived in the same apartment almost thirty five years, since before my mother was born. My grandmother followed him and put her arm around him. A few moments later, they called our house in Zagreb.

"Hedi, we'll come soon," said my grandmother over the telephone. "We're ready." My grandfather was still staring out the window.

My mother was worried they might change their minds. She urged her parents to pack and leave immediately.

"You must leave tonight," she said. "It is impossible for you to remain in Vienna, not even for one more day. Before long, it will be too dangerous to cross the border with your new visa. If you get arrested at the border, it will be the same as if you get arrested in Vienna. Please start packing. Leave tonight."

My grandmother hung up and told Grossvater about the conversation.

"What do you think, Jakob?"

"Emma, I think we should leave soon."

VIENNA: MAY 9, 1939

The Maccabi-Wien, the Jewish Sports Center in Vienna where Lisl and Bruno first met, planned a group escape from Vienna on a Danube excursion boat. The escape was to take Jews to Sulina, a Romanian port on the Black Sea. The trip was seventeen hundred miles on the Danube, and the boat had room for one hundred fifty refugees. From Sulina, the refugees were to board a freighter to Palestine.

Tante Anna had a friend who worked at the Maccabi Youth Center office, who knew Lisl was anxious to go to Palestine to join Bruno. On May 9, Tante Anna answered the phone. It was her friend, telling her a space on a riverboat was available for Lisl if she was still interested. The next day, Lisl picked up her papers for the trip, which was scheduled to leave from a pier on the Danube in three days.

VIENNA: MAY 12, 1939

With her permit and instructions in her hand, Lisl said good-bye to my grandparents. She had asked her cousin Lilly to go with her to the designated meeting place. The passengers were to meet at midnight.

Lilly, and Lisl, carrying just a knapsack, took several trams to get to their designated meeting place. As they got close, they saw the group Lisl was to join on a narrow street next to a large building. Lisl introduced herself to the group's leader, a Maccabi guide, who took her permit and gave her a blank light blue card with a string attached to put around her neck. It was her pass for the riverboat. Lilly stayed with Lisl as long as she could. At sixteen, Lisl was very young to be making such a long trip by herself.

The group included men, women, boys, girls, and babies. They were told they would board buses to get to the riverboat, which was tied up in the Donaukanal (Danube Canal) a man-made canal that flows through the city of Vienna to the Danube. Also tied to the canal walls were many barges, fishing boats, and pleasure boats.

Examining the faces in the crowd, Lisl and Lilly realized they did not know anyone. It was a mix of young and old, dressed for travel and carrying a minimum of luggage, mostly small suitcases or rucksacks. Though it was spring, they all wore warm clothes for cool nights on the river.

Two buses appeared and turned off their engines. The travelers were silent, knowing the consequences if they were discovered by the Nazis. In the middle of the night, Nazi patrols, SS, the local police, or even Hitler Youth could appear at any moment. The Maccabi guides gave instructions with hand signals.

"Lisl dear," Lilly whispered in her ear. "It looks like you are in good hands. These people know what they are doing."

Lisl put her arms around Lilly. "Good-bye, Lilly," she said, "and good luck on your trip to England."

The buses left at twenty minute intervals. Lisl, on the second bus, found herself sitting next to a girl about her age. No one talked on the trip to the Donaukanal, which took less than fifteen minutes. When the bus stopped, they saw their boat, silent and dark.

"I don't see the bus that left before us," Lisl whispered to her new acquaintance. The girl was quiet. The moon was high, giving them enough light to go aboard. The Maccabi guides got off first and led the passengers up the gangplank. It was a perfect night, thought Lisl.

"Look," whispered Lisl again to her silent friend, "the name of the boat is *Helios*. I was on this boat a few years ago."

Lisl had tears in her eyes. She thought of her parents in a distant and strange land and felt very much alone. She missed Bruno and couldn't wait to see him, but she was also thinking about the happy boat trip she took on the *Helios* with her mother and our grandmother several years before.

"Shhhh," said one of the Maccabis.

The group walked single file up the gangplank, holding on to a rope. The people who were on the first bus were already aboard. One more bus had yet to arrive. Silently, they were led to their sleeping quarters. Lisl and her friend settled in a corner at the end of a hallway. It would be their home for the next three weeks. They placed their backpacks on the wooden floor next to the wall and sat down, leaning against them. The next busload came, and in thirty minutes the *Helios* was untied and it slowly went through the canal to the Danube, keeping its engine noise to a minimum.

Four Maccabi guides sailed with the refugees. One quietly gave orders. There would be silence and darkness. Smoking was forbidden. Luggage and rucksacks were not to be unpacked. The *Helios* moved slowly down the canal to the Danube, keeping its engines as quiet as possible.

Lisl wanted to tell her new friend about her trip, four years earlier, when she, my grandmother Emma, Tante Anna, and Lisl's mother, Gisela, took the *Helios* to the cherry blossom festival in the Wachau region of Lower Austria.

"What's your name?" whispered Lisl.

"Hannah Levy. What's yours?"

"My name is Lisl Wertheim. How old are you?"

"I just turned seventeen. And you?"

"Sixteen."

When the *Helios* got to the Danube, it picked up speed. Lisl and Hannah were given sleeping bags and water and enough vitamin pills to last the trip. Each passenger paid the same amount of money, but young people slept on the floor and adults got berths in the cabins, which were usually occupied by tourists. They were all fed three meals a day. In her backpack, Lisl had an assortment of sweets my grandmother baked for her, and some salami and biscuits.

The *Helios* had to sail thirty three miles, a five-hour trip, before it could cross the border into Pozsony, Hungary. Once the *Helios* was in Hungary, a neutral country, the Nazis were not in control, and the refugees would be free. The SS *Helios* sailed slowly until it approached the Hungarian border, still dark and silent.

Suddenly, the ship's lights came on, and its horn blasted short sounds. The passengers cheered and hugged each other. They were out of Austria, no longer under Nazi control. They were free. The *Helios* sailed on through Bratislava and then to Budapest, one hundred fifty miles from Vienna, where it docked.

The local Jewish community was expecting them. Men, women, and children met them with food and wine and treated them like old friends. The refugees did not speak Hungarian, but the Hungarians spoke enough German to make them feel welcome.

The four Maccabi guides said good-bye to the passengers, left the *Helios,* and boarded another boat to go back to Vienna. Getting to Sulina was now a reality. The massive Danube, the second largest river in Europe, had become their lifeline. Flowing from west to east, it starts in Germany and runs about eighteen hundred miles east through Austria, Hungary, Yugoslavia, Bulgaria, and Romania, and ends at Sulina on the Black Sea. From Budapest, the boat sailed fifteen hundred miles to Tulcea in Romania and anchored. Two days later, they got word that the Panamanian ship had arrived in Sulina, and the *Helios* sailed the final one hundred miles to the Black Sea.

SULINA: JUNE 2, 1939

As the *Helios* tied up near the Panamanian freighter, all the refugees were on deck. Lisl looked in amazement at the name painted on the side of the big boat: *SS Lisl.* It was her name.

The *Helios's* passengers had another two-day wait before changing ships. During that time, they learned they would be on the last transport out of Sulina headed for Palestine. The *SS Lisl* was old and the refugees would be its final cargo. They also learned two hundred additional refugees, already in Sulina, would board the ship with them for the final leg of their trip.

SULINA: JUNE 4, 1939

Three hundred refugees were on the *SS Lisl* for the trip to Haifa. A tugboat tied up to the *SS Lisl's* port side and pulled the ship sideways out to the Black Sea. Once in open water, the tugboat was untied and the *SS Lisl* picked up speed and headed to the Bosporus Straits in Turkey, about two hundred miles away. The Black Sea was rough, it rained most of the time, and the majority of the passengers were seasick.

When the ship approached Istanbul, which was patrolled by the Turkish Navy, the passengers had to hide below deck until they reached the Bosporus Straits. The *SS Lisl* was supposedly carrying corn.

Istanbul sits on the banks of the Bosporus, which is a narrow strait connecting the Black Sea and the Aegean Sea, which flows into the Mediterranean Sea.

The ship passed through the Bosporus Straits without interruption and cruised into the Aegean and on to the Mediterranean. The sky was blue, it was warm, and the bright sun felt good after the gloomy sail on the Black Sea. The ship headed south to Haifa.

Unlike the *Helios*, the freighter had no cabins or sleeping quarters. The refugees slept on straw mattresses on the floor in cargo holds. The youngest lived in the lower hold while adults slept above them, one floor below deck.

Sanitation facilities were primitive. There was water for drinking but not bathing. Food was scarce. The five-day trip seemed like an eternity. Hours passed slowly with people talking or looking out to sea.

By now, Lisl and Hannah were good friends. They had been together more than three weeks. In Sulina, the girls had purchased a bottle of cognac, which they were finishing when someone yelled, "Land, land."

The ships engines stopped, and the *SS Lisl's* loudspeakers blared, "We are in the waters of Palestine!"

The city of Haifa could be seen from the bow.

> Haifa was first mentioned in Talmudic literature around the 3rd century. It was ruled by the Byzantines until the 7th century; then by the Persians; then by the Arabs; and in 1100, by the Crusaders, after a battle with its Jewish and Muslim inhabitants. In 1761 the Bedouins destroyed and rebuilt the city and that was the beginning of its modern era.
>
> After 1775, Haifa remained under Ottoman rule until 1918, except for the year 1799, when Napoleon Bonaparte conquered Haifa as part of a campaign to occupy Palestine and Syria. He failed, and withdrew the same year. By the beginning of the 20th century Haifa had emerged as an industrial port city and growing population center. Haifa was home to approximately twenty-thousand inhabitants, eighty-two-percent Muslim Arab,

fourteen-percent Christian Arabs, and four-percent Jews. The Jewish population increased steadily with immigration from Europe. Palestine had become a British Mandate.

HAIFA: JUNE 9, 1939

When the ship dropped anchor, young men and women from the Haifa-Maccabi Center appeared in rubber rafts and tied up to the *SS Lisl*. The Maccabi volunteers climbed aboard.

A British coast guard cutter came next. A dozen sailors also boarded the *SS Lisl*. Some met with the ship's captain. Others walked around the deck inspecting the passengers. The refugees began to worry. Thirty minutes later, the British returned to their boat, and slowly the cutter began circling the *SS Lisl*.

This was not the first ship the British had intercepted. On April 20, the *SS Assimi*, with four hundred seventy refugees aboard, was held captive off Haifa. During the first night, ninety passengers were unloaded to safety by Maccabis. On the second night, one hundred ten people made it to land under British gunfire. The British then seized the ship and put the captain in prison. He was later released and sailed his ship back to Europe with two hundred seventy refugees still aboard.

Eventually, the British allowed dozens of ships with thousands of Jewish refugees into Palestine. This was the beginning of Theodore Herzl's dream of a Jewish state in Palestine.

For three days, while the *SS Lisl* lay at anchor, the Jewish Joint Distribution Committee (JDC) negotiated with British authorities, and by the end of the third day, the passengers were given permission to disembark. At that point, a woman's voice came over the loudspeakers. She was singing the 'Hatikvah', the anthem of Eretz Israel (Land of Israel). The Maccabis who were on board rose to their feet and sang along. The refugees also stood up. Most recognized the music, but few knew the words. They all knew it was to be their new national anthem.

The British cutter turned and went back to Haifa. Then a pilot boat tied up to the port side of the *SS Lisl* and guided it into Haifa's harbor. The passengers were packed and anxious to get off.

Hundreds of people greeted the ship at dockside. As the refugees got off, some were met by relatives and friends. The rest were greeted warmly by members of the JDC. Each passenger had a home to go to, and in an hour, the dock was empty. Eretz Israel had just added three hundred and fifty Jews to its population of one hundred and fifty thousand.

HAIFA: JUNE 14, 1939

The day the passengers got off the *SS Lisl*, a family from Haifa was waiting for her. Lisl, who had been assigned this family by the JDC, was invited to live with them. The host family was poor, and their house was small, but Lisl was able to take a bath, something she hadn't done in weeks. They gave her eggs and cucumbers for breakfast, which were good, but not Viennese. They gave her hand-me-down clothes, and she shared a room with two other refugee girls.

After three days with her hosts, Lisl packed her things and set out to find Bruno. She knew he lived in Rosh Pina, a Jewish settlement village in the Upper Galilee, which was the center of the Betar Zionist movement. She went to the JDC office and asked how she could get to Rosh Pina, but the agency was reluctant to help.

Lisl pleaded with the JDC, which finally gave in. There was no bus from Haifa to Rosh Pina, so they gave her money for a taxi. When she got to the taxi stand, a stranger spoke to her in German. He asked her where she was going, and said he also was on his way to Rosh Pina.

"Would you like to share a cab?" he asked. He held out a bag of Lebanese apples and offered her one. "My name is Avi."

Lisl accepted both offers, grateful to be traveling with someone who spoke German. "My name is Lisl," she said. "My boyfriend lives in Rosh Pina. I've come from Vienna to be with him."

When their taxi got to a British checkpoint at the city of Tiberias, Avi told Lisl not to speak. A British policeman opened the rear door of the taxi and asked the two passengers for their identification papers. Avi showed a badge, and Lisl saw that he had a gun in his belt, under his jacket. The policeman told the taxi to proceed. Avi then told Lisl he was a Jewish detective and worked for the British police He was on his way to visit his girlfriend who lived in Rosh Pina.

When they got to Rosh Pina, a beautiful town just north of the Sea of Galilee, the detective paid Lisl's taxi fare and told her how to find Bruno's address.

Rosh Pina, the Hebrew name for 'cornerstone', was a thorn in Jewish-British relations because years before, its lands had been bought up by Jews from Safed, a nearby town, who became successful farmers. The Rosh Pina settlement angered the Arabs in neighboring villages, and they frequently attacked the Jews when they left their settlement. In 1938, a young member of the Betar movement retaliated with force. He was captured by the British military and became the first Jewish settler in Palestine to be hanged by the British.

Lisl soon found Bruno's house. It was a dormitory that belonged to Betar. She went inside and found teenage boys and girls, some whom she knew from Vienna, but Bruno was not there. Two minutes later the front door opened, and he walked in.

VIENNA: JULY 11, 1939

Lilly had been standing in line at the British Consulate since 5:00 a.m. She held two places for Herta and Uncle Fritz, who showed up together at 9:00 a.m. Herta hadn't been feeling well for weeks and was pale and thin. Fritz looked good as always. His black hair was smoothed back and his mustache well-trimmed. He was handsome and, like his brother Gustl, attracted many women.

Lilly was not the first in line that day. Hundreds of people had been standing on the sidewalk in front of the consulate for twenty four hours or more. My uncle and cousins had passports they got years before for vacation travel throughout Europe so once inside the consulate, their applications were processed quickly. They also had an affidavit from one of Herta's friends in London that guaranteed financial backing for the three of them. Without such an affidavit, the British would not grant visas. Uncle Fritz, Herta, and Lilly got their visas. Now they had to set a departure date.

VIENNA: JULY 12, 1939

The next day Lilly and Herta went to my grandparents' house to tell their parents, Tante Anna and Uncle Pepi, about their plans.

"Mutti," said Lilly, "we are ready to leave. We will take a train to Paris and then change trains for Calais, to take the ferry across the English Channel."

"When are you leaving?" asked Uncle Pepi.

"Fritz is buying train tickets right now. We will probably leave tomorrow or Friday. It depends on Fritz. He has some unfinished business to take care of."

Tante Anna and Uncle Pepi hated to see their daughters leave but knew it was inevitable. At least they would be traveling with Fritz. My grandparents wished them good luck, and Lilly and Herta said good-bye to everyone.

The next day, Uncle Fritz said good-bye to his parents and with two suitcases in hand, took streetcars to the Westbahnhof to meet Herta and Lilly. They easily got through the Nazi control station and got on the train. They arrived in England on July 15.

BERLIN: SEPTEMBER 1, 1939

Hitler invaded Poland after Germany and the Soviet Union, previously bitter enemies, signed a nonaggression pact.

LONDON AND PARIS: SEPTEMBER 3, 1939

France and Great Britain declared war on Germany. The Germans won a quick victory in Poland, occupied the country, and went on to defeat and occupy Norway and Denmark. World War II had begun.

ZNOJMO: SEPTEMBER 12, 1938

The German Army now occupied Znojmo.

"Bibi," said my uncle, "will you please call Heli into the living room? We need to talk."

Heli and Bibi sat down on the sofa and Uncle Josef looked at them. "The situation in our country has become intolerable," he began. "The Nazis have control of Austria and the Sudentenland. They just invaded Poland, Denmark, and Norway. And now France and England have declared war on Germany."

"What do you think will happen here?" asked Heli.

Bibi answered her question. "If the Nazis treat the Jews of Czechoslovakia the way they treat the Jews in Austria and Germany, we have a terrible situation ahead of us."

"You both understand the danger," said Uncle Josef. "We must act immediately. Bibi, I want you to go to Palestine, and Heli, you should go to Ireland. I have friends there you can live with."

"Okay, I will go to Prague and try to make the arrangements, but what about you?"

"I have to stay here as long as I can. I promised your dear mother that I would take care of your grandmother."

"No, Papa, I will not leave you," said Heli. "You have an invitation from an American university in Ireland to teach there. Only if you go with me, will I try to get to Ireland."

"I would really like for all of us to go to America," said Uncle Josef, "but the United States still will not accept refugees."

That afternoon, Heli and Bibi went to Prague. Heli's application for a visa to Ireland was denied. Bibi, however, got a tourist visa into Austria and Italy with his Czech passport. His destination was Genoa where he planned to take a boat to Haifa. He left the next day.

The only members of the Lampl family left in Znojmo were Uncle Josef, Grandmother Sara, and Heli.

VIENNA: SEPTEMBER 20, 1939

Uncle Pepi's orders from the IKG came in the mail. He was to report to the Aspangbahnhof for his transport to the Judenreservat in Poland at once. He packed two suitcases, a backpack, and two small boxes. Tante Anna went to the train station with him. The Nazis, both SS and civilians, all wearing swastika armbands, shouted at the crowd of Jews that congregated for the transport. The Jewish men were insulted, bullied, and humiliated and so were the wives and children who had come to say good-bye. Uncle Pepi's throat was dry, he could hardly speak. He kissed Tante Anna.

"Mutti, come soon, you will find me for sure." He believed a new life was waiting for them in Poland.

"My love, I am sure I will find you just as I found you when you lay wounded in Jaegerndorf," said Tante Anna, referring to his military service during World War I. "On the first possible transport, I will follow."

They looked at each other, embraced, and kissed each other good-bye. Six hundred and seventy two men boarded third-class cars. Seats were first-come, first-served. Then the SS guards chased the women and children away.

Tante Anna went home with many questions on her mind. Would she be allowed to follow Pepi? Would there really be a new life in Poland? Was it possible the Nazis were moving Jews to Poland as a goodwill gesture? Or was it all just lies?

Tante Anna.

Wertheim butcher shop: an employee, Lisl's mother Gisela, her father Heinrich, and employee.

From left: Heli, Lilly, and Lisl.

Uncle Fritz and Mädi.

Chapter 13

PARIS: SEPTEMBER 26, 1939

Three weeks after the war began Uncle Gustl went to the French Army recruiting station. It was Monday morning, and there was a long line of men on the sidewalk.

"What's going on here?" he asked the man ahead of him.

"We are all enlisting to fight the Germans," was the reply.

"How long have you been waiting?" asked Uncle Gustl.

"I've been here several hours. There is only one recruiter inside, and they say it takes about thirty minutes to process each guy."

"Bonjour (Good day)," the recruiter said when my uncle finally got inside.

"Bonjour," said Uncle Gustl, "I'm here to enlist."

"Monsieur, may I see your identification papers."

Uncle Gustl removed his Austrian passport from his jacket and handed it to the man.

"You are Austrian," said the recruiter. "Only French citizens can enlist in the French Army."

"But there is a difficult war going on. If you sign me up, you'll get a good soldier."

"I am sorry, but I can't. The only possibility is for you to join the French Foreign Legion. They have no restrictions on nationality."

The recruiter returned Uncle Gustl's passport and called the next volunteer. As he left, he asked the recruiter for the address of the nearest Foreign Legion office. My uncle was concerned. He knew mercenaries and hoodlums from all over the world served in the Foreign Legion. But he decided he would find out more.

Two hours later, Uncle Gustl was in Melun, on the outskirts of Paris. As he approached the address he'd been given, he found another line of men on the sidewalk. A sign on the building read Foreign Legion War Volunteer Office. He listened to the men talking and identified them by their accents. There were Austrians, Germans, Czech, and Polish men among the group. He thought many were Jews. Contrary to the French Army, the Foreign Legion enlistment staff welcomed everyone and processed them in minutes. Uncle Gustl soon was an enlistee in this uncertain group.

"Monsieur Jellinek, congratulations. Welcome to the Légion Étrangère. Report on October 10 to Larzac. There you will undergo medical, intelligence, and physical fitness tests. Bring one suitcase only."

Uncle Gustl was told Larzac, which he'd never heard of, was sixty miles west of Bordeaux and that it was the Centre D'induction de la Légion pour les Ressortissants Étranger (Induction Center of the Legion for Foreign Nationals).

In the two weeks before reporting to Larzac, Uncle Gustl closed his shoe repair shop, moved out of his apartment, and stored his belongings. He also wrote letters, explaining his plans, to his family in Vienna.

LARZAC: OCTOBER 10, 1939

Uncle Gustl took a train to Larzac. He arrived at night, was assigned a barracks, and was issued bedding.

The next morning, he woke up with a start in his new surroundings. He sat up in bed and thought about his situation. He was no longer Gustav Jellinek. He was now Legionnaire 88508. There were many new legionnaires in his barracks, most between ages twenty and forty. In addition to the men he'd seen in the recruiting line, there were a number of Frenchmen. Lawyers, judges, doctors, intellectuals and artisans, and skilled and unskilled workers were among the new recruits. They were all given uniforms. Then came an announcement over the loudspeaker.

"All legionnaires. Fall out to the quadrangle."

The recruits got out of bed, got dressed, and quickly left their barracks. The dirt quadrangle was about half the size of a football field. It was surrounded by four barracks. Standing in the center of the quadrangle, on a three foot high wooden box, was a legionnaire sergeant, very tall with an enormous black beard. Four hundred new legionnaires were ordered to stand at attention, one hundred in front of each barrack.

"Those who have a driver's license move to the east side of the quadrangle," yelled the officer. "This is the east side," he yelled again, pointing to his right.

"Those with good handwriting go to the north side in front of me," he said.

"Anyone who is a good athlete, go to the south side," was his next direction. He pointed to his back.

"The rest of you, line up over here on the west side."

Uncle Gustl and a young recruit who stood next to him slowly backed away from their group and, without being seen, went behind their barrack. Uncle Gustl was remembering advice from his Uncle Pepi, a corporal during World War I. "Never volunteer."

From behind the barrack, the two new recruits listened to the sergeant's next order.

"The ones with the driver's licenses will push wheel barrows. The ones with good hand writing will clean latrines. The good athletes will clean the streets. The rest of you start picking up rubbish around the post."

Uncle Gustl and his new friend hid the rest of the day. The next day, they learned these meaningless assignments were meant to kill time until final orders were issued. After three days of hiding, they got caught, and for the next three weeks, were made to clean streets. Finally, the new legionnaires were transferred to Marseille by train.

MARSEILLE: NOVEMBER 1, 1939.

Uncle Gustl had never been to Marseille, and he liked it. The sandy beaches reminded him of holidays on the Italian and French Rivieras.

The legionnaires moved into barracks, each of which had fifty double bunks, two commodes, and four washbasins. The urinal was a sheet metal wall fifteen feet long, with running water and a cigarette butt clogged drain. Ventilation came from one small open window. The odor was disgusting.

The first day in Marseille, the recruits were taken to the Saint-Jean Fortress, an abandoned citadel overlooking the Mediterranean, at the entrance to the Marseille harbor. The fortress dates to the 12th century when it was the command post of the Hospitallers of Saint John of Jerusalem. Its high square tower was built by King René in the 15th century.

They were led through a dark, narrow tunnel about thirty yards long and made to climb almost two steps to a large flat roof. From there, they could see the opening of the harbor and the Mediterranean Sea. Looking down, they saw the water's edge, large boulders, and rocks. The rocky coast was beautiful, thought my uncle, very different from other Mediterranean beaches he'd been to. His view was soon interrupted.

The sergeant ordered the men to drop their gear and follow him down the same stairway toward a second tunnel, which led to a beach on the other side of the citadel. There, they were told to pick up rocks and carry them up to the top level of the fort and throw them over the wall to the rocky shore below. The legionnaires repeated this exercise for four hours and went back to their barracks.

The group was in Marseille for three weeks with daily assignments, all meaningless. The men took written exams, physical fitness tests, and were given marching lessons. No one could leave the compound.

When Uncle Gustl passed all the requirements, he had to sign a contract saying he would serve five years in the French Foreign Legion, wherever it needed him. His orders were to join the Third Foreign Infantry Regiment in Oujda, a city founded in the 10th century in eastern Morocco, about nine miles west of Algiers. But before he went to Morocco, he was transferred to the Fourth Foreign Infantry Regiment in Castelnaudary for four months of basic training. Castelnaudary is in the province of Cassoulet in the south of France.

MUNICH: NOVEMBER 8, 1939

Nazi Party members gathered in a beer hall to commemorate the failed putsch (overthrow of a government) of November 9, 1923. Adolf Hitler was the main speaker. He was scheduled to begin his speech at 8:30 p.m., and it was meant to end at 10:00. Hitler decided to begin his speech half an hour earlier so he was finished at nine and left. Twenty minutes later, a bomb exploded and destroyed the beer hall. Hitler had escaped an assassination attempt. Nine people were killed.

ZNOJMO: NOVEMBER 13, 1939

It had been six months since Uncle Josef Lampl had been imprisoned for three weeks by the Gestapo. In the morning mail was a letter ordering him back to Gestapo headquarters. He was imprisoned for one week this time, then released. When he went home he told Heli if he was called again he would never return to the Gestapo.

ZURICH: WEDNESDAY, NOVEMBER 15, 1939

Hansi wrote to his parents in Koprivnica about his life in Zurich. Nothing was new since his last letter. The Jewish agency was taking care of him and had found him a job in a shoe repair shop, and he was making new friends. Karli was doing the same. Once again, Hansi urged his parents to send Gerti to England with the Red Cross. He was afraid that his parents might go to Turkey as they had suggested in one of their last letters. He told them they would not be happy living in that culture.

VIENNA: NOVEMBER 19, 1939

"Dear Anna," wrote Uncle Pepi, "I am well. I hope the same for you. Kisses to all of you. Yours, Josef. PS, At the next opportunity, I will write more." The letter had been opened and resealed.

"He is alive!" Tante Anna screamed to my grandparents. It was a month since she'd said good-bye to her husband. "He is alive!"

Tante Anna had been told three days before that Hans Wolf, who had been on the transport to Poland with Pepi had somehow returned to Vienna. With her letter in hand, she went to his home.

"Herr Wolf, I have a letter from Pepi," she said. "He is alive and well. Can you tell me more? And how were you able to return to Vienna?"

"Frau Weininger, our train stopped in a small village in Poland, and everyone had to get off. Our luggage was loaded onto horse carts and driven away. Artisans were led to another train, and the rest of us were chased into the woods."

"We ran through the woods not knowing which direction to go. Some of us were lucky and found railroad tracks. I jumped on a freight train that went to Austria, and others begged for rides on trucks to get to Vienna. I heard some shots while I was running. When I last saw your husband he was tired and hungry, but he was still alive."

Tante Anna went back to my grandparents' house but before she went up the stairs she was stopped by the building's caretaker.

"Frau Weininger," he said, "two minutes ago, a policeman came and asked for you. It was about your husband. I told him you were out. He just left."

Tante Anna ran out to the street, hoping to catch up with the policeman. She ended up at her neighborhood police station and went to the officer behind the desk.

"I am Frau Weininger. Do you know anything about a policeman looking for me at Kaunitzgasse 16?"

"No, I don't. All the officers are out patrolling the streets. They won't be in here until tomorrow morning. Come back after 8:00 a.m. Maybe I'll have an answer for you."

Early the next morning, Tante Anna and my grandmother went to the police station. The officer behind the desk told them the policeman who'd been looking for her the day before had a telegram for her, and it was being delivered at that moment.

"You should hurry back home," he said.

When they got back to the apartment, there was a telegram stuck in the door. Tante Anna ripped it open and read it out loud to my grandmother.

"You may come to the police station to collect the belongings of your deceased husband." There was no further information.

Tante Anna broke down and cried uncontrollably. My grandmother took her sister in her arms and tried to console her.

After a sleepless night, the two women went back to the police station to pick up Uncle Pepi's belongings. In a paper bag were a key ring, a tie, shoelaces, a cigarette case, and a journal with a few family photographs inside. It described Uncle Pepi's trip to Poland and the towns his transport train had passed through. The last entry was written when he was in Uljanow, a small town in eastern Poland. There was a hole through the middle of the journal. Tante Anna was hysterical, not knowing the cause of her husband's death.

My grandparents tried to convince her that Uncle Pepi had died in a hospital. The hole in the notebook, my grandfather suggested, was to hang it on a nail over Uncle Pepi's hospital bed. But my grandparents already knew the truth. Grossvater had heard earlier that day that Josef Weininger was shot in the woods. The paper bag with Uncle Pepi's things had been collected by Jews who were ordered by the Nazis to dispose of the bodies. Unknown to the Nazis, the Jews gave the belongings of the murdered men to sympathetic Poles, who sent them back to Vienna.

Tante Anna did not believe my grandfather. The hole in the journal had clearly been made by a bullet. She needed to know the truth.

CASTELNAUDARY: NOVEMBER 22, 1939

Sixteen weeks of grueling and arduous training in the art of warfare began for Uncle Gustl. He lost his identity and was at the mercy of a drill sergeant twenty four hours a day. He could not eat, bathe, or sleep unless the drill sergeant told him to, and he was made to perform physical activities that made no sense. Each recruit was given a handbook that explained everything they had to accomplish to graduate from basic training, including intense field exercises designed to test the new recruits for placement in their final regiments.

Chapter 14

VIENNA: DECEMBER 24, 1939

Tante Anna, at age fifty one, was a widow. She mourned Pepi and began to live in fear. She was terrified she would be arrested and sent to a concentration camp like Matthausen or Wöllersdorf in Austria. She was lonely, couldn't sleep, and thought about suicide. Life in Vienna was now impossible for her. She decided to go Zagreb to join us.

The IKG was processing thousands of Jews to get them out of Vienna. Tante Anna went to the IKG where she met a Viennese Nazi on the street who, for a bribe, told her he would guide her across the Austrian border into Yugoslavia. She never went into the IKG office and agreed to pay the man two hundred Reichsmark.

The day before Christmas she took a few belongings, said good-bye to my grandparents, and met the guide near the train station. He had two other couples with him. The Nazi took them by train to Graz, an industrial city in Austria about halfway between Vienna and Zagreb where he led them to a police station. The five were searched thoroughly.

In her bag, Tante Anna had packed a small Torah about the size of an eyeglass case that had been a gift from my grandmother. (Torahs contain Jewish law and teachings, and the books of Moses). A policeman unrolled it and asked what it was. She told him it was a talisman, a small object intended to bring good luck and protection to its owner. To her surprise, he gave it back, disappointed that she had nothing of value with her. The police then confiscated the escapees' passports.

Their Nazi guide then led them on foot to a nearby farmhouse where another Jewish couple with a baby was waiting. That night, they slept in the farmhouse; and the next day, they got ready for the one hundred sixty seven mile trip to Zagreb. The guide did not go with them. Two young men in their twenties took his place. They started the journey in a horse-drawn hay wagon. The young men sat on the seat and the eight refugees bounced along in the back.

Their first destination was a town called Spielfeld, thirty miles from Graz. It was cold and snowing. The drivers took the cart into a stable full of lambs and told the Jews to stay inside. Two days later, after sleeping on straw, and out of food and water, it stopped snowing and the young men came back. They got into the wagon and continued their trip, uphill through deep snow. They were all weak and cold, and the baby was crying.

Suddenly, the men stopped the cart.

"We are not going any farther unless you give us more money."

The refugees had no money but gave the men a few trinkets and personal items. Tante Anna gave them a small mirror and her hairbrush. They continued and eventually came to a farmhouse where they were met by barking dogs. The farmers, alerted by their dogs, came out and invited them inside, where there were eleven more Jews from Germany and Austria; men, women and children. They were given food and water. There were now nineteen people in the group of refugees. The Yugoslav border was fifteen miles away, and then it would be another fifty one miles to Zagreb.

SPIELFIELD, AUSTRIA: DECEMBER 26, 1939

Their young guides left, and just before nightfall, two men appeared with two more horse-drawn wagons. The plan was to leave at dusk.

As they piled into the carts, it began to snow again. It would be a cold trip. The refugees snuggled close together in the back of the wagons. Tante Anna looked at the children sleeping in their parents' arms. Next to her was a blind boy who had been helped into the wagon by another boy.

"My name is Anna," she said, putting her arm around his shoulder. He was shivering.

"My name is Klaus Herbst."

"How old are you?"

"I am fifteen."

"Where are you from, Klaus?"

"I'm from Leopoldstadt. Do you know where that is?"

"Yes. I also am from Vienna. Are you traveling alone?"

"Yes. My parents disappeared in Vienna, and my uncle sent me to Graz to join this group."

"Stay close to me, I will take care of you," she said.

Heavy snow covered the road to the border. Their journey ended at a railroad switching station where a stopped train blocked their way. The guides told them to get out of the wagons and crawl beneath the railroad cars to the other side. Tante Anna took Klaus' hand and helped him under the connector between two trains. On the other side of the tracks was a large warehouse. It was 8:00 p.m. They had crossed into Yugoslavia in a deserted area without border guards. The group slept in the warehouse that night. The next morning, a truck arrived to take them to Zagreb.

"Attention please," said the truck driver, in German. "Be careful when you climb into the back. Take a seat on the benches. There is food and water for you. It will take about two hours to get to Zagreb."

Tante Anna again took Klaus's hand, and they all climbed into the back of the truck. Their trip would soon be over. An hour later, they heard cars pass the trucks.

"We must be on the main road now," said Klaus. "I hear the cars."

"Yes," said Tante Anna. "We are getting closer to Zagreb."

Another hour went by and the truck stopped and someone opened the back flap. The refugees looked out and cheered. "It's Zagreb. We are really here."

ZAGREB: DECEMBER 28, 1939

"You are at the Zagreb railroad station," said the driver. "Go to the kiosk across the street and wait. Someone will come to help you. I will call to tell them you are here. I wish you all good luck."

In minutes, four taxis arrived at the kiosk. Three women got out of one.

"Please listen," said one. "My name is Ingrid. This is Stella, and this is Milka. We are with the Zagreb JDC. The taxis will take you to our office and we'll answer all your questions when we get there."

When they got to the JDC office, they were told to wait outside while fifty refugees from Germany, who arrived an hour before, were being processed.

Tante Anna wanted to call my mother and went looking for a telephone. She was stopped by a man in civilian clothes who stuck his hand in front of her face.

"Identification papers," he said.

Tante Anna was frightened. "I do not have any papers," she said. "I just arrived here, and I am waiting to get into the Jewish Agency."

He showed her a badge. "Come with me. You are under arrest."

Tante Anna began to cry. "Please," she said, "I will do anything for you, wash stairs, sweep roads, anything, but please don't send me back to Hitler. I have a blind boy I am watching out for. He needs me."

He grabbed her by the arm and took her to a police station where he put her in a cell with several other women.

"Who are you?" asked one of the women in Croatian.

"I don't speak Croatian," said Tante Anna.

"Where are you from?" asked another woman, this time in German.

"I am from Vienna."

"Vienna? You must be a Jew."

"It's none of your business who I am. Please leave me alone," said Tante Anna.

Some of the women had bloody scars. They must have been beaten, thought Tante Anna, now feeling desperate. But Tante Anna was lucky. A friend of my parents from Vienna had watched her being arrested from the other side of the street. She recognized her and immediately called my parents.

"Anna is in Zagreb," she said. "She was just arrested."

This was good news, and bad news. Tante Anna had made it to Zagreb, but was in jail. My father called the police station and was told since Tante Anna was in the country illegally she would have to go to court.

Two days later, she went before a judge. My mother and father were in the courtroom. She hadn't bathed, her clothes were dirty, and she had lost ten pounds during the last seven days. Her only suitcase had disappeared. The judge spoke to her in German and she told him her story, about Pepi, and about her difficult escape from Vienna. The judge was sympathetic and released her.

"Anna, Anna," said my mother.

She turned around, hearing her niece's voice.

"Hedi, Robert, you found me."

My mother hugged and kissed her aunt while my father watched, smiling. Then he greeted Tante Anna with another big hug.

"Servus, Anna," my father said. "It's so good to see you. I'm sorry about Pepi." He had not seen Tante Anna since before he was arrested and taken to Dachau.

"Servus, Robert," answered Tanta Anna. "It's good to see you too. How are the boys? How is my Pommynko? How is little Peter?"

"Everyone is fine, Anna. Let's go home. A neighbor is watching the children. You must be hungry."

"Yes, I am starving. And I need a bath and some clean clothes."

Tante Anna rested a few days at our house and then looked for work. She took part time jobs as a laundress, cook, and she cleaned houses. She had worked hard all her life in the butcher shop and didn't mind the menial jobs she was doing. They kept her from thinking about Pepi. When she came home at night, she was tired and was in bed before anyone else.

Thousands of German and Austrian refugees had converged in Zagreb since 1936 when Hitler began his rise to power. Zagreb had become a city where Jewish families settled temporarily, while most tried to immigrate to Palestine. Zagreb Jews and Christians helped them financially. Yugoslavs in other major cities, including Sarajevo and Belgrade did the same.

ZAGREB: FEBRUARY 19, 1940

The war in Europe did not keep my parents from trying to live the lifestyle they had in Vienna.

"Hedi," my father said. "We have to do things like we used to. I don't mean everyday things. Regardless of what is happening in Vienna and Germany, I am earning good money, and I want to take a vacation."

"Where?" asked my mother.

"There is a village in the Dolomite Mountains called Grajnska Gora. It is supposed to be very beautiful, and the skiing is superb right now. I want to take a few days off from work and go there."

"What a good idea," said my mother. "Pommy hasn't been on skis in two years. He'll have fun, and Peter is old enough for sledding."

"Good, then I will make the arrangements," said my father.

"Robert, do you think it is right for us to go skiing while my parents are still in Vienna?

"Hedi, what can we do for anyone right now? I hope your father and mother can come soon, but in the meantime we have to continue to live. We need this vacation."

That weekend, we went to the Dolomites for four days. My parents bought me new knickerbockers and leather ski boots just like theirs, which they brought from Vienna. We rented skis and bamboo poles. They even found a tiny pair of skis for Peter, who was now two.

We stayed in an alpine inn that served hearty breakfasts and dinners, and had musicians playing at night. The snow was good, and the sun was bright. It was a perfect ski weekend. It reminded us all of the good times we used to have.

MARSEILLE AND OUJDA: MARCH 12, 1940

Uncle Gustl's basic training was over. He was sent back to Marseille to board a French freighter to Oujda. The crossing took twelve hours, docking in Casablanca. The legionnaires were then taken by truck to the Third Foreign Infantry Regiment headquarters in Oujda. New uniforms were issued. None of them fit properly. The next day, he was sent to a military training center specializing in desert warfare. Eight weeks later, his company was transferred to Fez, the third largest city in Morocco with a population close to one million. Uncle Gustl was assigned to the quartermaster general's engineering department. Building roads was their specialty.

FEZ: MAY 1, 1940

The group of recruits from Paris was still together, but now the number of legionnaires had doubled. In Fez, they joined another group of French Foreign Legion members from all over the world. Some were mercenaries, others hoodlums, and criminals.

Drills were held each morning before the soldiers were sent to build roads. For any infraction the platoon's drill sergeant imposed severe penalties, including walking six miles with a full backpack and a weapon, to cleaning latrines for twenty four hours. The platoon leader was a thief who stole gear from the men and then demanded bribes to give the belongings back. My uncle was promoted to private second class.

"Jellinek, report to headquarters!" The announcement was made just before drills early one morning.

"I wonder what they want from me?" said my uncle, to no one in particular. He got dressed and, before breakfast, reported to company headquarters. Two other soldiers had also been called. The sergeant in charge told the men to change into dress uniform and report immediately to the colonel's home. They were given a car and the colonel's address. Uncle Gustl was assigned to be the driver. He had no idea why he was given these orders, but he welcomed the diversion.

He got into his green and red dress clothes. His white kepi, the traditional legion dress cap, with its skirt to protect his neck from the hot sun looked good on him. Displayed on both the kepi and the jacket was the legion insignia: a grenade with a hollow center bearing seven flames, two of them pointing down. Young, tall, and handsome, Uncle Gustl was elegant in this outfit. The three legionnaires took the military car and went to the colonel's house.

Private Jellinek rang the doorbell. An African legionnaire private opened the door and, in French, Uncle Gustl introduced himself and his fellow soldiers. They were led into the foyer of a large house, more beautiful than any he'd seen in Vienna or Paris, and told to wait.

Uncle Gustl was surprised when, instead of the colonel, a woman appeared. The three legionnaires sprang to attention.

"At ease, please," said the woman in French. "I am Annette Brougui. I am Colonel Brougui's wife. I do not give military commands so please make yourselves comfortable."

"Thank you, Madame," said Uncle Gustl, in nearly perfect French.

My uncle had seen Colonel Brougui at the military base. He was at least sixty. Annette Brougui looked about half his age and was striking. She was slim and shapely, with long black hair and very long legs. Her white silk blouse was unbuttoned low enough to show cleavage, and she was wearing a dark red cotton skirt. Her lipstick was the color of her skirt. In her high-heeled shoes, she was almost as tall as Uncle Gustl, who was six foot three. She was smiling.

"What is your name, Private?" asked Madame Brougui.

"Gustav Jellinek, Madame." He tried not to smile back.

"When did you join the legion?" asked Madame Brougui.

"I joined in Paris when the war broke out," answered my uncle, wondering if she knew he was a Jew. He thought how lucky he was to be away from his daily routine and in the company of this beautiful woman. He couldn't help himself; his face broke into a big smile.

Madame Brougui then explained why the men had been sent to her house. She was throwing a big party, and she wanted them to serve the food and wine.

"Have you ever done anything like this before?" asked Madame Brougui.

"Madame, I come from Vienna, and serving wine is every Viennese man's specialty. I can serve very well."

The other two men said that they had never been waiters before, but they would do their best.

The colonel's wife looked directly at Uncle Gustl.

"I don't think you will have any problem working for me," she said.

Then she looked at the other men and told them they should go back to the post. She thanked them for coming and said she would explain her party plans to Private Jellinek, who would be in charge of the duties for all three of them.

"When is the party?" asked Uncle Gustl when the others were gone.

"It will be in two weeks. Come, I'd like to show you the kitchen and where the party will be held. Then, during the next two weeks, I'd like you to come back a few times to meet the cook and the kitchen help. But today, could you drive me into the city?"

"Yes, Madame," he replied. He could not believe his good fortune.

"Private, here are the keys to my Citroen? Go outside, and I will be out in a few minutes. The car is on the right side of the garage."

Uncle Gustl found the black, four-door sedan, and started the engine. He was impressed. He'd never driven a car like it. The interior was black leather, and the legroom, in front and back, was greater than any car he'd ever driven. He drove to the front of the house, got out, and waited for Madame Brougui. When she came out, he opened the rear door for her.

"Merci," Madame Brougui smiled.

"Where are we going?" asked my uncle.

"Please take me to the Casbah."

FRANCE: MAY 19, 1940

The German armies overran the Netherlands, Belgium, Sweden, and Norway. They broke through France and reached the English Channel.

DUNKIRK: MAY 26, 1940

When war broke out against Germany, the British Army was sent to help the French, Belgian, Dutch, and Polish armies (Allied Forces) fight the Germans in France. The Allied high command had underestimated the strength of the Germans. Overpowered, the Allies were ordered to retreat to the French port of Dunkirk on the English Channel.

When they got to Dunkirk, the troops were attacked by the German air force and became trapped. The British launched a rescue mission to evacuate the Allied soldiers by sea. A huge fleet of vessels, including tiny tugs, barges, lifeboats, private craft, and navy destroyers, was sent to Dunkirk.

The rescue ships approaching Dunkirk were easy targets for the German Stuka bombers. The harbor was under constant bombardment. The Germans had also planted mines, leaving little opportunity for the Allies to enter the harbor. The smaller boats, piloted by civilians, had the task of picking up soldiers on the beaches and the harbor and transporting them to the British navy ships waiting offshore. Of the eight hundred fifty vessels that took part in the rescue, two hundred thirty five were sunk.

The British lost more than sixty eight thousand men at Dunkirk, but seven hundred and fifty thousand troops were evacuated. It was a colossal rescue mission.

OSWIECIM, POLAND: JUNE 14, 1940

Oswiecim had become the site of an immense concentration camp. The Germans renamed the town Auschwitz. The first transport into Auschwitz contained Polish political prisoner who were murdered immediately. Soon after, Soviet prisoners of war, Romas (Gypsies), Jews, and prisoners of other nationalities were also taken to Auschwitz.

PARIS: JUNE 16, 1940

The Germans occupied Paris. French resistance was almost nonexistent. German soldiers and the SS roamed the streets of the French capital just as they had in Vienna. Unlike the Viennese, a massive exodus of Parisians began. Thousands of people were leaving the city by foot, car, train, or any other means available to them. They were heading for places unknown.

ZAGREB: JUNE 20, 1940

The train carrying my grandparents Jellinek from Vienna was due to arrive at any moment. It was 6:00 p.m. We stood waiting anxiously on the platform. I watched the train roll in and saw people eating in the dining car. When it stopped, we walked toward a car where passengers were getting off. I began to run.

"There!" I yelled. "There they are!" I turned around to make sure my parents heard me. They were following me, my father carrying Peter. I rushed straight to my grandfather. He picked me up with one swoop, and I wrapped my arms around him. My grandmother put her hand on my shoulder and said, "Servus, Pommy."

My parents caught up to us. My grandfather put me down and everyone hugged. My grandmother picked up Peter and kissed him.

"Servus, Hedi," said my grandfather. He stroked her hair and held her close to him. Then he and my father shook hands.

"Let's get your luggage," my father said.

"This is all we have, Robert. We had to leave our apartment in a hurry, and we spent the last week in the Lichtensteinerstrasse with friends. All we have left are these two suitcases."

PARIS: JUNE 22, 1940

The French Parliament signed an armistice with Germany. Vichy, a town southeast of Paris, became the seat of the French government, but under Nazi control. Vichy ruled a zone in Southern France. It was called Régime de Vichy, or Vichy, and was commonly known as L'État Français (The French State). It was a Nazi puppet state, collaborating with the Germans. General Philippe Pétain was named head of state along with the French colonies Morocco and Algeria.

LONDON: AUGUST, 1940

Germany attempted to bomb Britain into submission during night time raids. Meanwhile, the German Army landed in North Africa.

FEZ: AUGUST 22, 1940

Uncle Gustl's affair with Annette Brougui had been going on for more than three months. The colonel's wife arranged for him to work at functions and parties and he became her driver, often taking her into the city. The hotel they frequented was in the center of the Casbah. Comfort and privacy were ensured by the hotel's owner, who took a liking to Uncle Gustl. The colonel's wife was two years older than my uncle. They were fond of each other and enjoyed a similar sense of humor.

Their relationship, however, was soon over.

A French Army officer was also attracted to Madame Brougui, and he was persistent. He found out about the affair and asked his Foreign Legion counterpart to keep Uncle Gustl in camp and far away from Madame Brougui. They never saw each other again.

At this point, the legionnaires stationed in Fez had not engaged in warfare with the Germans, and they were asked if they would prefer to be sent somewhere else. Uncle Gustl went to his commanding officer, Madame Brougui's husband, and requested a discharge so he could go to Bordeaux to join the Free French Movement and fight the Nazis. His request was placed on the first page of a three page document.

"Sign all three pages," the colonel ordered. Two pages were blank.

"Sir, why do you want me to sign blank pages?" asked Uncle Gustl.

"Do as you are told!" ordered Colonel Brougui.

Uncle Gustl signed all three pages and the next day he got his orders. The request on page one, to be discharged, was denied, and the colonel had filled the blank pages with orders sending Uncle Gustl to a labor camp on the edge of the Sahara desert where a railroad was under construction. His entire unit was demobilized, and he alone was sent to the desert to build the railway. In exchange for his affair, he was given hard labor.

A few months later, he became ill and was sent back to Fez to a new unit, the Ninth Company of the Foreign Infantry Regiment.

VICHY: OCTOBER 3, 1940

The Régime de Vichy, the French state collaborating with the Nazis, passed its own version of the anti-Jewish Nuremberg Laws. It deprived French Jews of their citizenship and forbade them from voting.

VICHY: OCTOBER 22, 1940

Twenty nine thousand German and French Jews from Baden, the Saar, and Alsace-Lorraine were deported to Vichy by the Nazis. They were sent to concentration camps in Poland.

WARSAW: NOVEMBER 16, 1940

The Nazis established a ghetto of more than three hundred fifty thousand Jews in Warsaw, the capital of Poland. The Jews represented thirty percent of the city's population. They were forced to wear white armbands with a blue Star of David. The Nazis kept the Jews from the outside world by building a ten-foot high wall, topped with barbed wire. It was closely guarded to prevent movement between the ghetto and the rest of Warsaw. The ghetto was rundown, dilapidated, and rat-infested, with starvation and disease. Later, many were taken to concentration camps.

KOPRIVNICA: JANUARY 26, 1941

Edith ran up the stairs to her family's second floor apartment. She had just come back from Koprivnica's Jewish agency. She was excited.

"Papa," she said, "we can go to China. Chinese visas are available at the agency."

"What do you mean?" asked Uncle Otto.

"We can leave Koprivnica," she answered.

"Have you heard about this Otto?" said Tante Frieda.

"Papa, there is nothing to do here. My school is terrible. You and Mutti don't speak the language. It is time to leave."

"Edith is right," said Tante Frieda. "Otto, it's time to go. We cannot live here any longer."

Uncle Otto lit a cigarette.

"What do you think the Hackers will do? What about Papá and Mamá? We can't just leave them here alone."

"Grete and Heinrich haven't said anything about leaving. We should go to Zagreb and talk to them and to your parents," suggested Tante Frieda. "But no matter what they do, we must leave. Papá and Mamá should come with us."

"The newspapers say Hitler plans to conquer all of Europe. Yugoslavia doesn't have a chance against the Germans. It's just a matter of time before they come here. This could be our chance to get away, but are we sure we want to go to China?" asked Uncle Otto.

"No other country is accepting refugees," said Edith. "China is our only hope."

"It could take a year to get there," said Uncle Otto. "And then what? What will we do in China?"

"I heard that we would have to go to Genoa, just like the Wertheims did," said Edith. "Genoa has many ships going to China."

"Has anyone heard from Gisela and Heinrich?" said Uncle Otto. "We must talk to everyone immediately. Let's try to convince them all to leave as soon as possible."

The next day, Uncle Otto met with my grandparents and the Hackers. They said they knew the danger, but would not leave Koprivnica.

Edith persisted, and her parents finally agreed. Four days later, they were packed and ready to say good-bye, but they worried about getting into Italy without Italian entry visas. The Jewish agency could not issue visas, but it did, however, offer advice. They were told that the Mussolini government was part of the Axis powers (Germany and Italy) and without visas, they could not enter Italy legally. Crossing the border illegally could get them arrested. They were told to stay away from large cities on the Italian border, such as Trieste, and to plan carefully so they could cross into Italy in the countryside where they would be less conspicuous.

Unable to find an immediate solution to their travel plans, they decided to first go to Zagreb. We met them at the train station and took them to our house. Several days later, they moved into a boarding house near us. Meanwhile, there were rumors that Germany, Italy, and Hungary were about to invade Yugoslavia.

Chapter 15

ZAGREB: APRIL 2, 1941

The rumors were true. Germany invaded Yugoslavia. The Luftwaffe (German Air Force) bombed Belgrade, the capital of Yugoslavia, leaving terrible destruction. The Yugoslav Air Force was all but wiped out on the ground. The Luftwaffe Stukas machine-gunned pedestrians in Sarajevo, killing hundreds. Then air raids began over Zagreb.

The city became dark. Streetlamps and all indoor lighting were prohibited. Blackouts were mandatory. Black paper covered automobile headlamps, with only a slit in the center to identify them as moving objects. Windows were also covered with black paper. We used small candles at night with shades over them, so the light shone directly onto the floor. Our house was not hit. I never saw a bomb explode near us. But I heard them, and when the bombing stopped, I snuck outside and saw beams of light in the sky searching for German bomber planes.

HAIFA: APRIL 6, 1941

Lisl and Bruno were married. Lisl changed her name to Alisa. Bruno became Arie. They took the name Amidror as their family name. They were now Alisa and Arie Amidror.

ZAGREB: APRIL 7, 1941

"Hedi," said my father.
"What is it, Mutsch?"
"I am going to enlist to fight the Germans."
"Robert, that's impossible. You can't do that. What is going to happen to us if the Germans win this war? What if you are captured or killed?"

"Hedi, I have to go. I am going to the enlistment office to make some inquiries."

"Please don't. You're upset. Wait until tomorrow. You'll calm down."

My father was stubborn. He left the house and came back two hours later.

"Hedi, they don't want me. I'm too young for the army."

"What do you mean 'you are too young'? You are thirty nine. How can you be too young?"

"They said I never served in World War I, and they only want people with fighting experience."

"Good!" said my mother. "But now we have to talk about what's going on here. We have nightly air raids. Every night, we have blackouts. What's going to happen if the Nazis occupy Zagreb?"

ZAGREB: APRIL 10, 1941

The Germans took over Zagreb. Ante Pavelić, a Croatian right-wing leader who was in exile in Italy, returned to Zagreb with the approval and support of the Nazis. He then proclaimed Croatia an independent state. Pavelić had been exiled from Yugoslavia in late 1934 after he was accused of taking part in the assassination of Yugoslav King Alexander. The king was murdered while on official business in Marseille in October of that year.

ZAGREB: APRIL 11, 1941

"Hedi," my father said, "it's getting worse everyday. We have to find a way to leave, and Vati and Mutti have to come with us."

My mother was worried. She did not think my grandparents would leave Zagreb, especially since we didn't know where we'd be going. She kept me home from school that day. My father did not leave the house, and my grandfather listened to the radio constantly. The broadcasts said the Germans were all over Yugoslavia and would occupy the entire country in just a few days.

When we left Vienna, we thought we would never again see SS and German soldiers. It had been two and a half years since we had seen a Nazi. Zagreb had been a safe place for us, but it was now just another place where we would be hunted by Nazis.

Zagreb, on the other hand, had become very comfortable for the Wehrmacht, the SS, and any other Germans in uniform. Without any opposition, German soldiers could steal or confiscate anything they wanted. They also indulged themselves at café houses and bars, drinking, and eating a combination of Austrian and Hungarian delicacies they hadn't had in months on the battlefields.

My parents let me play soccer that afternoon when my friends came home from school. A hard kick went three feet over my head, and I chased the ball. The ball was rolling toward the street. I stopped short at the sight of three German soldiers. As the ball rolled near them, a soldier stopped the ball and with his right foot kicked it back to me. It came straight at me, but I was too scared to move. I stood still, staring at the soldier who had kicked it, while the ball rolled past me. He laughed, and they left. In a minute, they were out of sight.

I turned and looked at my ten-year-old friends. They were in a huddle, one with the ball in his hand. They were as afraid of the Nazis as I was, and they weren't Jewish. I crossed the field and went home and never went back to school in Zagreb.

BELGRADE: APRIL 12, 1941

Ten days after the massive bombing, Belgrade, the Yugoslav capital, surrendered to the Germans.

ZAGREB: APRIL 14, 1941

Uncle Otto told Tante Frieda he thought he had found a way for them to get out of Yugoslavia.

"I talked to a man at the café who told me we should go into Italy from Kanal. It is a very small town. We can get there by train through Lyublyana. When we get to Kanal, we only have to walk several miles until we reach the Soča River. The other side of the river is Italy."

"Without Italian visas," said Uncle Otto, "we will have to sneak across."

"I will do the talking," said Edith. "I've heard enough Italian to get by."

"I'm worried about the visas, but I guess the worst that can happen is for us to get arrested, and that can happen here too," added Uncle Otto. "The man in the café said a town called Cividale is about six miles from the river. He thinks it would be possible for us to stay there before continuing to Genoa. He said Cividale is a friendly town with a large German-speaking population. It is a crossroad for merchants and traveling salespeople."

BELGRADE: APRIL 17, 1941

Yugoslavia surrendered. The Wehrmacht took three hundred thirty four thousand Yugoslav prisoners.

KANAL: APRIL 23, 1941

The train stopped in Kanal for five minutes to uncouple two freight cars and allow passengers to get off. The Weisses started walking west. It was lunchtime, and few people were out. The small town had only a few dirt roads, and they followed the largest one. Ten minutes later, they were on the other side of town following the only road out of Kanal. They each carried a small suitcase. Edith, in a bright print dress, also carried a backpack with water, and some bread and cheese. In an hour, they reached what they hoped was the Soča River.

"Papa, look over there at that bridge. It looks like it has a guard house. This must be where we cross the river."

They dropped their bags on the ground and sat out of sight on a large rock. Tante Frieda opened Edith's knapsack, and Uncle Otto cut slices of bread and cheese with his pocket knife. While they ate, they discussed how they would cross the bridge. Uncle Otto said he thought it would be easier for Tante Frieda and Edith to get past the border guards if he wasn't with them. He suggested that he stay behind and cross later in the dark. They all agreed.

Tante Frieda gave her husband a kiss on the cheek. "We'll wait on the other side," she said.

He watched his wife and daughter until they were out of sight. When they approached the bridge, they were met by two Italian border guards. "Arreto (Halt)," said one of the guards in Italian, "your papers, please."

"I'm sorry," said Edith, in Italian, "we do not have visas, but here are our passports."

The guard looked at the Yugoslav passports and seemed unconcerned. "We cannot let you over the bridge without a visa," he said, "but the river isn't very wide. Look for a farmer with a boat. You can pay him to row you across."

The Italian guard was friendly, and they believed him, but they wondered why an Italian border guard would be so helpful. Italy was a fascist country, and Mussolini was a ruthless dictator and an ally of Hitler.

My cousin took her mother's hand and said, "Come Mama, let's get Papa and look for someone with a boat."

They walked back to where they'd left Uncle Otto, but he was gone.

"He must have swum across," said Tante Frieda.

They followed the riverbank about two hundred yards and found a woman fishing. There was a small rowboat nearby. Edith approached the woman and in Croatian said, "Hello, can you row us across the river?"

The woman, in Slovenian, asked Edith to repeat the question. Very slowly, Edith repeated her question, and the woman understood. She put down her fishing rod.

"Are you sure you want to go to the other side? That's Italy you know, it's a fascist country."

"We know," Edith continued, "but we must get across. We can pay you."

"No, no, I don't want any money. You look like nice people. Are you refugees?"

"Da (Yes)," said Edith.

The woman walked to the boat and put oars in the locks. My aunt and cousin put their suitcases in the boat and climbed in. The woman pushed the boat from the bank and jumped inside. Standing, she pushed the boat with one oar until it floated, then sat down to row. They were on the other side in less than five minutes, and Tante Frieda and Edith climbed out.

"Thank you very much," said Edith. "Good-bye, thank you again." She shoved the rowboat away from the riverbank, and their new friend waved and rowed the boat back to the other side.

Then Uncle Otto appeared.

"Papa how did you get here?" asked Edith, hugging her father with relief.

"Otto, did you swim across?" asked Tante Frieda. "No, your clothes are dry?"

"I went to the bridge and asked the guards if someone spoke German. One of the guards understood me and called the sergeant. I told the sergeant if he didn't let me cross the bridge, I would never see my wife and daughter again. I gave him a pack of cigarettes, and he let me go." Edith smiled and gave him a kiss. Tante Frieda hugged him.

"Otto, I'm so glad you're alright, let's go find Cividale."

They walked on the only road from the bridge for about three hours and then saw a sign that told them they were entering Cividale. Rolling hills surrounded the city. Passing monuments that were hundreds of years old, they followed signs to Centro Cita (City Center). Soon they were at the Piazza del Duomo (Square of the Dome) in the center of Cividale.

Circling the piazza were restaurants with outdoor patios. People at the tables watched them as they walked through the square with their suitcases.

"Are you new in town?" asked a man as they went by his table. It was 4:30 p.m. and he was drinking a small cup of coffee.

"I am sorry," said Edith in Italian. "We do not speak much Italian. Do you speak German?"

"I speak German," said another man at the next table.

"We are traveling through and need a place to stay," explained Edith.

"Where are you headed?"

"We are going to Genoa."

"Genoa, that's a long way from here, why Genoa?"

"We want to take a ship to China," answered Edith.

When they heard China, a group at another table looked at each other in astonishment.

"Sit down and have some food," said the German-speaking man. "When was the last time you ate?"

They sat down, and another man joined them.

"My name is Antonio DiSena. I also speak some German. Are you refugees?"

"Yes," said my uncle. "I am Otto Weiss. This is my wife Frieda, and my daughter Edith."

"Let's order some food and talk about where you might stay," said Signor DiSena. The waiter came and he ordered for all of them.

Uncle Otto had taken with him from Zagreb several thousand dinars, but they needed to be frugal if they wanted to go as far as China. Tante Frieda spoke for the first time.

"Signor DiSena, thank you, but we do not have a lot of money, and we have no lira yet."

"Don't worry about the money. It is more important to worry about the Carabinieri (Italian police). If they discover you, they will put you in prison. Where did you come from?"

"We left Vienna in 1938," said Uncle Otto. "We were living in a small town in Yugoslavia, but now the Germans control the country, so we had to leave. We cannot stay in Europe. That's why we are going to China. Some of our family is already there."

"You are Jews, yes?" said Signor DiSena.

"Yes," said Tante Frieda, almost in a whisper. She looked around but saw no reaction from any of the Italians.

"China is so far. Why don't you go to England or America or someplace else closer?"

"China is the only country in the world that will take Jewish refugees," answered Uncle Otto.

Antonio DiSena looked puzzled. "It's hard to believe that China can be your only destination?"

"We could try to go to Palestine, but it is more difficult," said Uncle Otto. "It is easier to get on a freighter to China."

The waiter brought the food. It was a full meal, soup, roast chicken and vegetables, and a carafe of red wine. When they finished, Signor DiSena invited them to stay at his house.

"Come with me, I live nearby," he said. "You can stay with us. Frau Weiss, please let me carry your suitcase."

The house was on a street behind the Piazza. It had a sign on the front, Pensione DiSena. Signor DiSena's home was a bed-and-breakfast, known in Italy as a pension.

Signor DiSena introduced the Weisses to his wife, Signora Maria-Grazia DiSena, who warmly invited them into the house. The pension had five guest rooms and a bath on the second floor, and one bedroom in the attic. They were offered the attic, which had four small beds, a washbasin, and three chairs. They were told to use the toilet on the second floor.

When Edith inquired about the nightly rate, Signora DiSena asked Edith and Tante Frieda if they would help her with chores in exchange for room and board. They gladly agreed to clean rooms and change beds, and do the daily food shopping. The signora said most of her customers were traveling salesmen who only stayed one night, so beds needed to be changed every day. There were always a lot of sheets and towels to wash. Tante Frieda said she would help with that too. Edith asked to do the grocery shopping.

CIVIDALE: MAY 16, 1941

Slavko Losic first noticed Edith at the outdoor market in the Piazza. He saw her three days in a row and on the fourth, waited for her at her favorite vegetable stand. He was twenty two.

"Hello," he said, "my name is Slavko."

"Hello, I am Edith."

Slavko paid for his groceries and waited for Edith to finish her shopping. She had three bags of vegetables.

He asked her where she was from and why she bought so much food every day.

"Why do you ask?" said my cousin.

"I see you here every day. I would like to get to know you."

"That's nice. Thank you," said Edith.

"There is a little café around the corner. Would you have some coffee with me?"

"Yes, but I don't have much time. I work in a pension, and I need to take this food back soon," replied Edith.

Slavko took two of Edith's shopping bags, and they walked to the café. For the next several weeks, Edith and Slavko met each other every day at the market and then had coffee together. Eventually, Edith asked Slavko to come home with her to meet her parents.

BERLIN: JUNE 6, 1941

Ante Pavelić, the Croatian right-wing leader, meets with Adolf Hitler.

CIVIDALE: JUNE 16, 1941

Edith and Slavko had fallen in love. Slavko was Jewish with a background similar to Edith's. He and his parents came to Cividale from Djakovo, a town in Yugoslavia one hundred twenty miles from Koprivnica. They were also heading to Genoa, but their plans were to take a ship to Palestine.

MOSKOW: JUNE 22, 1941

Germany, breaking a nonaggression act between the two countries, invaded Russia. The German invasion began on an eighteen-hundred-mile front from Finland to the Black Sea. The biggest military operation in history, it included three million five hundred thousand German soldiers, three thousand three hundred and fifty tanks, and nearly two thousand aircraft. The Russian Army was unprepared for the surprise assault and could offer only limited resistance with its ill-prepared soldiers, inferior tanks, and unready aircraft. By the end of the first day, the Luftwaffe had destroyed eight hundred Soviet aircraft on the ground at sixty airfields, and four hundred in the air. Germany was now at war on its Eastern and Western fronts.

ZAGREB: JULY 7, 1941

Ante Pavelić was rebuilding the 'Ustaša', the Croatian nationalist Far Right movement that had been founded in 1929. The Ustaša was becoming an active military group, recognized by its distinct brown uniforms. The Ustaša worked hand in hand with the SS. Its mission was the death and destruction of Serbs, Jews, Gypsies, and Communists. The name Ustaša had become synonymous with terror and genocide. Its soldiers built concentration camps to imprison their opponents. The first camp was built on the banks of the Sava River, sixty miles south of Zagreb. It was named for the town it was in: Camp Jasenovac. Five more camps were soon added.

Croatia was now dependent on Germany for survival and was another Nazi puppet state.

The refugee population in Zagreb had increased by the thousands. Yugoslav Jews who had been in the country for many generations were being persecuted, along with the new refugees. The Ustaša, in their notorious brown uniforms, roamed the streets arresting Jews, Serbs, and Gypsies at will and sending them to Jasenovac, which was known as a destination with death.

Chapter 16

ZAGREB: JULY 13, 1941

Hansi's parents and his sister Gerti moved from Koprivnica to Zagreb. My parents found them a small apartment not far from where we lived.

ZAGREB: JULY 15, 1941

"Hedi, do you remember Samuel Weisberg?" my father asked during dinner.

"I met him someplace, but I don't remember where."

"I know him from the shoe business. He has lived in Zagreb all of his life. I called him and asked his advice about leaving Yugoslavia."

"Really, what did he say?" My mother stopped eating and put her knife and fork on her plate.

"He said we should get Bolivian passports and go to Portugal to try to get to America. Samuel knows someone who used to work at the Bolivian Consulate."

"Why Bolivian passports?"

"Bolivia is neutral country, so if we have Bolivian passports, we do not need visas in Europe. That means we can travel all the way through Italy, France, Spain, and into Portugal."

"Robert, this is an interesting possibility. What else did he say?"

"Samuel said his friend at the consulate has blank passports and an embossing machine he stole during a Nazi bombing raid. When someone wants a passport, all he does is paste a photo in it and imprint it with a seal. He wants ten thousand dinars, in cash, for two passports. Samuel says he will contact him tomorrow if we want."

"We have to do this," said my mother. "It could be our only way out of here."

"Samuel also told me that Lisbon is a major escape for refugees to America and other Western countries. Portugal adopted a policy allowing thousands of Jewish refugees to enter the country.

"I will call Samuel in the morning. Why don't you talk to your parents and Anna about coming with us?"

"I will do that," said my mother. "We will need new photos."

"I think the photo store where I have my pictures developed can take passport photos. I'll call them right away."

We didn't waste any time. The next morning, the four of us had passport photos taken.

My grandparents would not leave. They believed they were too old to be harmed by the Nazis. Grossmutter insisted they would be safe because she was born a Czech, as was Tante Anna. They were determined to stay in the apartment. They had enough money, and Tanta Anna was working so they could pay their rent and buy food.

ZAGREB: JULY 18, 1941

My father and Herr Weisberg arranged to meet at a café in the center of Zagreb. My father got there first and ordered coffee. A few minutes later, his friend arrived and sat down. He looked around to see if anyone was listening.

"Robert, you are looking well. We don't have much time. Do you have your photos and the money?"

My father passed him an envelope with the four passport pictures and ten thousand dinars.

"Wait here, I'll be right back."

Herr Weisberg went to the back of the café and into a small room where a man was sitting at a desk piled with blank passports. He gave him the money and the photos, and five minutes later, he was back at my father's table.

"I can't believe it was that easy," said my father.

My father looked at the passports and quickly put them in his pocket. Both were embossed with the official Bolivian seal. My mother's passport included the photos of me and Peter. In just fifteen minutes, we had become Bolivians and had new Spanish names. Our last name was now Valles. My first name was Ernesto, Peter was Pedro, and my father was Roberto. My mother became Hedviga instead of Hedwig. During the period we used our new names, I don't ever remember being called anything but Pommy.

ZAGREB: JULY 20, 1941

It took one day to pack. My grandparents and Tante Anna helped us. In the front hall there were two suitcases of clothing and three small trunks packed with the same things we had shipped from Vienna: reels of film, a projector and screen; and my mother's sheet music and her accordion; the tennis racquets; my electric train and a few toys for Peter. He was now three and a half, so his stroller was left behind.

My mother tried to call the Hackers to say good-bye, but there was no answer. She dialed a second and third time, and still there was no answer.

"Robert," my mother said, "I called Heinrich and Grete three times, but they don't answer. It is strange they are not home at nine on Sunday morning. I'm going to walk over to see them."

It was a ten minute walk from our house across a canal to the Hackers' apartment. When my mother got to the canal, cars and people were waiting on both sides of the bridge. It was closed off on both ends and Ustaša soldiers were on the bridge, yelling at civilians they had captured that morning.

"Line up against the wall!" screamed a soldier.

My mother slowly moved closer. There were about thirty men, women, and children, lined up against the bridge's railings, facing each other. Ustaša soldiers were pacing back and forth in the middle.

"Get close to the wall and face the water! Turn around and face the water!"

My mother stood paralyzed. Heinrich and Grete Hacker and my cousin Gerti were among the captives.

"Grete," she screamed to my father's sister, "Heinrich, Gerti!"

A stranger touched her elbow and gently pulled her away.

"Don't look," he said in German. "Turn your back."

"I can't. My husband's sister and family are on the bridge."

"Please turn your back to the bridge," he repeated.

My mother watched as soldiers put black hoods over the captives' heads. Then they pulled swords from their sheaths.

"Oh, my God." said my mother, covering her face with her hands. "They can't do this!"

The stranger held on to my mother's arm. An Ustaša officer yelled a command for the captives to bend at the waist over the wall.

Within seconds, the Ustaša soldiers had decapitated everyone on the bridge, their heads falling into the water.

My father's brother-in-law, Heinrich Hacker, age fifty three, was dead. My father's sister Grete, (Hansi's mother) age forty three, was dead. My twelve-year-old cousin Gerti was dead. And my mother had seen it all.

She was led away by the stranger, who was trying to keep her from becoming hysterical.

"Where do you live?" he asked softly, putting his arm around her shoulder.

"Five streets from here, on Gajdekova Ulica."

"Come, I will take you home."

My mother could not imagine how she was going to tell my father, or anyone else, what she had just witnessed.

KOPRIVNICA: JULY 21, 1941

It was Monday, 10:00 a.m. Grosspapá Marcus and Grossmamá Hermina Weiss heard the familiar sound of trucks and Ustaša soldiers screaming in the street below their Florijanska Ulica apartment. They did not dare look out the window. This was an everyday event. Living in fear of being arrested was now a way of life for everyone in this small town, Jews and non-Jews alike. This time, however, it was different. The soldiers' voices were at their door. A rifle butt slammed against it, forcing it open.

Two Ustaša men with rifles across their chests walked in and grabbed my grandparents. They forced them down the stairs onto the street.

A truck with an open back was parked in front of the house. There were already a dozen people in the back. Grosspapá and Grossmamá, age seventy-two and sixty-nine, were pushed up onto the truck. Someone in the back helped my grandmother. They sat down, holding hands.

Grosspapá and Grossmamá were among two hundred and twelve Jews arrested that day in Koprivnica and taken to the Jasenovac concentration camp one hundred twenty miles away. It was a six hour drive on back-country roads. The truck had no food or water and not so much as bucket to use for a toilet.

ZAGREB: JULY 21, 1941

It was Monday afternoon, the day after the massacre on the bridge. My mother was in a state of shock and unable to talk about it. She decided to wait until we were safely out of Zagreb to tell my father about the deaths of his sister and her family.

A taxi took us to the train station. Our destination was Split, a popular Yugoslav seaside resort on the Adriatic, about one hundred eighty miles southeast of Zagreb. Herr Weisberg had suggested that we take a ferry from there to Fiume, a city on the Adriatic, Croatia's largest seaport. From there, we could cross into Abbazia. This itinerary, he said, would keep us out of big cities, such as Trieste, which were overrun with Nazis and the Ustaša.

We got on the train, now traveling as Bolivian citizens. It took close to four hours to get to Split. There were no Ustaša or Italian checkpoints along the way. When we got to Split, my father went into a bank to change our dinars into lira. Then we checked into a hotel that had been recommended by Herr Weisberg.

"Mutsch, I have something to tell you," said my mother as she unpacked a suitcase.

My father looked at my mother. She looked worried.

"Robert, I am pregnant."

"What?"

"I am pregnant," she repeated.

"Hedi, a baby, how is this possible? I thought we were so careful. Do you feel okay?"

"Yes, I am fine. But I wish it hadn't happened. We have no choice. I cannot have a baby now. We can't travel this way. We need to find a doctor who will end this."

My mother went to the hotel's receptionist who gave her the name of a Jewish doctor. That night, she went to his office. Three hours later, she took a taxi back to the hotel. My father helped her into bed, and she fell asleep, almost immediately.

The next morning, while my father took me and Peter to breakfast, she called Grossvater Jakob to tell him we had safely arrived in Split.

"Hedi, I have been trying since yesterday to reach Marcus and Hermina to tell them you left Zagreb. They don't answer the phone, so I called their friend, Andre Volnic, about an hour ago. He said they were put in a truck and taken away by the Ustaša."

My mother was tired. She was weak from the procedure in the doctor's office the night before. The deaths of Tante Grete, Uncle Heinrich, and Gerti, and now, the news about my grandparents was too much to comprehend. How could she possibly tell my father about all of this? The last two days had been extremely difficult.

The next day, Tuesday, we took our trunks and suitcases and boarded the ferry to Fiume where we met with a landlord, also recommended by Herr Weisberg, who rented us a small furnished apartment. We went out to dinner, and when we got back, my mother sent Peter and me to bed. She closed our bedroom door and went into the small living room. She sat down on an overstuffed chair, lit a cigarette, and crossed her legs. She took a deep breath and looked at my father.

"Mutsch, I have terrible things to tell you."

"Hedi, what are you talking about?"

"Mutsch, your parents were arrested. My father told me when I called him yesterday. They must have been taken to Jasenovac."

My father sat still for minute. Then he stood up, walked to the window, and stared out to the street. He had tears in his eyes. Jews did not leave Jasenovac alive. No one left Jasenovac alive.

"We should have made them come with us," he said.

"Robert, there is more," said my mother. Then she told him about the killings of his sister, brother-in-law, and niece.

"Grete, Heinrich and little Gerti are gone. Robert, I saw it happen."

My mother got up and put her arms around my father. He held on to her. They stood together, sobbing.

"How do we go on?" said my father after a long silence.

"I don't know," said my mother, "but for our children, we have to . . . somehow we have to."

CIVIDALE: JULY 25, 1941

Two Carabinieri knocked on the door of the DiSena Pension. Otto, Frieda, and Edith Weiss were arrested. The Carabinieri loaded them into a truck and drove them to their regional headquarters in Udine, thirty miles away. Someone in Cividale had reported them to the police. They spent the night in jail, all in the same cell.

In the morning, a guard unlocked the cell door and told them to follow him. He led them to a room where they were interrogated and issued a lasciapassar (identity pass), which officially admitted them to Italy, and gave them permission to travel to other parts of the country. The identity pass was a means for the Carabinieri to keep track of refugees. My uncle, aunt, and cousin were then released. They took a bus to Cividale and went back to the DiSenas pension. Their personal belongings had not been touched.

ZURICH: AUGUST 6, 1941

Hansi checked his mail. He usually got a letter from his mother every week, but it had been almost three weeks since the last letter. He was worried. Every day, the Swiss newspapers had reports of Nazi atrocities in Poland, Germany, and Austria, and now they were writing stories about persecution by the Ustaša in Yugoslavia. Hansi followed the war closely, reading all he could about fighting on various fronts. He believed his parents were still in Zagreb, and he kept writing letters, urging them yet again to send Gerti to England with the Kindertransport.

He did not know that the transports had ceased in late 1939, after ten thousand refugee children from Central Europe had been taken to England.

Hansi was terribly worried and becoming depressed. It was affecting both his work and personal life.

FIUME: AUGUST 6, 1941

We had been in Fiume two weeks, but it seemed a very long time. My parents were not themselves, and I didn't know why. They were sad and quiet, and my father rarely left the house.

"Robert," said my mother as she cleared the breakfast table, "it is time to move on to Abbazia. Let's pack our things and go."

Until now we had traveled by train or boat but this time, to get to Italy, we had to walk over a bridge that was guarded on the other side by Carabinieri. It wasn't far, but it was impossible to hand carry all our belongings.

"We need a wagon," said my father. "Pommy, do you want to come with me to the hardware store?"

We bought a sturdy, wood, flat top wagon with large wheels. My father piled the trunks on top and tied them down with a rope. We began walking to the bridge, my father pulling the wagon. My mother carried a suitcase, and I carried the other. In twenty minutes, we were there. It was hot, and we were all perspiring. We got halfway across the bridge when my father suddenly stopped.

"That's enough," he said.

"What's the matter?" asked my mother.

"I can't pull this another step. We have to get rid of some of these things."

"You are right, let's open up the trunks and take out the things we absolutely need."

In the middle of the bridge, my parents opened the trunks, and repacked one with my mother's sheet music, the reels of film, the Leica, the tennis rackets, and my electric train. The accordion was in its own case.

The wagon was two thirds lighter, and we kept going. Left behind on the bridge were two trunks, and an odd assortment of personal belongings. Suddenly, my mother stopped short.

"We are not going back for any of those things," said my father.

She looked at him. "Here we are escaping from the Nazis and carrying all these meaningless things. It is ridiculous. Why are we carrying these tennis racquets?"

With that, she opened the trunk, took out the rackets, and threw them into the river. "There!" she said.

My father said nothing. The tennis racquets were a symbol of our old life. Letting them float away was the beginning of a new life, wherever that might be. We continued and crossed a red-white-and-green line (the colors of Italy) which was painted on the road from one side to the other. It was the Italian checkpoint. Two Carabinieri guards stopped us, and my mother gave our passports to one of them.

"You cannot cross," he said, passing them back to my mother.

My mother stood her ground. "We are Bolivians," she said confidently, "and we do not need visas."

The guards ignored her.

She tried another approach.

"Please," she said. "We had to leave our apartment in Fiume, and we cannot go back. We have to find a place to live."

The guard looked at us for a moment, and then told the other Carabinieri to take us to a courthouse, which turned out to be a three-minute walk from the bridge.

We were taken before a magistrate, a man in his sixties who sat behind a large desk. The magistrate peered over his glasses and smiled. He didn't say a word, but he picked up his pen and wrote on our passports that we had permission for a three-week stay in Abbazia.

My parents had been to Abbazia before on vacation. It was known for its splendid beaches, and was a favorite resort for the aristocracy in the Austro-Hungarian Empire. With its beautiful old villas and grassy parks, the town had a special air of elegance. We were soon checked into two adjoining rooms in a small hotel in the center of the town.

Carabinieri, Italian State Police.

ABBAZIA: AUGUST 8, 1941

My father found an old synagogue. He went in and talked to the rabbi about his sister and parents. That night, for the first time in three years, we attended Friday evening services as a family. The rabbi prayed for the well-being of my grandparents and the souls of my aunt, uncle, and cousin. Following the service, the rabbi and others came to us and expressed condolences and their hope we would someday see my grandparents again. That's when I learned the fate of the Hackers and my grandparents. I cried myself to sleep that night.

The next morning, we all walked to a beach just two blocks from our hotel. For the next few weeks, we spent a lot of time on that beach. It seemed we were putting the past behind us.

ABBAZIA TO VENICE: AUGUST 22, 1941

Our three weeks in Abbazia were almost up. No one had any information about my father's parents. They had just disappeared.

Leaving the wooden wagon at the hotel, we took a train to Venice. It took two hours, a short trip compared to the others we had taken since October 1938. When we got off the train, my father went to the ticket counter and purchased second-class tickets to Lisbon. We planned to say in Venice until Friday.

Then we boarded the Venice Grand Canal water ferry. We got off near the Piazza San Marco and went to a hotel my parents had stayed in several times while on vacation.

During those four days, my parents talked a lot about what lay ahead of us. The trains to Portugal went through northern Italy, then through Vichy, the part of France that was friendly with Germany. Our trip would then take us to Spain, a country still recovering from a three-year civil war that had ended in 1939. Spain was in an economic recession, and famine was widespread. Spain's head of state, Gen. Francisco Franco, was sympathetic to Hitler and was making it difficult for Jews to travel through the country.

It would take almost four full days to travel the fourteen hundred miles from Venice to Lisbon. Without our Bolivian passports, the trip might not have been possible. But my parents were certain they would get us through France and Spain, and then to Portugal. The plan was to stop in Madrid to visit a Jewish agency to see if it could give us more information on how to get to America.

Before we left Venice, my father went to a bank and changed our Italian lira into American dollars so he had currency that was accepted everywhere.

VENICE TO MADRID: AUGUST 25, 1941

Our journey to Portugal began with the water ferry taking us to the train station. We boarded the train to Madrid at 10:00 a.m. Two Carabinieri officers occasionally walked through the cars, but they paid no attention to us. The trip to the French border took eight hours. At the border, a French guard walked through the car, checking passports. He looked at ours and moved on without saying a word.

A vendor came through, and we bought lunch and dinner. We were alone in a compartment with eight seats, four seats on each side, so there was plenty of room for us to stretch out to sleep that night. The next day, at the French and Spanish border, we had to change trains. The rails on Spain's railroad tracks were wider than the rest of Europe, so all other European trains had to stop there and turn around.

We arrived in Madrid at 3:00 a.m. on Sunday, walked to a nearby hotel, and registered for one room. On Monday, we all went to HIAS, the Hebrew Immigrant's Aid Society, that was known worldwide. It was packed with refugees from all over Europe, each asking the same question: how to get to America. The answer given by the HIAS was one we already knew: we had to get to Lisbon first.

We were told there were a few ships bound for North America from Bilbao on Spain's northern coast, but it was a long way from Madrid to Bilbao, and there were no assurances of us getting aboard a ship there, because of an overwhelming demand. We were also advised that many Spaniards were unemployed and starving, and impatient with refugees.

MADRID TO LISBON: AUGUST 26, 1941

We took an 11:30 a.m. train to Lisbon. There were no Gestapo, no Ustaša, no SS, not even a Spaniard to check our passports. We had a three-hour ride to the Portuguese border. Then it would take two hours to get to Lisbon.

We sat in a second-class eight-passenger compartment already occupied by two men, who were smoking. My mother lit a cigarette and sat back and relaxed. During our time in Spain, the only thing we could get to eat was corn bread and green beans. My parents were anxious to get out of the country.

The train moved out, and we were headed for our last European destination. It was a good feeling.

It started to rain, a downpour. I looked up and saw water seeping through the ceiling. My jacket was wet. My father took two umbrellas from one of the suitcases and gave one to my mother. My mother and I sat under it, and Peter and my father shared the other, for three hours. Spain was not maintaining its trains. As we approached the Portuguese border, my father became concerned about the American dollars he was carrying.

"Hedi," he whispered to my mother, "I could be searched by the Spanish border guards. If they discover the money, they will steal it for sure."

"I could put the money in my underwear," my mother whispered back.

"You'd probably be the first one to be searched."

"I could carry the money," I said into my mother's ear, trying to keep the two strangers from hearing me. "Look at my pockets. They can hold all of the money." I had seen the packets of money my father had in rubber bands. My mother looked at me. I had two pockets in my pants and two on my jacket, one on the inside.

"Robert, a ten-year-old is less likely to be searched than an adult. I think it's a good idea," said my mother.

"Pommy," said my father, "let's go outside for some fresh air."

There were several people in the aisle, looking out the windows. We went inside the toilet compartment. My father took the money from his pants, and we put it into my pockets. Then we went back into our compartment. Within an hour, the train slowed down. We were at the Spanish-Portuguese border. Again we had to change trains, because the Portuguese tracks were not the same width of those in Spain. We walked across the Spanish border without anyone even noticing us.

Then we walked into Portugal through a small tunnel-shaped wooden structure, which was manned by Portuguese border guards. They took a quick look at our Bolivian documents and motioned us on. As we passed through, we went by a shop that immediately caught my attention. It had the most amazing array of food: breads, pastries, meats, cheeses, butter, and all kinds of fruits and vegetables. It was incredible. We were just a few footsteps out of Spain, and we could buy all kinds of food. Twenty feet behind us, there were only green beans and corn bread.

"Papa," I asked, "can we get something to eat?" My father took Peter's hand, and my mother and I followed them inside where he bought us sandwiches, sodas, and pastry for dessert. We sat on a bench to eat while we waited for the train to Lisbon. It was sunny and warm, and we were hungry.

It had been days since we had such good food. Lisbon was only three hours away. By that time I had emptied my pockets of the money I was carrying. I was not rich anymore.

ZAGREB: AUGUST 27, 1941

Tante Anna cleaned a dentist's office three times a week. One day, a thirty-six-year-old woman came in for an appointment. Her name was Ivka Kostelic, and it was the second time Tante Anna had seen her. The two women got into a friendly conversation, in German. Ivka invited her to her home to meet her mother, who was ill and partially paralyzed from a stroke.

A few days later, Tante Anna rang the doorbell, and the Kostelic family cook opened the door.

"Are you the nurse we advertised for?" she asked, in Croatian.

"No, I am a friend of Ivka. My name is Anna Weininger."

"I am sorry, Ivka is not here," said the cook.

The elder Frau Kostelic overheard the conversation and called to Tante Anna to come in.

"Ivka has told me all about you," said Frau Kostelic, who was lying on a large chaise lounge in the living room. "I'm sorry my daughter isn't here right now. She should be back soon. Please sit down."

Thirty minutes went by, and Tante Anne said she would come back another day when Ivka was home.

"She is always here to help me with lunch," said the elderly woman. "Why don't you come for lunch tomorrow?"

The next day Ivka and her mother asked my aunt to move in with them. She could help take care of Frau Kostelic. Tante Anna welcomed the offer, and soon Tante Anna was like one of the family. Grossmutter Emma and Grossvater Jakob, who were still living in our old apartment, visited often, and Grossvater entertained them on Ivka's piano with Viennese waltzes.

Chapter 17

LISBON: SEPTEMBER 11, 1941

Portugal did not participate in the war. It remained neutral, and Lisbon, its capital, was a safe place for refugees, as well as spies and criminals. More than one hundred thousand Jews traveled through Lisbon in 1941 and 1942. But Portugal would not give them permanent residency or allow them to work. The HIAS office in Lisbon helped refugees find housing, set up soup kitchens for the poor, and it found schools for children to attend.

We moved into another small apartment. As soon as we were settled, my mother went to the post office and called her parents in Zagreb.

Grossvater answered the telephone. My mother told him about our trip to Lisbon and gave him our address. Grossvater told her that Tante Anna was living with the Kostelics, and that he had received a letter from her brother, Gustl. He gave my mother his Foreign Legion address.

"I am afraid I have no news about Robert's parents," he said.

It had been eight weeks since the deaths of the Hackers.

I was sent to school. This time, the teacher spoke only Portuguese, and once more, I learned nothing. My parents had little to do, and spent most of the time reading German-language newspapers and talking with other refugees. We had been in Portugal two weeks and still had didn't know how to get to America. There had not been a ship headed in that direction since we arrived.

"When Pommy gets home from school, we should go to the American Consulate and see if they can help us out," said my mother. "Robert, tomorrow is Friday, and before you know it we'll be here three weeks, still not knowing what to do."

We all went to the consulate that afternoon, but my mother was the only one who went inside. Ten minutes later, she came out.

"They say it is impossible for us to go to America without a sponsor," she said. "The official I spoke with suggested we try to go to another country. He said that now, Chile, the Dominican Republic, Uruguay, Cuba, Mexico, and Argentina, are all easy to get into."

"Cuba and Mexico are the closest to America," said my father. "The Cuban Consulate is just down the street. Let's go there."

The embassies and consulates in Lisbon were in the same area. The buildings were large and beautiful, with flower gardens and ornamental trees. We walked by several, and in a few minutes were at the Cuban Consulate. We all went inside, but again it was my mother who did the talking. She was told our Bolivian passports would admit us to Cuba, and all we had to do was fill out a few papers. Outside on the sidewalk, my father looked at my mother.

"We know nothing about Cuba. Is this really a good idea?" he said.

"Robert, we can't stay here. We should go there and try to get to America from Cuba. It's a lot closer than Portugal."

The next day, we all went back to the Cuban Consulate. My parents filled out some forms, were issued visas, and told where to go to purchase passage. The next scheduled ship from Lisbon to Havana was almost three months away, on December 7. Lisbon would be our home for much longer than we expected.

ZAGREB: SEPTEMBER 14, 1941

Tante Anna was preparing Sunday lunch for the Kostelics and Grossvater and Grossmutter, who were expected at noon. It was 1:00 p.m., and they had not arrived. The doorbell rang. Ivka went to the door, expecting my grandparents, but there was a woman standing there. She was crying.

"Miss Kostelic," she said, "there was a raid last night on the Gajdekova Ulica. Many Jews, including your friend and her husband, were arrested."

"That can't be possible," said Ivka. By now, Tante Anna was also at the door. She had heard the conversation. Her face was pale.

"Ivka," asked Tante Anna, "would you please go to Emma and Jakob's apartment to see if you can find out more?" Tante Anna couldn't believe what she'd heard. Had her sister and brother-in-law been arrested too?

Ivka immediately got her coat and left. Tante Anna sat down on the sofa next to Frau Kostelic's wheelchair. Ivka's mother reached for Tante Anna's hand and held it tightly.

"Anna dear, everything will be all right. The woman probably made a mistake. Your sister and her husband could have been delayed for some other reason. Wait and see."

The two women sat holding hands, waiting for Ivka to return.

It was a thirty minutes to Gajdekova Ulica. Ivka walked quickly. As she got close to my grandparents' house, she looked around, searching for any clue as to what had happened. There was no one else on the street. A few yards from the house she stopped, worried. Then she pushed my grandparents' doorbell. The building had buzzers in each apartment that opened the front door to let visitors in. There was no response, and she tried a second and third time. She tried another apartment, and a man opened the front door.

"Hello," he said.

"I am sorry to bother you, but I am looking for the Jellineks. There doesn't seem to be anyone home."

"They've been arrested. The Gestapo took them to the old school. It's two streets behind here." He abruptly shut the door in Ivka's face.

Ivka placed her hand over her mouth. Then she looked up into the sky. "What am I going to tell my dear friend? What am I going to tell Anna?" she whispered to herself.

Ivka went home and found her mother and Tante Anna still sitting in the living room.

"Anna," said Ivka, "many Jews were arrested. The Gestapo took them all to a closed-up school." She took off her coat and sat down next to Tante Anna.

"I must go to that school right away!"

"No, Anna, it's impossible. I am not letting you go. It's too risky. I will not let you out of my sight!"

"But I have to find Emma, she is my sister." Tante Anna was now in a panic. She picked up her purse and walked to the door.

"Anna," yelled Ivka, "you will be arrested too. Please don't leave the house."

Tante Anna stopped and went back to the sofa. She began to cry. Ivka tried to console her. Then Tante Anna wiped away her tears and stared across the room, motionless. The three women sat silently. Eventually, Ivka went into the kitchen and made tea. No one was hungry for lunch, which still sat in the oven.

The following morning, Ivka went to the school with a bag of food, hoping to somehow see my grandparents. As a non-Jew and lifelong resident of Zagreb, she felt safe. The four-story school building had been deserted for years. It was surrounded by a three-foot stone wall. On top of the wall was a chain link fence, two feet high. The entrance had a wrought iron gate, wide enough for a truck. German soldiers were stationed at the gate, and at intervals around the building. They would not talk to her. She couldn't see anyone through the windows.

Disappointed, she went home, but during the next few days, she went back, hoping to learn something about my grandparents. Her visits were unsuccessful, and when she went home, Tante Anna was waiting at the door. Ivka was worried about her friend. She wasn't eating or sleeping and was becoming withdrawn.

ZURICH: SEPTEMBER 18, 1941

Hansi's last letter to his parents was returned, marked "Undelivered," by the Zagreb Post Office. The next morning, Hansi did not get out of bed. He stayed there the entire day and night, didn't eat, and he didn't answer the telephone. Karli tried to reach him and became concerned. The two young men talked almost daily.

Karli went to Hansi's rooming house the next day after work and found his friend in bed, soaking wet with perspiration and unable to speak. He called an ambulance. When the emergency medical people arrived, they said Hansi appeared to be suffering from severe depression and needed to see a doctor. Hansi met with a psychiatrist for the next four months, all the time praying he would hear from his parents and young sister. He blamed himself for his family's disappearance. Eventually he was able to return to work.

ZAGREB: SEPTEMBER 19, 1941

Ivka went again to the school and found it empty. There was no one inside, and the guards were gone. A woman passing by told her the Gestapo had taken everyone away in trucks. Ivka went home and told Tante Anna the bad news.

Before they had a chance to talk about it, the doorbell rang. It was Klaus Herbst, the blind boy who was in Tante Anna's group from Spielfeld, Austria, to Zagreb. He was accompanied by another teenage boy, who was acting as his guide. Klaus told Tante Anna and Ivka that he was one of the prisoners in the school, and he was kept in the same room as her sister.

"Anna," said Klaus, "I met Emma and Jakob. She told me where you were living. I bring you greetings and kisses from them. The Gestapo released me yesterday because being blind, I was an inconvenience. I can't stay because my friend has to get home. If it's okay, I will come see you again. I hope everything will be all right."

Klaus and his friend left, and Tante Anna turned to Ivka.

"What do you think will happen to them?"

"Anna, I don't know. They are old and of no use to the Nazis. Maybe they will be taken care of by someone," answered Ivka, fully aware she was speaking empty words.

Tante Anna thought about Pepi. She still couldn't imagine how someone could shoot him as he ran through the woods. She thought of the Hackers dying on the bridge. How could people do these awful things?

"Poor Emma and Jakob," she said to Ivka. "How can they endure this imprisonment? Emma is seventy one, and Jakob is three years older. How dreadful it must be for them. Do you think they are in Jasenovac?"

"The Ustaša takes its prisoners to Jasenovac, but it was the Gestapo that took Emma and Jakob," answered Ivka. "I think the Gestapo usually takes its prisoners to Germany. They could have sent them to Dachau or Auschwitz in Poland."

Tante Anna knew a trip to Germany or Poland took many days. Only cattle cars were being used to transport prisoners. She doubted there was much food and water for the prisoners, and certainly there were no toilets. How could her sister, at her age, survive such a trip?

ZAGREB, SEPTEMBER 26, 1941

Tante Anna and Ivka went to our old apartment and asked the caretaker if he knew where my grandparents' possessions were. The caretaker took them into the basement where they found several boxes, marked Jellinek. Sorting through them, they found letters and an address book. Tante Anna took the address book, and a few personal things, home with her and found Uncle Gustl's Foreign Legion address and our address in Lisbon. She wrote letters to both my mother and her nephew, telling them about my grandparents.

LISBON: OCTOBER 4, 1941

"I'm going to the post office to call my parents," she said. "We should have had a letter from them by now. It's been more than three weeks since I talked to them. I'll be back soon."

My mother placed the call to Zagreb, but it didn't go through. A telephone operator came on the line and told her that the number my mother gave her was no longer in service.

She left the post office and slowly walked home, wondering what to do next. Her parents were obviously not in their apartment, and she knew Tante Anna had moved out, but she didn't know how to reach her.

"Robert," she said as she came in the door. "I'm afraid there is more bad news. My parents' phone is disconnected, and I don't know how to reach Anna."

JASENOVAC: NOVEMBER 7, 1941

Grosspapá Weiss had been in Jasenovac since July 21. He had not seen or heard from Grossmamá since they got off the truck that took them there. When they arrived at the camp, most of the prisoners were executed. Those who were spared were professionals, such as doctors and pharmacists, and tradesmen, who could be of use in the camp. Living conditions were terrible. The barracks were filthy and cold, there was no medicine for the sick, and there was very little to eat.

Jasenovac records show that Grosspapá was murdered on November 7, 1941.

Grossmamá most likely died in nearby Camp Stara Gradiška, where the women were incarcerated.

THERESIENSTADT: 1941

Theresienstadt, a small town thirty six miles northeast of Prague, had been turned into a Jewish ghetto. As in the Warsaw Ghetto, all Jews were cut off from the outside world.

PRAGUE: MONDAY, DECEMBER 1, 1941

Lilly wrote from London that she had found Heli a job as an au pair. She urged Heli to come at once. Heli went from Znojmo to Prague to apply for a visa, but was again denied. Discouraged, she went home to Znojmo.

LISBON: DECEMBER 7, 1941

We were among three hundred refugees who boarded the SS *Colonial* to Cuba. It was a Sunday. Newspaper headlines and special radio broadcasts that day announced that Japan had attacked the United States at Pearl Harbor. The United States immediately declared war on Japan. Boarding the ship with us that day were Stevo, Anka, Slavko, and Djuro Singer, Yugoslav Jews from Belgrade. Eventually, we would become good friends.

On board, my mother, Peter, and I were assigned bunks in the women's dormitory. For the entire trip, I was surrounded by women all ages, often half dressed in girdles and bras. At first, I wanted to hide under the bedcovers. That afternoon, two boys approached Peter and me.

"My name is Slavko," said the older one, who was a year younger than me.

"I'm Pommy, and this is my brother Peter, he is almost four years old."

"This is my brother Djuro," said Slavko. "He is four too. Come with us. I want to show you something." Slavko led the four of us up a stairway to a balcony. "Look at this," he said, pointing at nude women taking showers.

Djuro and Peter paid little attention, but Slavko and I stood enthralled for a few minutes until one of the women chased us away, just as the loudspeakers announced it was time for dinner.

The dining hall was huge, but not big enough to accommodate all the passengers at the same time. We were divided into groups alphabetically. The Singers and the Valles were in the same group. By the third day, we ate all our meals together.

The weather was cold, and we spent very little time on deck. The ocean was rough and, at times, waves went over the ship's deck. None of us had been at sea before, and many people were seasick. Others got sick watching others being sick. The stench was awful. After a few days of constant rolls, an old Polish lady in our section died. We watched as crew members took her body to the top deck, wrapped in cotton from head to foot like a mummy. The crew put her in a wooden box with some rusty chains inside and nailed it shut. The Singer brothers and Peter and I watched as they slid the coffin overboard. It took a while to sink. It floated for a while with air bubbles coming out and then slowly sank. Later on, Slavko told me he was having nightmares about the old lady drifting to the bottom of the ocean.

During the long days we spent together aboard the *SS Colonial,* Slavko and I talked a lot. His family had fled from Belgrade to Lisbon.

"Did you have bombings in Zagreb?" asked Slavko during one of our conversations.

"Yes, but I only heard them, I never saw an explosion. We had lots of blackouts."

"We had some very scary times in Belgrade," boasted Slavko. "I woke up one morning as my mother was yelling for us to get dressed. There was a crack in the plaster moving across the ceiling of my room. The four of us rushed across the street to a house with an underground garage. We huddled in the back of the garage while the Germans bombed a Yugoslav military post down the street. We were lucky we didn't get blown up. The Stukas made shrieking noises when they dropped the bombs, and then it was quiet. A few seconds later, a big explosion blew out the garage door and hurt everyone's ears."

I was fascinated. "We never had anything like that. We were lucky."

"How did you get to Lisbon?" asked Slavko.

I told him the whole story, including the part where I carried thousands of dollars across the Portuguese border.

"How about you?" I asked.

"We went to Rome first. Then we took an airplane to Lisbon, but it landed in Madrid first. In Madrid, we had a scary incident. A Spanish policeman got on the plane and looked at all the passengers. Then he pointed to my father and told him he had to get off because some important person needed his seat. My mother started to cry, and my father got mad. He said he had a wife and children, and he would not leave them. Then a priest came from the back of the plane and said he would give up his seat. The priest got off, the important person got on, and my father did not have to get off, so it worked out all right."

During our voyage, Slavko's father arranged for a young woman to teach some of us Spanish. There were six people in our group. Weather permitting, we sat on deck for our classes. My mother, who had a talent for languages, took part. She already spoke Italian and French and a little Croatian. By the time we arrived in Havana, her Spanish would be good enough to converse with the Cubans.

THE *SS COLONIAL*: DECEMBER 9, 1941

The ship's engines stopped, and the ship slowed down and came to a stop. I asked my mother if I could go on deck to see what was going on. She told me to look for my father so he could go with me. On my way to the men's dormitory, I ran into Slavko and his father, and together we found my father. He was already on deck with many other passengers.

In the water about a hundred yards away was a German U-boat. It was sitting still. Approaching us was a small launch with a German officer and six sailors aboard. They all carried guns.

Just two days at sea, we became aware we were in waters with German submarines. Passengers feared the worst. Would we be ordered back to Europe, or worse, would they torpedo our ship?

The Germans came aboard and did a quick inspection. The *SS Colonial* flew a Portuguese flag and carried no weapons. The Germans gave the captain permission to continue and went back to the submarine. The U-boat then slowly submerged and disappeared.

BERLIN: DECEMBER 11, 1941

Germany and Italy declared war on the United States. The United States and China declared war on Germany and Italy.

THE SS COLONIAL: DECEMBER 15, 1941

"Attention please!" blasted the loudspeakers. The announcement was made first in German and then repeated in Polish. "We will dock in Havana this afternoon." There was no announcement in Spanish.

Passengers applauded and cheered. Passengers went on deck. Then someone shouted, "Land! It must be Cuba."

We were more than three thousand miles from the nearest Nazi.

The ship slowed down, and some people went below to pack. By the time they returned to the deck, a tugboat was headed toward us. The passengers cheered again. After ten days of bouncing around the ocean, the sea was calm. Then the ship stopped, and the tugboat moved alongside. The crew threw ropes overboard, and the *SS Colonial* was tied to the tugboat. A uniformed sailor came aboard, and another shout of joy broke out. The sailor waved and smiled. A few minutes later, the tugboat began towing the ship into Havana.

We were towed past a large castle into Havana harbor, then to a pier. It was warm and sunny. Cuban dock workers tied up the *SS Colonial*, and suddenly there was silence aboard the ship. The refugees hugged each other, and some cried. My father held my hand, and my mother picked up Peter. It had been five months since we left Zagreb.

Immigration and health inspectors came aboard. We formed lines to be interviewed. It was our turn. Would the Cuban authorities accept our Bolivian passports?

My mother, holding our passports, was nervous. The immigration officials were speaking Spanish. We were supposed to be Bolivians, and my father spoke no Spanish. Would the Spanish she learned on the boat be enough?

"Señor y Señora Hedviga y Roberto Valles de Bolivia, y los hijos Pedro y Ernesto? (Mr. and Mrs. Hedviga and Roberto Valles of Bolivia, and sons

Pedro and Ernesto?)" asked a handsome Cuban officer sitting behind a table. "Buenos días."

"Buenos días, señor. Nosotros hablamos solo un poco Español (We only speak a little Spanish)." said my mother. "Porque no vivimos en Bolivia hasta muchos años (Because we did not live in Bolivia for many years)."

The official smiled, and winked at my mother. Then he stamped our passports. "Bienvenidos a Cuba (Welcome to Cuba)," he said.

"Bienvenidos?" my mother said. She did not understand the word.

"Si, si (Yes, yes)," he said.

My mother turned to my father, took Peter's hand, looked at me, and said, "Let's go. He knows we are refugees."

We carried our luggage down the gangplank. The Singers followed us, and another family we had met during our voyage followed them. They had two boys who stood out from the rest of us because they were always dressed in black pants and white shirts, and they spoke Polish and a funny kind of German. Yiddish, they called it. The boys and their father were never without a yarmulke (a skull cap). On the pier were two long tables. We went to a table with a sign reading Centro Israelitico (Jewish Center).

It had been almost four years since the Anschluss and three and a half years since my father was released from Dachau. We still did not know what had happened to my two sets of grandparents. We still had not heard from Uncle Otto and Tante Frieda. We knew Hansi was in Zurich, Uncle Gustl was in North Africa, Lisl was in Palestine, and her parents were in China. We had heard Uncle Fritz, Lilly, and Herta had safely gotten into England. We thought Tante Anna was still in Zagreb, but had no idea where Heli was. My mother wrote a letter to Uncle Gustl in care of the French Foreign Legion Postal Annex in Fez to tell him we were in Cuba.

Our family was scattered all over the world, and we were about to begin a new life in a country with customs and a climate very different from Europe. Even the food was different.

There were only eight thousand Jews left in Vienna. When we left in 1938, there were more than two hundred fifty thousand.

HAVANA: JANUARY 15, 1942

It was Peter's fourth birthday, and my mother invited the Singers for dinner. I helped decorate the living room with balloons and paper streamers. Anka Singer baked a chocolate cake. She put five candles on top, four for Peter's birthday, and a fifth representing life. The eight of us filled our small

Uncle Otto, photo from Yugoslav passport.

Tante Frieda, photo from Yugoslav passport.

dining room. We were gradually settling into our new life in Cuba, but America was for both families the ultimate destination.

We were living in a furnished apartment above a restaurant that we found through the Jewish Center the day we got off the boat. Our address was Calle 21 and J.

The living room, dining room and two bedrooms had balconies that overlooked tables on the sidewalk below. Peter and I used to throw spitballs at people sitting at the tables. We were never caught. The restaurant was also a grocery store. I ate my first Oreo cookie there. The cookies were displayed in a tall glass jar and cost two cents each. My parents enrolled me in the English-speaking Herbert Spencer Academy, and my father was interviewing for work in diamond-cutting factories.

WANNSEE: JANUARY 20, 1942

Fifteen high-ranking Nazi and German leaders held a conference at a villa on the Wannsee, a lake outside of Berlin. The topic of the meeting was the Final Solution to the Jewish Question in Europe. The 'final solution' was the Nazi code name for the deliberate and carefully planned destruction of all European Jews. Nazi killing squads were already executing Jews in parts of Russia and Poland. The Wannsee Conference declared formally that Germany was committed to murdering the entire Jewish people, and all Jews in Nazi-occupied Europe would be taken to extermination camps in Poland.

On the agenda was 'methods of killing and extermination'.

ZAGREB: FEBRUARY 11, 1942

Newspapers reported that every person in Zagreb had to be registered with the police. German authorities declared that people who had unregistered Jews in their homes would be executed. Ivka refused to register Tante Anna even though her neighbors knew she was living with the Kostelics.

"Ivka," said Tante Anna. "I must register to protect your mother. She is frail and cannot escape."

"No, Anna, I will not let you. Also, you must not go to work. The dentist might disclose you. You should not even go on the streets until this war is over."

Tante Anna could not be persuaded to stay in the house. She took daily walks to the market for groceries. On one of those walks, she ran into someone she knew.

"Viktor Schlesinger?" asked Tante Anna.

"Frau Weininger, what a surprise. How are you? I heard about your husband. I'm so sorry."

"I am fine, thank you. What are you doing in Zagreb?"

"I think I am doing exactly what you are doing here, Frau Weininger."

"Herr Schlesinger, I did not think you were Jewish," said Tante Anna. "Why did you have to leave Vienna?"

"You are right, I am not Jewish, but I am anti-Nazi, and the Nazis found out. If I hadn't left, I would have been arrested. I am in Zagreb just for the day. I live in Odra, a small village about eight miles from here. I fix up houses for farmers in that area and have become friendly with Tito's partisans."

"Tito?" asked Tante Anna.

"Josip Broz Tito. He was in the Yugoslav Army. He is a Serb communist who is organizing men to fight the fascists. They call themselves partisans."

"I thought Gen. Draža Mihailović was forming an anti-Fascist army."

"Yes, you are right. He and his group are called Chetniks. Mihailović too was in the Yugoslav Army. He and Tito keep their armies hidden in the mountains and forests. They are both fighting to liberate Yugoslavia from the Nazis and the Ustaša."

This was the first Tante Anna had heard about partisans.

"It is good to see you again. Here is my phone number. Why don't you come visit me when you come back to Zagreb? I live with a lovely family, and it is safe there. And please, call me Anna."

Twice in the next two weeks, Victor called on Tante Anna, bringing her fresh eggs, cheese, and sausages from Odra. On the second visit, he told her and Ivka that he could no longer live in Odra.

"It is too difficult for me there," he said. "Would you consider renting me a room?"

Ivka said yes, and Victor said he would move in three days later.

"Everyone in Zagreb has to register with the police," said Ivka. "Do you think you could get false documents for Anna stating that she is from Odra?"

When Victor returned three days later, Tante Anna had a new identity. She had become Victor's sister, Anna Schlesinger of Odra.

CIVIDALE: FEBRUARY 22, 1942

Uncle Otto, Tante Frieda, and Edith's plan to China had changed. They felt safe in Cividale, were not threatened by Fascists, and there were no Nazis in that region of Italy. The DiSenas appreciated the chores Tante Frieda and Edith did daily. Only Edith had learned to speak Italian, but the DiSenas spoke enough German for most conversations. Uncle Otto was bored and restless but spent a lot of time walking the DiSena's two dogs. Eventually, he began to show symptoms of dejection.

"Do you worry about having us here with you for so long?" asked Edith one morning.

"Yes, a little," said Signor DiSena. "But we do not think about it much. We do not like your enemies. Most Italians are different from Germans and Austrians. We don't hate Jews. I'm glad you found safety here."

There were two loud knocks on the front door. Antonio DiSena opened the door and faced two Carabinieri guards who said they had orders to drive the Weiss family to the train station to join other refugees. Signor DiSena explained that Uncle Otto and his family were his guests. They had Yugoslav passports and were welcome to stay as long as they liked. But the guards went to the third floor and told Tante Frieda and Uncle Otto to pack their things.

Uncle Otto became very upset and sat down. Tante Frieda gave him a glass of water, and Edith walked into the room. She asked the Carabinieri where they would be going and was told they were being taken to the Udine railroad station, the same place they had been taken when they were arrested six months before.

The Weisses packed quickly, uncertain of what would happen next. The DiSenas hugged them on the way out the door. Uncle Otto was shaking.

"They released you after only one day the last time," Signora DiSena whispered in Edith's ear. "Be strong."

"Wait one minute please," said Signor DiSena. He walked into the kitchen and returned with a bottle of his best red wine.

"Otto," said Signor DiSena. "Please take this. It will make you relax."

My uncle's eyeglasses were wet from tears. He put the wine into his suitcase and followed the Carabinieri to their police car. The DiSenas stood speechless as they watched them drive away.

An hour later when they got to the Udine train station, they found many police cars and vans full of Jews arriving from different parts of Italy and France. All the refugees were being directed to trains which were headed to various destinations in Italy.

Slavko and his parents had also been arrested. They were being sent to Ferramonti di Tarisa in Cosenza on the southern tip of Italy.

The Weisses were put on a train to Arzignano, a small town near the city of Vicenza in northern Italy.

As she was boarding the train, Edith saw her boyfriend getting on a train on the next track.

"Slavko," she yelled.

"Edith," he shouted back. "Write to me through the Red Cross in Switzerland. We are going south to Ferramonti. It is a long way from here. Edith, please write to the Red Cross."

"Yes, I will write as soon as I can," Edith yelled back.

"Edith," Slavko yelled in Italian, "Ti amo."

Their trip to Arzignano took ten hours, with stops in Venice and Padova. It was late at night when the train arrived. The two end cars with the Cividale prisoners were uncoupled, and policemen from Arzignano got on board. They gave the refugees sandwiches and drinks, and told them they would spend the night in the cars.

Early the next morning, the cars were unlocked, and the prisoners were allowed off. They were marched across the street to the town's soccer field, where a local policeman stood on top of a wooden box with a megaphone in his hand. The sixty prisoners gathered around the policeman. Tante Frieda was holding Uncle Otto's hand. Edith had their two suitcases.

"Attention: everybody!" He spoke Italian, and a civilian translated his words into German. Uncle Otto recognized the interpreter as one of the prisoners who had been on the train.

"In Arzignano, there are several ways for you to live, all under the supervision of the local police. This is not a prison. You will be assigned to houses. Some of you will live with other prisoners. Others will live with the homeowners themselves."

"Otto," whispered Tante Frieda, "he said we will not be in a prison."

He squeezed his wife's hand. "Yes, Frieda, I am listening," he said.

"Papa," whispered Edith, "this is not a camp. We are going to live in houses. Do you think they will lock the doors?"

"There are three tables," said the policeman, pointing behind him. The translator was repeating every word. "One member of each family will go to the table that has the first letter of your last name and be assigned a house."

Uncle Otto went to the third table. He was first in line. He filled out some documents and was given a piece of green paper with an address on it.

"Read this," he said to Edith when he went back to the crowd. "I think this is where we are to live."

Edith looked at the slip of paper. It read Via Cavour 52.

"This looks like our new address," said Edith. "I wonder how we are supposed to find it."

In less than an hour, all the refugees had an address. The policeman got back on his box.

"Those with a yellow paper, go to my left; the green ones to my right; the rest of you stand in front. The person in charge of your group will show you to your houses."

Within minutes, Uncle Otto's group was walking toward Arzignano's city hall in the Piazza Libertá, Arzignano's main square. At the Piazza they turned right and walked two minutes to a narrow street with old stone houses abutting one another on each side. It was Via Cavour. They stopped at number 52 and the leader asked which of them were Weisses and the Ostrovkys.

"You will live here," he said. "The door is open. Good luck."

Italian concentration camps, sometimes referred to as displaced persons camps, were not at all like the German camps. They were unoccupied residential houses, empty villas, and even movie houses. They were furnished, and accommodated anywhere from six people to two hundred. The Italians called it domicilio coatto (forced housing).

Chapter 18

HAVANA: FEBRUARY 25, 1942

My mother went to the American Consulate to inquire about visas to the United States. She was told that since we came from Europe, we needed passports from a European country. Our Yugoslav and Austrian passports had expired, which meant we had to apply for new ones.

During our travels in Europe, American immigration policies had kept refugees from applying for visas. Now, ironically, our false Bolivian passports, that had gotten us out of Europe, became an obstacle to emigration out of Cuba.

Though we were legally citizens of Austria, the country was now considered part of Germany and was at war with the United States, so my parents decided not to reapply for Austrian passports. Instead, they sent a letter, along with the expired passports, to the Yugoslav Consulate in Washington requesting renewal. At the same time, they made an appointment at the American Consulate in Havana with Vice-Counsel Charles Anderson.

FERRAMONTI: FEBRUARY 26, 1942

Slavko Losic and his family were placed in a camp with Italian Jews, and non-Jewish Italian political prisoners. In the Ferramonti camp were many professionals, including physicians, dentists, university professors and rabbis. When the town's inhabitants found out about the talented prisoners, they began sneaking into the camp at night to see doctors and dentists, who were more skilled than their own. This camp too was very much different from those in Germany: the inmates were allowed to establish schools and even synagogues.

HAVANA: APRIL 15, 1942

My father had become a diamond cutter and was employed by one of twenty six industrial diamond companies run by Belgian and Dutch Jews. Each day he stood with a magnifying glass in front of a dozen cutting machines the size of shoeboxes, which were mounted on a workbench. High-speed three-inch rotating blades cut the diamonds one at a time. It took hours to cut one diamond to perfection, and his earnings were dependent on the number of diamonds he could cut per day. My father worked hard and was making a good income.

The Austrian Jews, as did the Germans, Polish, and Czechs, kept to themselves. They formed cliques and clubs where they got together to socialize. There was also a sizeable native Jewish community, but the Cubans had little to do with the refugees. The Austrians' social club, established before we arrived, was called Asociacion Austria Libre (Association Free Austria). My parents became members.

The club's hall had two grand pianos set on a small stage. At one of the Austria Libre social events a man was at the piano playing Viennese music. My mother saw that he had no sheet music and was playing from memory, often improvising. She was impressed. Only an accomplished musician could do that.

"Robert," she said, "he is really good."

"Yes, he is. Let's go to the piano and watch him."

The piano player was about forty, approximately my parents' age. He wore glasses, and sometimes closed his eyes while he played. He was clearly enjoying himself.

When he stopped, he looked at my parents.

"Guten Abend (Good evening)," he said.

"Guten Abend," answered my mother. "You play very well."

"Thank you. Is there something special you'd like to hear?"

"Whatever you wish to play is fine with us," she replied.

He smiled and continued playing parts of operettas and arias, and some Mozart and Schumann. He jumped from one piece to another in perfect harmony. When he stopped, he asked my parents if either of them played the piano.

"I do," said my mother.

"Can you play four-handed?"

"Yes."

"Sit down," he said.

My mother sat down on the bench and, following the sheet music in front of her, began to play. She played the chords on the lower keys, and he played the melody on the higher keys. Within minutes, there was a small crowd around the piano.

"What is your name?"

"Hedi."

"I'm Fritz."

"Servus, Fritz," said my mother.

"You are good, Hedi. Let's show them what we can do."

Together they played waltzes, sonatas, Hungarian dances, and Viennese songs for almost an hour, as if they had played together forever.

"Let me introduce you to a few Cuban songs that I find delightful," said Fritz.

He got out some sheet music and started to play Cuban music. The people around the piano loved it: some began to dance. Soon, my mother joined in.

My father stood next to her. He was happier than he'd been for a long time. My mother had a radiant smile, and Fritz was enjoying his new keyboard partner. She improvised as well as he did, and played the piano with passion.

When they finished, everyone applauded, and Fritz Kramer formally introduced himself to my parents. He had been a professional musician in Vienna: an accompanist to singers, and a piano teacher. He arrived in Havana several months before us. Fritz and his wife, Marta, and my parents established an immediate friendship and sat down to have a drink together. Before they left the hall that night, my mother told them she also played the accordion.

"Would you play in front of an audience?" asked Fritz.

"What do you have in mind?" asked my mother.

ZNOJMO: APRIL 20, 1942

Heli's father opened another letter from the Gestapo, ordering him to report the following day. He turned pale, and his hands were shaking. He sat down.

"Heli, I told you I will never go back," said Josef Lampl. "Please allow me to die as a free person, not as a slave. I cannot go back to prison for the third time."

Heli bent over and kissed him, then left the room. She knew what he was about to do.

Uncle Josef injected himself with an overdose of morphine he had purposely saved from his veterinary practice. He died within minutes. He was fifty six years old.

Three weeks later, Heli and her grandmother, Sara, received letters telling them they would be transported on May 18 to Theresienstadt.

THERESIENSTADT: MAY 19, 1942

The Theresienstadt Ghetto had been turned into a concentration camp, but prisoners had the freedom to walk around some parts of the old town as they did when it was still a ghetto. The only difference was that the Nazis were now murdering selected prisoners by taking them into nearby woods to be shot.

Conditions in the old, dirty, and neglected buildings were appalling. Everything was filthy, including the utensils they had to eat with. Roaches covered the walls. Mice and rats ran along the floors. Close to fifty nine thousand Jews were crammed into what was once small, walled town of thirty five hundred people. Many died, four thousand in one month alone.

Heli was assigned work digging in a potato field. At dusk, she went back to the room she shared with her grandmother. Sara was sick and very weak. My great-grandmother died that night in her sleep. She was eighty one.

Though her grandmother was gone, Heli was grateful the older woman did not have to suffer anymore at the hands of the Nazis. She was even optimistic she could survive the concentration camp.

One night, she was standing in line for supper when she thought she recognized a doctor she knew from Prague. He approached her.

"Heli, I am Jiři Ganz. You remember my sister? Her name is also Helena. I am working here as a doctor, so they give me special privileges. Could we get together sometime?"

Dr. Ganz had a reputation in Prague as a flirt who had many girlfriends.

"Yes, but where?" said Heli.

"Would you meet me for coffee tomorrow at 7:00 p.m., in the café on the next block?"

"Yes, I can do that."

"Good," said the doctor again. "I will be there."

Heli met him at the café, and she had a friend with her.

"This is my friend Jani," she said.

The doctor was surprised. He had expected an evening alone with Heli. When the night was over, he escorted them back to the women's quarters. He asked Heli out again, but said he'd like her to come alone.

"That will be fine, but I want you to know that I am not an easy girl," she said.
Two weeks later, after several dates, Dr. Ganz met Heli outside the café.
"Heli, will you come to my room? I have something to tell you."
Heli agreed. When they got to his room, he sat down.

"I heard you are on a list of prisoners who will be taken to another camp," he said. "Heli, please marry me. If you do, you won't have to leave here."

Heli was surprised at the marriage proposal. She wasn't in love with Dr. Ganz and didn't know him very well, but she feared the alternative. During the past few weeks, prisoners had been taken away from Theresienstadt by train, and nobody knew where they had been sent. It was rumored they were transported to camps, to be put in gas chambers.

"You are sure that if I marry you, I won't have to leave?" Heli asked.

"Yes, people are sick and dying here and the Nazis need me to take care of their guards," said the doctor.

"Okay then, I will marry you."

Dr. Ganz stood up and held her hands.

"I am very happy," he said. "Give me your identification number and don't worry about anything. You must go now before we are caught together in my room."

The next day, Dr. Ganz told her to go to the administration building and tell the clerk she was his fiancée. The clerk would take her off the transport list.

"Before you go, Heli, we need to set a date for our wedding. What do you think about next month?"

"That's fine, Jiři," said Heli. It was the first time she had called him by his first name, and she decided she was beginning to like her fiancé. Three weeks later, they were married by a rabbi in a simple ceremony. By that time, they knew the trains from Theresienstadt were heading for Auschwitz.

ARZIGNANO: MAY 21, 1942

Since their arrival in Arzignano, Uncle Otto had been unable to sleep or eat. He had lost thirty pounds. Tante Frieda took him to a doctor, who sent him to the Manicomio Provinciale (mental hospital) in Vicenza, ten miles from Arzignano. The diagnosis was severe depression. Edith and Tante Frieda tried to get permission to go visit him, but their requests were denied by Arzignano police.

HAVANA: MAY 26, 1942

In less than three months, we had received new Yugoslav passports. Once again, we were the Weiss family. The American Consulate had helped us fill out applications for visas, and we had gotten our first refusal from Washington. It was disappointing, but not a surprise. We were advised to reapply. The Valles family from Bolivia no longer existed. My mother changed the spelling of her name from 'Hedi' to 'Hedy'. It sounded more American. It was also the way Hedy Lamarr, the famous movie actress, spelled her first name.

My mother was reading a letter from Uncle Gustl.

"Robert," she said. "Gus is very unhappy. The Foreign Legion has him doing hard labor. He says he is trying to get out of Africa. Is there any way we could get him a Cuban visa?"

"Do you remember the man we met at the Tropicana a few weeks ago? He used to be in the Foreign Service." said my father. My parents and their friends went frequently to the famous Tropicana nightclub, which was known as the Paradise under the Stars."

"Yes," she answered. "He told me he saw me play at the Rialto Theatre. Zwonko introduced us so he must know how to find him."

Zwonko Rosenberger was the father of Saša, one of my classmates. He had been a Yugoslav diplomat and knew Cubans in the Foreign Service. My mother called him the next day and three days later Zwonko gave her a Cuban visa for Uncle Gustl, which she mailed to him in care of the French Foreign Legion in Fez.

HAVANA: JUNE 12, 1942

After six months in Cuba, we moved into a large apartment at Calle 23 y Avenida de los Presidentes in Vedado, a quiet middle class suburb of Havana, not far from where the Singers lived. The street was a wide boulevard with a big grass strip in the center that became a playground for us and the Singer boys. The neighborhood pleased my parents because it was a bit like our neighborhood in Vienna.

My parents joined a tennis club. I had my first tennis lesson with Rogelio Fernandez Mira. I changed schools and went to the Academia Trelles, a private Cuban school, along with the Singer brothers and Saša. I immediately developed a crush on a pretty girl named Laura Dzierlatka. By now, I spoke good Spanish and was taking an English class.

Lunch at school was served in the dining room on large family-style tables. Table manners were strictly enforced. My table habits were European: knife in the right hand, and fork in the left. I had to change. Cuban customs called for switching the fork to the right hand to eat. Elbows had to be off the table, with our napkins resting neatly on our laps. The boys all wore jackets and ties.

My parents and other refugees formed a group called Asociacion Austria Libre of Cuba, which helped develop the Havana Philharmonic Orchestra. They hired Erich Kleiber, a Viennese-born conductor who had moved to Argentina before the Anschluss, to conduct the new symphony orchestra. Herr Kleiber was not Jewish but had worked in the Free Austrian Movement in South America, which had honored him with the title 'President of Honor' for his work on behalf of Jewish refugees.

Asociacion Austria Libre also gave Conductor Kleiber an honorary Cuban presidency award during a dinner at a restaurant called Wiener Küche (Vienna Kitchen), which was on the Prado, a main thoroughfare in Havana. My mother sat at the head table.

At the end of his acceptance speech, Herr Kleiber said: "I am now temporarily expelled from my country. But, wherever I am standing upon five planks of my conductor's desk, I am standing on Austrian soil."

ARZIGNANO: JUNE 20, 1942

Edith received her first love letter from Slavko. He said he longed for her and was trying to leave Ferramonti to get to Arzignano. But to do so, he needed a wife in Arzignano.

"Will you marry me?" he said.

ARZIGNANO: JUNE 27, 1942

Tante Frieda got a letter from Uncle Otto saying he would be released from the mental hospital on the following Tuesday, July 30. He asked to be picked up.

ROUEN: AUGUST 17, 1942

The United States conducted its first bombing raid of the war. B-17 bombers, known as Flying Fortresses, targeted railroad yards in Rouen, France, a city in Normandy sixty miles inland from French beaches on the English Channel. It was two years after the American War Department told President Roosevelt that the only way to win the war against Germany was to strategically bomb German military and industrial and civilian targets.

STALINGRAD: SEPTEMBER 14, 1942

The Russian-German battle for Stalingrad began. It was the turning point on the Russian front, and the bloodiest. The battle was marked by brutality and a disregard for military and civilian casualties on both sides. The Germans suffered eight hundred fifty thousand casualties. For the Russians, who also endured great losses during the battle, the victory at Stalingrad marked the start of the liberation of the Soviet Union from Nazi Germany. Two million casualties, both civilian and military, were reported among the Russians and Germans.

THERESIENSTADT: SEPTEMBER 18, 1942

Forty four thousand, six hundred and ninety three Jews from Theresienstadt had been sent to Auschwitz. Few survived the gas chambers. Daily, more Jews were being taken to the concentration camp.

CASABLANCA: NOVEMBER 8, 1942

Uncle Gustl was asleep in his hotel room. He was sick with a liver disease he probably got from insect bites in the desert and was getting daily injections at a military hospital. It was 4:00 a.m. A tremendous noise woke him up.

"The Americans are bombing the harbor!" he heard someone yell from the street.

He jumped out of bed and went to the roof of the hotel and watched American planes bomb Casablanca. The harbor was full of Allied ships. Uncle Gustl thought about the Cuban visa he had received from my mother and decided he had better get out of Morocco at once. When the bombing stopped, he went to the police station to apply for an exit visa to Cuba. He was told by a clerk his Cuban visa was a forgery.

He left and went to the hospital for his injection and told his story to the army nurse who gave him his shots. Her name was Marie St. Pierre.

"Marie," said Uncle Gustl, "I'm too sick to go back to the Foreign Legion. I need my shots every day. It looks like I'll have to stay in Morocco until the war is over. I don't know how I can get out of here. I am going to try and hide in the mellah (the Jewish quarters in Casablanca) and I will have to find a job."

"I may be able to help," she replied. "I'll make some phone calls. Let's meet for dinner tonight."

That night, she told Uncle Gustl she had found someone who would put him to work in the mellah as a leather cutter. The owner of the leather shop, however, would report him to the Foreign Legion police if he left without his permission. Uncle Gustl would be paid ten francs a day, half of which the owner would keep in case he died. That money would pay for his funeral.

"This is a slave contract," said Uncle Gustl. "It is barely enough to pay for a room. But I guess I have no choice."

It turned out that Uncle Gustl knew more about the leather business than the owner. A month later, Uncle Gustl got a promotion. He was now the shop's manager, in charge of making and selling the goods, which included leather jackets and skirts, handbags and briefcases.

One day a man came into the shop and, in German, told my uncle he wanted to buy a jacket. He was arrogant, and my uncle didn't like him. Uncle Gustl spoke to him in French and soon sold him a jacket, charging him twice the selling price. Uncle Gustl put the extra money in his pocket, feeling he'd just won a battle with the Germans.

That night, he took Marie to a nightclub, the Café Oriental. She was three years younger and very pretty, and the two had become close. They had dinner and danced. The club was full of an international mix of people, all dressed up. The piano player was American, a black man who played a mix of jazz and songs from American musicals. This was the first extravagance for my uncle since he left Vienna. Sitting at a table in a Casablanca nightclub with a beautiful woman, good food and French wine, listening to piano music, made him feel good. It didn't matter where the money came from.

"You are enjoying yourself," said Marie.

"I am, thanks to you."

"I am very fond of you, Gustl, and I am having a wonderful time."

He kissed her. "Will you come home with me tonight?"

She squeezed his hand and kissed him back.

ZURICH: JANUARY 11, 1943

Hansi had graduated from a shoemaking trade school in Zurich and was making a good living and saving money. He knew his parents and sister had perished but did not know how. He missed them but was corresponding with my parents in Havana, and Uncles Gustl and Otto.

Four-o'clock tea, after work, was a major part of his life, especially since he'd met Edith Bernheim. They saw each other frequently and soon decided to go 'steady'. She was a Swiss-born Jew.

ZAGREB: JANUARY 13, 1943

Viktor Schlesinger had become abrasive, and Tante Anna wondered if she could trust him. Ivka wanted to throw him out, but she was afraid he would tell the Nazis about Tante Anna, so she put up with him. Besides, he often rode his bicycle to Odra for fresh eggs and cheese, coming back with news about the partisans.

One day, he did not come home. After several days, Tante Anna and Ivka were concerned. If he had been arrested, they could be discovered. The Nazis would know Tante Anna's true identity, and Ivka would be arrested for harboring a Jew. Ivka quietly made inquiries and found out Victor and two dozen farmers involved with the partisans had been arrested and sentenced to death by hanging.

Ivka's mother died the next day. In spite of her illness, Mrs. Kostelic had always been an optimist, brightening everyone's outlook on the world around them. It was a huge loss for Ivka, and Tante Anna too.

CASABLANCA: JANUARY 14 TO 24, 1943

President Roosevelt met with British Prime Minister Winston Churchill in Casablanca to plan war strategies.

HAVANA: FEBRUARY 16, 1943

We had been in Havana fourteen months. Our second refusal from the American Consulate came in the mail. Again, it was not a surprise. The same thing was happening to many of our friends. The United States had quotas for refugees that were assigned by country of origin, and there were few visas available for Germans, Austrians, Poles, and Czechs. My parents reapplied.

ZAGREB: FERBUARY 17, 1943

A month after he disappeared, much to the surprise of Tante Anna and Ivka, Victor came home. He was bruised, dirty, and unshaven. He told them about his arrest.

"When I got to Odra," he said, "the Ustaša were there. They arrested me and some farmers I know. They beat us and told us we would be hanged because we were partisans. Someone called the Catholic archbishop in Zagreb, and he got us out of jail. The archbishop convinced the Nazis none of us had anything to do with the partisans and none of us was a Jew. I am lucky to be alive," he said.

ZAGREB: FEBRUARY 20, 1943

In a radio broadcast, the Gestapo and Ustaša both announced their intentions to immediately search for, and arrest, all Jews in Zagreb. All Zagreb residents were forbidden to leave their houses or look out their windows until the search was over. Viktor suggested they hide Tante Anna in a wardrobe if anyone came to the door. Ivka was nervous. She made herself a cup of tea and sat down in the living room. She felt the Ustaša could come to their building any minute.

At midnight, the doorbell rang. Tante Anna went into the wardrobe, and Victor shoved some boxes in behind her. Ivka went to the door.

"Ah, here you are. I was waiting for you," she said. "I will take you through my apartment. Look at anything you wish."

The three men at the door were in civilian clothes but said they were Ustaša. They were surprised by Ivka's reception. They inspected the apartment and found Victor asleep in his bed.

"Who is that?" asked one of the officers. "Do you have a Jew in the house?"

Ivka's heart was beating. "Certainly not," she said. "He is a good friend. He comes once in a while to bring me milk and meat from his farm. I went to the station to register him but was told not to bother since he only stays for one night. He rides his bicycle. It is in the front hall. He is not a Jew. He has documents to prove it."

The Ustaša finished their search, looking with flashlights into the closets. They said their search was over, and Ivka offered them a glass of water, which they accepted. Before they left, one of them asked Ivka to go on a date. She said she already had a boyfriend.

ZAGREB: FEBRUARY 21, 1943

Ivka opened the door for her landlord.

"I came to tell you I sold the house," he said. "I am sorry, but the new owner is a high-ranking Ustaša officer. You could be in great danger. He asked me about Anna. I didn't tell him anything, but he could get suspicious."

Ivka thanked him for the warning and called to Tante Anna. She told her the landlord's message.

"You have to leave Zagreb at once, Anna," said Ivka. "We cannot take any more chances."

"You are right, Ivka. We both will be arrested if I stay. I already know what I want to do. I am going to join the partisans."

"I will go with you to Odra," said Ivka. "I speak better Croatian than you."

ZAGREB: FEBRUARY 23, 1943

Tante Anna was ready to leave Zagreb. She had memorized everything she knew about her Schlesinger 'family' in case they were stopped on the way to Odra, and she had her documents saying she was Victor's sister. Victor had left the day before. He said he would meet Tante Anna and Ivka when they got to Odra, and would arrange for Tante Anna to stay with farmers he had once lived with.

Buses no longer went to Odra, so Ivka and Tante Anna packed small bags and rode their bicycles. They left before sunrise so no one would see them leave. A crate of Tante Anna's personal things were hidden in Ivka's cellar. The two women carried empty baskets so it would appear they were going to a farm for food. To their surprise, no one stopped them.

As planned, Victor met them and introduced Tante Anna to the farmers as his sister. Early the next morning, Ivka, who stayed with Tante Anna that night, went back to Zagreb. Viktor met Tanta Anna for breakfast and told her when she was ready to join the partisans he would take her to them.

Tanta Anna settled in with the farmers and their three children, helping them with their chores. On Saturdays, Ivka biked the eight miles to Odra and stayed overnight, always relieved to find Tante Anna was safe. Every week she brought her a few personal things, and a bag of bandages and medicine. Victor said they would be helpful when she joined the Partisans. On her third visit, Ivka saw fourteen men and women hanging from trees in a field alongside the road. One was pregnant: all were nearly naked. When Ivka got to the farm, Tante Anna told her the Ustaša were killing, on the spot, everyone they suspected of supporting the partisans, stealing their clothes and shoes and leaving them to die naked.

A few days later, the farmer's wife told Tante Anna she did not believe she was Victor's sister and she had to leave. She thought she was a Jew, and if the Ustaša found out, her family would be killed. She also asked her why she was hiding bandages and medicine. Tante Anna immediately rode her bike to see Victor.

"The partisans are coming in to town tomorrow night to pick up food and supplies I have for them," said Victor. "You stay with me tonight, and maybe they will take you back with them."

The next night, Tante Anna waited for Victor to come home. By now, she had a huge carton of bandages and medications. Victor came home and told her to get her bag.

"They won't take you," he said. "They expect to meet up with Ustaša and Germans in route, and you would be a burden. They gave me money to go to Zagreb for more supplies, and they will be back next week to pick them up. But you cannot stay here. I am going to take you to a shed that's deep in the woods. Pack up some food. But leave the medicine and bandages here."

The next day, Viktor hired a horse-drawn carriage and went to Zagreb. Before he went back to Odra, he picked up Tante Anna's crate in Ivka's basement. When Victor got back from Zagreb, it was dark; and he went directly to the woods to give Tante Anna her crate, which had several blankets in it. He gave her enough food for several days and said he would be back as soon as he could.

A few days later, when Victor came back, he told Tante Anna the partisans still did not want her. They were looking for strong men.

"I found you another room in another village," he said. "Leave your crate here for now. I will bring it to you when I can."

My aunt was disappointed. She was ready to fight the Nazis.

ENGLAND: MARCH 12, 1943

Germany launched the first V-1 jet-propelled, pilotless bombs against England.

Chapter 19

ARZIGNANO: APRIL 8, 1943

Ten months after he proposed, Slavko was still in Ferramonti, unable to get a transfer to Arzignano. Finally, Edith and Tante Frieda convinced the Arzignano police to issue Slavko a transfer so the young couple could marry. They then went to the Podestà (Mayor's Office) which wrote the following letter to the police in Ferramonti:

"We inform you that the fiancée of Losic Slavko, Edith Weiss, daughter of Otto, has declared that the dossiers to get married with Slavko Losic have been dispatched to the rabbi of Verona."

Verona was the only city nearby that had a synagogue. For Edith's marriage, the police also authorized Uncle Otto and Tante Frieda to travel to Verona.

CASABLANCA: MAY 30, 1943

Uncle Gustl had recovered from his bout with liver disease. He was making more money, and had a car, but he was still in the mellah, afraid to leave because his boss would report him to the Foreign Legion. He had one day off a week and often went to a resort outside Casablanca. It had a large swimming pool that sat on the rocks above the shore. Marie had been transferred, and they had lost contact.

Every day he thought about ways to get out of North Africa. The American Army was in Casablanca so he decided to try to join. He went to the U.S. Army Headquarters and talked to a major who said he could not be a U.S. soldier, but he could apply for work as a civilian contractor. Uncle Gustl applied to be a clerk-typist, and was given a test. He typed as fast as he could with two fingers and got the job.

The next morning, when he did not show up at the leather shop, the owner called the Foreign Legion, which sent their police to his hotel. Before he was taken away, he called the American major he met the day before. The major got on the phone and demanded Uncle Gustl's release on the grounds he was a member of the American military. Uncle Gustl reported to his new job that day and never went back to the mellah. In a month, he was given a job as an interpreter with a pay raise. After four months, Uncle Gustl was promoted to administrative assistant, the highest-paid civilian rank in the American Army in North Africa.

ROME: JULY 25, 1943

Benito Mussolini's reign of Italy had ended. Mussolini was ousted by his own government and imprisoned.

FERRAMONTI: AUGUST 6, 1943

Slavko was told by the Ferramonti police that they had received his permit to go to Arzignano but in several weeks all Ferramonti prisoners would be released. Slavko wrote to Edith that as soon as he was freed he would take a train to Arzignano. He expected to arrive October 5. He asked her to set the date for their wedding.

Tante Frieda made the wedding arrangements with the rabbi of Verona and then sent him Edith's dowry, which synagogues required at that time. Tante Frieda bought white satin and began to sew her daughter's wedding dress.

CASSIBILE, ITALY: SEPTEMBER 8, 1943

Italy signed an armistice with the Allied Forces, which now occupied Italy south of Rome. Italian soldiers threw down their arms, happy their conflict was over. The German Army retaliated by arresting all the Italian soldiers they could find. The Italians were sent to prisoner-of-war camps in Germany, where many of them died.

CROATIA: SEPTEMBER 23, 1943

Tante Anna had lived in the same small village for five months, still posing as Victor's sister. The farmers she lived with were elderly, and Tante Anna did most of the farm chores. She also did most of the cooking and laundry. The farm was in a remote area, and she seldom saw Victor or anyone else. As far as she knew, very few people knew she was there. She was still intent on joining the partisans, but Victor had not been able to make that happen. One day she was hanging laundry when Victor arrived on his bicycle.

"It's time to go," he said. "Some of the partisans will come through here in about half an hour. There is room for you in the wagon. They are going back up into the mountains. This is your chance to get to the partisan camp. Get your things together."

Tante Anna had been packed for months. She and Victor went to her room and got her clothes and the carton of medical supplies she'd been hiding. Without saying good bye, they left the farmhouse and went to the road. The carriage came and they loaded her things and Victor's bicycle into it. The wagon was pulled by two horses and was loaded with supplies, including boxes of guns and ammunition. The two men aboard had rifles but were not wearing uniforms.

In thirty minutes they were above the village, halfway up the mountain. They stopped at a small house with a large pen, full of goats, in back. Two German shepherds greeted them cautiously. They were let in by a woman who had a rifle in her hand. The woman's husband and two teenage boys were eating at the kitchen table, all with guns by their sides. Tante Anna, Victor, and the two partisans were offered food and a glass of wine.

"Victor says you want to join us," said the woman. "You will have to learn to fire a gun. We will practice here starting tomorrow morning. There are blankets and plenty of room in the barn out back for the four of you to sleep tonight." She poured them a second glass of wine.

Tante Anna went to the barn with the men, who were exhausted from their trip. They had not slept in twenty four hours. Victor and the two men put the horses and the wagon inside so they would be out of sight. They all went to bed early, with Tante Anna wondering how long it would take to learn to fire a rifle. She was finally a partisan.

At midnight one of the boys came running into the barn. "Get up, we have to hide. The Ustaša are in the village. We heard gunshots."

The boys and their parents all carrying guns ran into the woods with the dogs. The two partisans picked up their rifles and handed one to Tante Anna and another to Victor. They followed the others into the woods. It was raining.

"Stay low," said Victor, "or you'll get shot."

The group huddled together, wet and chilled to the bone. Then there was thunder, and it began to pour.

"The gods are with us," said Victor. "The storm will keep them from coming up the mountain."

In the morning it was quiet. The group went back to the house and the barn, changed into dry clothes, and fed the dogs. Then they put their belongings and some food in the wagon, and hitched up the two horses. Tante Anna, Victor, the two boys, and their parents got in back. The other two soldiers got on the bench and took the reins. With the dogs following them, they headed higher up the mountain following a winding dirt path that was muddy from the rain the night before.

Several times they had to stop to move tree limbs, or push the wagon through the mud. Several hours later they came to a small clearing with four houses. Chickens and a few sheep and cows were wandering around outside their pens. A half dozen people came out to meet them, the men dressed in old Yugoslav Army uniforms. Viktor had been there before and knew them all. Once again, he introduced Tante Anna as his sister. Tante Anna's group was told they would occupy one of the houses.

They unloaded the wagon and took their things inside. Except for boxes of guns and canned food, the house was nearly empty. It had a few mattresses on wooden frames about a foot off the floor, which was covered with straw. There was no running water. Tante Anna put her things next to one of the beds and lay down. She'd been on the run since midnight. She fell asleep but woke up a few minutes later with a mouse creeping up her arm. She pulled the blankets over her head and went back to sleep. She would sleep that way for the next year.

Three families lived in the other houses. Between them they had ten children, four of them under twelve. Tante Anna was given the job of caring for the youngest while their parents and the older children went out on raids against the Nazis and Ustaša. Often, she was left alone with the youngsters for days at a time. Sometimes other partisans left their children with her too. She gave them basic care, and began teaching them lessons she had learned in school.

She was taught to handle guns but never had to fire one. Tante Anna became a partisan, but never took part in battle.

ARZIGNANO: OCTOBER 5, 1943

"Do you want me to go meet the train with you?" asked Uncle Otto.

"No," answered Edith, "I want to meet him by myself."

The last time she saw Slavko was in February 1942. Edith wondered if they would recognize each other. Standing on the platform, she heard the train from a distance. Seconds later, it pulled into the station and came to a stop. My cousin watched the passengers get off, her heart pounding. Slavko was the last one off.

"Edith!"

"Slavko!"

They hugged and kissed. "How soon will we be married?" asked Slavko. "I can't wait."

As they walked home, hand in hand, Edith explained that her wedding dress was ready and her dowry had been sent to Verona, but the rabbi was sick and the wedding date was postponed.

"The rabbi asked if we could wait until the end of the month," said Edith.

THERESIENSTADT: OCTOBER 12, 1943

As a physician, Jiři had been treated well in Theresienstadt. So Heli and Jiři were surprised when they got orders to report to a transport heading to Auschwitz. Three days later they boarded one of twenty freight cars, each of which held fifty people. They were allowed to carry one small suitcase and Jiri's medical bag. The train was guarded by the SS and Doberman pinschers.

ARZIGNANO: OCTOBER 22, 1943

The Arzignano refugees knew from shortwave broadcasts that the Allies had occupied southern Italy for more than a month, and heavy fighting was forcing the Germans to retreat. They feared that as they moved northward, the Nazis would kill every Jewish refugee in their path.

"If they come through Arzignano, we will be murdered. We have to leave quickly," said Uncle Otto at dinner. Slavko suggested they meet with some of their friends to plan an escape.

"What about the wedding?" asked Tante Frieda.

"We will have to delay it," said Uncle Otto.

There were more than six hundred Jewish prisoners living in eight towns in the province of Vicenza, twenty one of them in Arzignano. In addition to the Jews, there were political prisoners from Greece, Albania, and England. There was one American in the group. Most of the prisoners had access to telephones.

Uncle Otto and Slavko met with other men in his neighborhood to discuss ways of leaving. The men then called prisoners in the surrounding towns. After a week of planning, there were thirty people who were ready to escape. The plan was to go to southern Italy where they would be protected by the

Allies. They decided the only way to avoid the Germans was to somehow travel down Italy's Adriatic coast. It was not clear how to do that, but the first step was to get on a train and head south.

ALGIERS: OCTOBER 23, 1943

Uncle Gus was told he could join the British Army, so he resigned from his civilian job with the U.S. Army and took a train to Algiers. He went through basic training in Algiers and was given the rank of corporal. He had not been trained in warfare, so the British sent him to Cheshire in the Scotland Midlands, where he was put to work loading trains. He asked his superiors to assign him to the Intelligence Corps as a German-speaking soldier, hoping he would be sent to Germany as an interpreter.

Uncle Gustl in British Army uniform.

ARZIGNANO: OCTOBER 30, 1943

It took eight days for the refugees to get ready. Those from other towns went to Arzignano, and they all got on a train together, bound for Ancona, two hundred fifty miles southeast of Arzignano. The Italian police paid no attention to them. They were more concerned about their own fate at the hands of the Germans. They left a week before the date of Edith and Slavko's wedding.

The trip to Ancona required several train changes. On the final leg the train was packed with people who, like themselves, were trying to get closer to the Allies. At one point, a half mile from Ancona and with the Adriatic Sea in sight, the train suddenly stopped and conductors ran through the cars.

"The train cannot proceed. The Resistenza has sabotaged the tracks. We are near the line of battle. Everyone get off quickly!"

The conductor was referring to the newly formed Italian resistance movement of more than three hundred thousand freedom fighters who had joined the Allies in their fight against the Germans.

The passengers got off, many leaving some of their luggage behind. The Arzignano group got together and started walking along the tracks in the direction of the sea. In less than thirty minutes, they were in a small deserted harbor with a pier that extended about thirty yards into the water. There were five small boats tied to moorings, and one on the beach. Two boys were using a funnel to pour gasoline from large cans into the tanks of the boat that was on the shore. It was a double-ender with an open deck, about forty feet long. It had an inboard engine and a wheelhouse large enough for one person. Uncle Otto and Slavko approached the boys.

"What are you doing?" Slavko asked in Italian.

"We found this boat floating in the harbor, it looks in good shape. We got the gasoline from a German plane that was shot down. We are going to see if the engine will start."

"Where is the German plane?" asked Slavko.

One of the boys pointed northwest.

"It went down over there, about a mile from here," he said.

"That was hard work, carrying all that gasoline," said Uncle Otto. "Do you think you can get that engine running?"

"We will find out soon."

By now, Edith and some of the others had gathered around the odd-shaped boat.

"Could we pay you to take us south?" asked Edith.

The boys looked at each other and, almost in unison, nodded their heads yes.

"Where do you want to go?"

"We want to go south as far as we can," said Slavko. "How long will it take to use up the fuel?

"Probably about fifty hours, maybe more if the sea is calm."

"We need to leave soon," said Slavko. "Is there a place near here to buy food and water?"

"Up on that hill there is a store. You can buy lots of things there."

Edith and a few others left to find the store. When they got back they had enough food and water to last several days, and the boys were waiting inside the boat.

"What are your names?" asked Edith as the group handed their belongings to the boys.

"I am Marcello, and he is Francisco."

"How old are you?" she asked.

"We are both sixteen," said Marcello. "Can some of you men help push the boat into the water?"

"What will you do when we land somewhere?" asked Edith.

"Oh, we'll figure it out. People in our families live along the coast. Don't worry. We want to get out of the way of the Fascists too."

Five of the men pushed the boat into the water while others held ropes that were tied to the bow. Francisco started the engine, and everyone cheered.

The refugees took off their shoes, waded into the water and climbed into the boat. It was built for fishing, not for thirty two people, and it was a tight squeeze, with people sitting on their luggage. It had no toilet, only a bucket. The boys had a compass, but no charts, so they had to make sure land was in always in sight.

During that night and the next day on the water, the rudder chain broke several times, and water seeped in through several small cracks. The boys stopped the engine and went under the boat to fix the rudder, and the refugees took turns bailing with the toilet bucket. German planes flew overhead. Some of the passengers were seasick. But they all took it in stride.

Early in the morning of the second day Marcello said they were almost out of gasoline. Tense minutes followed as Marcello steered the boat to shore. The sun was rising, and there was not a cloud in the sky. He landed it on a beautiful sandy beach. No one said a word. They didn't know where they were, but all were in awe of the beauty surrounding them.

Francisco and Marcello jumped off and steadied the boat while everyone got off. The water was warm. The refugees gathered their belongings and gave Marcello and Francisco each a handful of lira. They said good-bye and then walked to a street that ran parallel to the beach. The sidewalk was lined with benches and straw umbrellas. It was early, and there were no cars or people in either direction.

Eventually, they saw the first sign of life. It was a policeman, and he was coming toward them. The refugees kept walking, wondering what would happen next. What would the officer think of this group of thirty men, women, and children who had not bathed in days, wearing dirty wrinkled clothes, and carrying wet suitcases?

They got a pleasant surprise. "Welcome to Bari," said the policemen. "You are fortunate. The Germans left yesterday."

Chapter 20

BARI: NOVEMBER 1, 1943

Bari was a city of two hundred thousand people, with a section of town that dated back to the Middle Ages. It had a major supply port that the Allies recognized as useful. Should they eventually occupy it, they wanted to preserve it as much as possible and they did not bomb it.

The British were in full force with their trucks, tanks, and artillery and the town's population had become accustomed to Jewish refugees who arrived in Bari almost daily from southern France and the Italian Alps.

The local police, with the cooperation of the British Army, created an internment program for incoming refugees in a former German prisoner-of-war camp. They named it Bari Transit Camp. It had small barracks, each with six bedrooms, a kitchen, and a bathroom. Food and clothing were provided. The Weisses and Slavko moved into the same building. My aunt and uncle shared a room, Edith shared a room with a girl her age, and Slavko was put in a room with a middle-aged man who'd come from Arzignano with them.

When the barracks filled up, refugees were moved into villas or summer homes the Germans had ransacked. What wasn't stolen had been destroyed. The houses were in small towns surrounding Bari. The local townspeople welcomed the Jews, who represented the end of Fascism.

Edith and Slavko began looking for work. Edith got a job almost immediately as an interpreter for the British, who paid her enough to provide for the rest of her family.

HAVANA: MAY 7, 1944

It was my thirteenth birthday.

Victory, a biweekly Havana newspaper which was published in Spanish, French, German, and English, ran a story that was copied from the *Nation,* an American magazine. The story reported that, for the first time since the war began, Germany was suffering a severe food shortage. Potatoes were being rationed, and Germans were allowed to buy only ten pounds per person, which would have to last them through the following winter.

HAVANA: MAY 12, 1944

I celebrated my bar mitzvah at the Vedado Synagogue on the Avenida de los Presidentes. I had studied hard, did a good job reciting my prayers, and gave a short speech in Spanish to congregants, friends, and my parents. I wore a white suit and tie, and was proud of what I had accomplished. So were my parents. Peter was six, and was also dressed in white. A luncheon was held after the ceremony for everyone who had attended the service.

ROME: JUNE 4, 1944

American troops occupied Rome. The city became a major destination for thousands of refugees, including many from Ferramonti. The U.S. Army was unable to cope with the massive number of displaced people and asked for assistance from Washington.

THE BEACHES OF NORMANDY: JUNE 6, 1944

The Allied invasion of Europe began with more than one hundred sixty thousand Allied troops, and thirty thousand vehicles, landing along a thirty-mile stretch of open Atlantic beaches and high cliffs. The Allies called it the Battle of Normandy, and D-Day. The French called it Jour-J or Le Choc. The French coastline was heavily fortified by the Nazis.

The majority of the troops who landed in Normandy were from the United States, Great Britain, and Canada. Troops from Australia, Belgium, Czechoslovakia, France, Greece, the Netherlands, New Zealand, Norway, and Poland also participated. The battle lasted nearly three months, far longer than Allied strategists anticipated, and more than fifty thousand troops were lost.

Among the Canadian soldiers who landed in Normandy on D-Day was Corporal Farish Donald Hemeon, husband of Verna and the father of my wife, Leslie Hemeon Weiss.

Uncle Gustl was sent from Scotland to train as an interpreter with the British Army intelligence group, whose specialty was interrogating German prisoners. To keep him from appearing Jewish and to protect him from the Germans, he had to give up his name. He changed it from Jellinek to Jerome. My uncle Fritz, who was first an air raid warden and then enlisted in the British Army, had already changed his name to Jenkins. My mother's brothers were now Gus Jerome and Fred Jenkins.

WASHINGTON, DC: JUNE 9, 1944

President Roosevelt for the last six years had repeatedly been informed of atrocities in Nazi concentration camps, but neither he nor his government considered the killing of millions of Jews a priority. Roosevelt's only concern was winning the war. With pressure from labor unions, which feared job losses if too many immigrants were allowed into the United States, his state department continued to refuse visas to European Jews.

On Friday, June 9, at the urging of Congress and major U.S. Jewish organizations, the president established the Oswego Emergency Refugee Shelter at Fort Ontario, an abandoned army camp in Oswego, New York. The Haven, as it was called, was considered a token gesture for Jewish refugees, who at the end of the war would be sent back to their own countries.

BARI: JULY 4, 1944

A notice on a bulletin board in British headquarters said President Roosevelt was inviting one thousand Jewish refugees to the United States to live in a temporary haven in Oswego, New York. Edith was one of the first to see the bulletin. Without asking Uncle Otto, Tante Frieda, or Slavko, she wrote their names on a form posted next to the notice. She then left her office and ran home to tell her parents.

"I have some wonderful news. I signed us up to go to America."

Edith was out of breath.

"Edith," Uncle Otto said, "what are you talking about? Frieda, get her a glass of water."

"I don't need a glass of water. Please listen. I signed us up to go on a ship that will leave Naples for America on July 21. Only one thousand refugees can go."

"But thousands will want to go," said her mother. "What makes you think we can get on?"

"I was the first one in Bari to sign up," said Edith. "I think we have a good chance. The British really like me, and maybe they can help. I put Slavko's name on the list too."

Uncle Otto took off his glasses. Accustomed to his mood changes, Tante Frieda took his hand.

"Otto, this could be a very good thing," she said. "Please don't get upset."

Edith took his other hand and kissed him on the cheek. "Papa, I have a feeling we will be on that ship."

"I hope so," he said. "It's just that we have had so many disappointments."

"I have to get back to work," said Edith. "Mama, if you see Slavko before I do, please tell him the good news."

Slavko and Edith had been engaged for two years but never had an intimate relationship. They lived in the same house, but Slavko always slept in his own room. He was shocked that night when Edith told him she had placed his name on the list of people to go to the United Sates.

"Edith, I don't want to go to America. I want to go to Palestine, as soon as possible."

"You want to go to Palestine?" Edith was also shocked.

"Yes, what made you think I didn't?"

"I don't know what to say," said Edith. "I thought we would get married, and go America together to start a new life."

"What would I do in America? I don't speak English. I don't even speak Italian. Edith, I love you, but I can't go. I want you to go with me to Palestine."

"Slavko, let's wait until we hear if we are accepted, and then we can talk about it again. Please think about it."

Edith had a sleepless night. She worried about her father's mental health if they were not accepted, and she did not know how she could separate from Slavko if he wouldn't go with them.

The next day when Edith went to work, the sergeant in charge of her office was waiting for her.

"Edith, I can make sure you get on the boat to America," he said. "I hate to see you go, but I am very happy for you and your family."

RASTENBERG, GERMANY: THURSDAY, JULY 20, 1944

A bomb exploded at Adolf Hitler's headquarters. It was the third attempt on Adolf Hitler's life. He sustained minor burns and a concussion. One of his senior officers, Col. Claus Schenk von Stauffenberg, was accused of planting the bomb, was arrested, and was hanged, along with others who were suspected of participating in the plot.

Tensions in Germany were growing. Hitler trusted no one. The Nazis were now in a two-front war, with the Russians in the East, and with the Allies in the West. The British Air Force, with fifteen hundred heavy bombers and some four thousand fighter planes, was strategically attacking oil fields and airports in Germany and Austria and the Soviet Army was about to control southern Poland.

NAPLES: JULY 22, 1944

Ruth Gruber, an assistant to the American secretary of the interior, arrived in Bari to supervise the transport of refugees to Oswego, New York. She did not approve of the U.S. Army trucks that were waiting to take the refugees to Naples, where they would board their ship. Instead, she arranged for three trucks owned by the Jewish Brigade, a part of the British Army stationed in Palestine. Each truck displayed a large Mogen Dovid (Star of David) emblem on the side.

Riding in a truck operated by Jewish soldiers was a unique experience for the Jews of Bari. The soldiers spoke Hebrew to each other and addressed the refugees in Yiddish or, depending on where they came from, in Polish or German. It took two days over mountainous terrain to get to Naples.

Slavko refused to go. When they got to Naples, my cousin and her parents were among nine hundred eighty two displaced persons who boarded the American troopship *SS Henry Gibbins*. Not everyone was Jewish. In the group were seventy three Roman Catholics, seven Protestants, and twenty eight Greek Orthodox refugees, all invited guests of President Roosevelt.

The ship also carried a thousand wounded American soldiers, and was part of a convoy crossing the Atlantic Ocean. The ship was full, with people sleeping in three-tiered bunks about two feet apart. The American GIs were segregated from the refugees.

NEW YORK: AUGUST 3, 1944

Ten days on the Atlantic was difficult for the refugees, few of whom had been at sea before. Uncomfortable sleeping quarters, strange food, and an unpredictable future created stress among them. Many were seasick. A German air raid and submarine sightings made things worse.

Their were spirits lifted when on August 3, the *SS Henry Gibbins* pulled into New York Harbor, with the Statue of Liberty in full view. The wounded soldiers who could, went on deck with the refugees. It was a spectacular entry to the United States of America. In unison, the refugees and soldiers cheered at the sight.

The soldiers were met by ambulances, army doctors and nurses, and hundreds of relatives.

The refugees were taken immediately by train from New York City to Oswego, where they were met by military police and driven by truck to Fort Ontario, an abandoned army camp. The camp was gated and surrounded by a chain link fence with barbed wire on top. Many of the refugees gasped. It looked like a concentration camp.

Inside the barracks small rooms had each been furnished with army cots, a table, and two chairs. A communal bathroom was at one end of the building. It was bare, but safe, and thousands of miles from Nazism.

Nine hundred eighty two people from many parts of Europe were now free in their own community, behind a barbed wire fence in a former U.S. Army camp.

AUSCHWITZ: OCTOBER 23, 1944

When they were taken to Auschwitz, Heli and Jiři were separated. Heli had been in the concentration camp for a year, and it had been a struggle to survive. Along with the other women, she often was beaten with horse whips. Jiři was shot a month after they got there, but Heli was not aware her husband was dead. There were rumors circulating that the Russian Army was advancing in Poland.

American planes flew over Auschwitz, day and night. The Nazis tried to protect the concentration camp from being bombed by giving everyone civilian clothes so they wouldn't look like prisoners. They did not want to lose their crematoriums.

Some of the prisoners were moved to other locations, Heli among them. She was put on a boxcar with sixty other women. There was not room for everyone to sit. There was a bucket of water for drinking, and another to urinate in. It was dark inside the car. Three days later, the train stopped at a German arms factory in a small town near the Russian border. The women got off the train. All were hungry, and many were sick. Heli had a fever.

They were stripped of their clothes and made to stand naked while barbers shaved their heads. Heli took the only two things she had left, a small watch and her wedding ring, and pushed them into her rectum. After they were shaved, the women were forced to take outdoor cold-water showers. It was the end of October, and the temperature was in the forties. Heli fell unconscious as she left the shower. The other women dressed her in one of the striped uniforms they had been issued and got her on her feet, and into the barrack they'd been assigned to. They put her to bed.

The next morning, the women were sent to the factory, where they joined two hundred Czech, Polish, and Hungarian women who were manufacturing bullets. They worked twelve-hour days. Every morning they were asked if anyone was sick or pregnant. If the answer was yes, the woman was shot.

NAZI ARMS FACTORY, POLAND: NOVEMBER 1944

The Russian Army was advancing. The Germans decided to move everyone from the factory so the prisoners could not reveal that it manufactured munitions. Two days later Heli and more than six hundred other women were sent by train back to Theresienstadt.

Heli was met by old friends who took her in. She was thin as a skeleton and very weak. Her friends gave her warm clothes, fed her hot soup, and kept her hidden until she regained her health. In the meantime, the Germans learned the International Red Cross was coming to Theresienstadt and the Nazi soldiers fled. The Russian Army came the next day and liberated Theresienstadt.

The Russians lifted all restrictions, freeing the Jews to go where they could. Heli returned to Russian occupied Prague with only the clothes on her back, her watch, and her wedding ring. She went to the home of an elderly aunt who had kept some of Heli's family's belongings. Her aunt invited her to stay for a few days. Heli then sent a telegram to her brother in Palestine. That's when Bibi learned of his father's suicide.

Heli began searching for Jiři. When they married in Theresienstadt, they agreed if they were ever separated, they would meet again in Prague after the war. Heli made contact with everyone they knew, hoping someone had heard from her husband. One of them was Otakar, an old friend. Otakar had no word from Jiři, but he invited Heli to his house for dinner.

CROATIA: JANUARY 4, 1945

Tante Anna had been with the partisans and their ten children for sixteen months. The children were now better educated than their parents, and people in surrounding villages often left their children with her for lessons.

Occasionally, Victor, who was back in Zagreb with Ivka, paid a visit. The partisans had intensified their fighting with the Germans, but had suffered heavy casualties.

Victor arrived one day and told Tante Anna she was needed at a partisan first aid station.

"There is only one doctor, and she is overworked and needs help," he said.

Tante Anna took a few things and went with Victor to the doctor's office, which had been converted to a first aid station. He introduced her to Dr. Ursula Ratoff. The doctor told her she could live with her and several other women who were caring for babies of partisans who had been killed. One baby was sick and near death and needed constant attention. His name was Mariantschek.

My aunt began helping with the children and soon was helping Dr. Ratoff patch up wounds in the first aid station. With her care, Mariantschek recovered, but another baby contracted typhus and died. Tante Anna washed the dead child and buried it.

Two months later, fighting in the area increased and Tante Anna and the other women took six children and fled. Tante Anna carried a baby in her backpack and another in her arms. The women walked to a nearby village with a small medical clinic and left the babies with a nurse. Tante Anna decided it was time to go back to Zagreb.

She was walking through the village, looking for a place to sleep for the night, when a woman ran up to her and took hold of her hands.

"The war is coming to an end," she said. "It will finally be over. Budapest and Vienna have been occupied by the Russians. It just came over the radio."

Soon everyone in the village was on the street, some of them firing guns into the air in celebration. Tante Anna could not grasp the news. She could not imagine the war was over. She asked the woman if she knew a place she could stay for the night, and the woman invited her in.

"I have an extra room," she said. "Please stay with me. My name is Petra."

The excitement in the village soon ended. The war was not yet over, and Tante Anna decided to delay her trip back to Zagreb.

WARM SPRINGS, GEORGIA: APRIL 12, 1945

President Franklin D. Roosevelt died. Vice President Harry S. Truman was sworn in as president of the United States.

The statue of Moses erected by the Zagreb Jewish Community. The inscription reads "In memory of the Jewish people who were killed by Fascists." Photo taken in 2007 by Ann Bromberg.

DACHAU: APRIL 29, 1945

The United States Army liberated Dachau.

HAGANJ, YUGOSLAVIA, APRIL 29, 1945

The war news got better every day, and Tante Anna decided it was finally safe to go home. She had been in the village Haganj four months. By now, the partisans were going home, the fighting in Yugoslavia was over, and the Ustaša was on the run. It would be just a matter of time before they would be rounded up and put in prisons. Shortwave radio said it would be just days until Germany officially surrendered.

My aunt found a truck driver who agreed to give her a ride to Zagreb. On the way to the city, they drove by large groups of German soldiers being marched to prisoner of war camps, each with just one young partisan guarding them. The road was blocked in many areas where soldiers had fallen to the ground in despair. The prisoners looked defeated, weak and tired, and put up no resistance. Many had no shoes. They had traded them for bread.

These Germans had wreaked havoc on Yugoslavia, occupying every city and town, but the tables had turned.

When Tante Anna got home, she was met by Ivka and Viktor. It was an emotional reunion.

"Anna, my dear friend, at long last you are back with us. It has been two years." said Ivka. "We must celebrate."

"First, I need to find my children," said Tante Anna. "I think Lilly and Herta are still in England. I wrote to them several times to let them know I was with the partisans, but I don't know if they ever got my letters."

"We should contact the Red Cross," said Ivka. "Maybe they can help."

Two weeks later, Tante Anna got a telegram from Lilly. Lilly was safe and healthy, but her oldest daughter, Herta, had died of a blood disease. She was thirty-three.

BERLIN: APRIL 30, 1945

Adolf Hitler committed suicide with his own gun.

EUROPEAN ALLIED COMMAND, MAY 8, 1945

General Jodl, the German chief of staff, signed Germany's unconditional surrender to the Western Allies at 12:41 a.m. The war in Europe was over. This date would be remembered as V-E Day (Victory in Europe Day).

JAPAN: AUGUST 6, 1945

The United States Army Air Force dropped an atomic bomb on the city of Hiroshima. Three days later, an atomic bomb was dropped on the city of Nagasaki.

OSWEGO: OCTOBER 6, 1945

In the fourteen months she was interned at Fort Ontario, my cousin Edith wrote daily about her reflections on her life, and what she wished for. Her mother suggested she write a short story. She did, and this touching story was published in *Child Life Magazine* in 1944. It read as follows:

> Fourteen months have elapsed since we arrived here. Fourteen
> months in Oswego, New York, at Fort Ontario, which was once an

Cousin Edith in high school graduating gown.

Cousin Edith in Yugoslav countryside.

Cousin Edith, fourth from left, front row: Class of 1945, Oswego.

Army camp. Our small group of nine hundred eighty two persons, coming from many different parts of the world, has formed a community here. A community, which, as everywhere, has its joys and sorrows.

Walking through the camp you can hear many different languages, and our children speak Italian, German and English, all mixed up, which results in a strange kind of Esperanto. You can see the white barracks, the broad, green parade grounds where sports like baseball, volleyball, and football are played, the administration buildings, hospital, movie theatre, canteen, and recreation halls.

If you should come in about 8:00 a.m. you would meet our youngsters hurrying to Oswego's schools. As I am one of them, I know how they felt when they entered American schools for the first time. Most of us hadn't been to school for the last six years, and our European schools were very different from the American ones. We were not used to choosing our own subject, changing teachers and classrooms every period.

We stared at the jolly American girls in sloppy sweaters and socks to match, the boys wearing their shirts outside and trousers rolled up. Could we learn to become like them—happy and young and gay? If six years could be erased from my memories, the transformation would be easier. Before that I was a child who liked to play. I spent many a happy day skiing, skating, going to parties. But unfortunately those years between cannot simply be crossed out. For us, the refugee youth, the happy days of our childhood have vanished. We hardly even remember them, because of all the horrors that followed. That is just another result of the crimes committed by the Nazis. For isn't it a crime, nearly as bad as killing a human being, to kill his happy memories of the past? I think it is.

When I am praying for a better future, I am praying too that if I should ever have a child, my child will be like these carefree Americans whose minds are not harassed by six years of fear and oppression. But my days in Oswego High School were the happiest ones since I left Vienna, my hometown. And when I walked last June through the school's auditorium in white cap and gown, holding my diploma tightly, I felt proud, happy and thankful for having been given the chance to attend an American school, learn something about American life and traditions, and be graduated with one hundred sixty American boys and girls from my class. Maybe we should now return again to the Fort, where about 12:00 a.m. everybody is walking to the mess halls. The mail has already arrived and news, local as well as news abroad, is being excitedly discussed. Some have letters from relatives or friends in Europe, whom they thought dead, and you can imagine their happiness; others again have bad news that one more family member is missing.

Whatever the news, you will always find one or more groups discussing the burning question: 'When shall we leave the Shelter?' Someone has heard from a very sure source that it will only be thirty days longer; others again know positively that we shall still be here next summer. I may tell you confidentially that no one yet knows when we can go. It is quite possible, at least I hope so, that by the time you read this article the 'Fort Ontario Refugee Shelter' will be history. For that will mean that we are back in real life again, after an interlude for which we are grateful, but which, of course, cannot go on indefinitely.

There are days when I feel quite happy sitting in my barrack room, reading, doing homework, or writing letters, but there are also those when I begin to wonder if I shall ever have a real home again with everything that belongs to it. A home like those of my American schoolmates and the one I once knew—with a radio, a piano, a friendly white kitchen, and small things, tiny figures or books, lying on tables. But maybe, by the time you read this . . . who knows?

Here in the camp—while we wait—we go for walks in the evenings, or to movies or for a bit of square dancing. Yes, you might find it strange that in a camp of Europeans, square dancing has become popular with both young and old. You would laugh seeing our fathers and mothers dancing a Virginia reel. But they want to learn it; they want to do something which brings them nearer to the country they are living in. They have also courses in sewing, beauty culture, arts and crafts, carpentry, and other useful things, but the one which helps them most is the course in English.

So, one day passes much like another, and with every day we hope to be nearer to America; to this land of liberty and justice. Fourteen months ago we were Europeans. Today our only wish is to be one of you, to be an average American boy or girl, happy, young, and proud of this country.

Chapter 21

HAVANA: MARCH, 20, 1946

The phone rang in our apartment. My mother, now forty one, answered in Spanish.

"Hola."

"This is Charles Anderson from the American Consulate," he said in Spanish. "I wish to speak with Señora Weiss."

"I am Señora Weiss. Señor Anderson? How are you? Why do you call? Do you have visas for us?"

"Señora Weiss, are you still in the same apartment?"

"Yes, we are"

"Your visa applications have been approved," he said. "You may travel to the United States to become permanent residents."

"Please Señor Anderson, could you repeat what you just said?" my mother asked.

"Señora Weiss, your visas are approved. You must come to the consulate as soon as possible with your husband and sons so we can stamp them into your passports."

"Sí sí, naturalmente (Yes yes, of course)," said my mother. Many thoughts raced through her mind. She had to get in touch with my father and tell him.

Eight months before, my parents had made a deal with Charles Anderson. Big apartments in good locations were scarce in Havana. They promised the vice consul our apartment in exchange for the visas.

"Señor Anderson, when do you want us to come?"

"Can you come tomorrow at 10 a.m.?"

"Yes, we will be there. Thank you very much Señor."

My mother was in a hurry to tell my father the good news. She could not wait until suppertime. He worked in Old Havana, and it would take close to an hour to get there. Peter would be out of school at noon and Bertha, our maid, had the day off. I would be in school until four. My mother called Anka Singer and asked her if she would take Peter home with her when she picked up Djuro.

"Anka, listen, I am so excited. I just spoke with the American Consulate, and they have our visas. We can go to America." My mother began to cry.

"Hedy, it is all coming together. I'm so happy for you."

"Anka, I am going to see Robert at the factory. I'll take the bus. I cannot wait for him to come home from work. I need to tell him now."

My mother left the apartment and went to the Avenida de los Presidentes to catch the bus. The bus route took her down the Malecón, a beautiful wide boulevard, about three miles long, that runs along the coastline to the old city. She admired the old buildings and statues that were Havana's landmarks. She smiled as she passed the famous Hotel Nacional where she and my father often went for dinner and dancing. She would miss this beautiful place.

When the bus stopped in the old city, my mother walked to the industrial section. She had been to the diamond factory before. An armed guard was at the door. He recognized her and gave her permission to go inside and speak to the receptionist.

"Buenos días, Señorita," said my mother, "I must see my husband, Roberto Weiss. It is very important."

"Can you tell me what this is about please?" asked the receptionist.

"It is very personal and very important," said my mother. "I came all the way from Vedado to speak with him. Please, will you get him?"

The receptionist left the office and came back a minute later, accompanied by a man my mother knew from social events. It was Anton Van Liempt, a Belgian Jew, who had been a diamond merchant in Antwerp. He was the superintendent of the plant.

"Hedy, what are you doing here?" he asked in German.

"Anton, it's good to see you," said my mother. "Anton, I must see Robert right away. Is it possible?"

"Is everything all right?"

"Yes, everything is very good. I must talk to Robert."

"Of course," said Anton, curious about my mother's visit. "I'll go get him."

A few minutes passed before my father appeared. He was alarmed at the surprise visit of my mother.

"Is something wrong? Are the children okay?"

My mother didn't know if she was going to laugh or cry.

"Mutsch, we are all fine." She began to cry. "Wir fahren nach Amerika (We are going to America)."

"Hedy, say that again."

"We are going to America. We got our visas. We are really going to America." She put her arms around my father, and he held her close. "I couldn't wait to tell you."

"How did you find out? When can we go?" asked my father.

My mother stopped crying and began to smile.

"Mr. Anderson called an hour ago. He said our visas were approved, and tomorrow at 10:00 a.m. we can go to the consulate to pick them up. It will take us a few weeks to prepare but we can probably leave next month."

"It's been so long," said my father. "I can hardly believe it. But, Hedy, I have to get back to work. My machines are running, and Anton is watching them. We'll tell the boys tonight."

"Mutsch, I also have to leave now. Peter is with Anka."

"What about the American? Does he still want our apartment?"

"Yes, he said so on the telephone."

"He can have it, and everything that's in it," said my father.

My mother left the factory and went to the Singers' home. It was not yet 2:00 p.m. Peter and Djuro were outside kicking a soccer ball. Anka had coffee on the stove and cigarettes on the kitchen table. They sat for more than an hour, smoking and drinking their coffee, while they reminisced about their lives during the last eight years.

HAVANA: APRIL 25, 1946

My mother helped Bertha clean our apartment for the last time. We packed only our personal things and our clothes, and left all the furnishings for Charles Anderson, who planned to move in the next day. Bertha stayed to say good-bye.

A friend drove us to the airport in his four-door Dodge convertible, a car in which I was a hero a year before. We were on the way to a beach for a picnic, and his small dog was sitting on my lap. The top of the car was open. Suddenly, the dog jumped out of the car. I had his leash in my hand and yanked him back in. I saved his life.

At the airport, we went through the customs inspection without incident. Then we boarded a Pan American DC-3 for to Miami. The plane had twenty one passengers and was full. We had never been in an airplane before. All of our travels had been by train, except for the ship we took to Cuba five

SS Colonial.

Banquet in Havana in honor of conductor Erich Kleiber. My mother at far right.

My father running diamond-cutting machines in Havana.

Peter at La Concha beach, Havana.

Peter, my mother, father and me, La Concha Beach, Havana.

years before. I sat next to my mother by the window. The windows on the DC-3s were small and round, like portholes. I sat amazed as we taxied down the runway and roared into the sky. I couldn't understand how such a large machine could get off the ground, never mind fly. The view of Havana was spectacular.

During the one-hour flight, all I saw was water. As the plane approached the Miami airport, we all peered out the small windows to get our first look at America. It landed at 10:10 a.m. We lugged our baggage through immigration and customs. The U.S. officials were courteous and waved us on, without so much as a question. After everything we'd been through, it seemed anticlimactic.

From the airport, we took a taxi to the Miami railroad station where my father purchased one-way tickets to New York City. Many people at the station spoke Spanish, and we had no trouble finding our train. By now, I spoke enough English to help. I had learned it in school, and had spent many hours reading American comic books, and listening to radio broadcasts from the United States.

We were experienced train travelers. I couldn't even guess how many train trips we'd taken since 1938. We checked most of our bags and boarded a train next to a departure sign that read 'Atlanta—Washington—Philadelphia—New York'. Uncle Otto had written that he would meet us. He and Tante Frieda and Edith had been released from Fort Ontario and were living in New York City. They had made arrangements for us to move into the Hotel Churchill off Broadway near West 72nd Street.

Our train did not have compartments like the trains throughout Europe. We sat across the aisle from each other in wide double seats, all facing front, my mother and Peter on one side, and my father and me on the other.

The train left on time, at 12:30 p.m. I remember looking around at other passengers who were reading newspapers and wondered how the St. Louis Cardinals were doing. I had always listened to their games on Havana radio. Many of the Cardinals played winter baseball in Cuba. Dick Sisler of the Cardinals was my hero. He hit more home runs in Cuba than any other player.

Thirty minutes after the train left the station, a very large man came through the connecting door in the front of the car. He was dressed in a two-piece blue uniform with shiny gold buttons and a gold badge, and a tall cap with a black brim and gold braid. I didn't know what to expect.

"Tickets please, get your tickets ready," he called out. He had an accent I later learned was Southern.

He went down the aisle chatting with everyone as he took their tickets. Then he got to us.

"May I have your tickets please?"

My mother was ready for the conductor. She first handed him our tickets, and then gave him our passports.

The big man smiled broadly. He looked at the passports, then at my mother.

"Hedviga Weiss. I like the name Hedviga."

"My friends call me Hedy."

He handed the passports back to her.

"Welcome to America Hedy. You don't need passports here."

Epilogue

This book has told the story of twenty-eight members of my family from Vienna and Prague, who were persecuted by the Nazis.

Ten did not survive the Holocaust. Nine were murdered by Nazis and the Ustaša. They were: my grandparents Emma and Jakob, and Marcus and Hermina; my father's sister Grete, her husband Heinrich, and daughter Gerti; Tante Anna's husband Pepi; and Heli's husband Jiři.

Heli's father, my great-uncle Josef, committed suicide.

The other fourteen members of my family died of natural causes. They are as follows: Hansi, who married in Switzerland and had one daughter; Edith, who married in the United States and had two children; Uncle Otto and Frieda who lived in New York City; my parents, Robert and Hedy, who lived into their eighties in Marblehead, Massachusetts.

Also, Uncle Gustl who married in London and had three children; Fritz, who never married but settled in Luton, England; Gisela and Heinrich who moved in 1948 from Shanghai to Israel; Heli's brother Bibi, who married in Israel and had two children; Tante Anna, who eventually moved into a retirement home in Zagreb and lived into her eighties, and her daughter Lilly, who married in London and had one daughter. Lilly's older sister, Herta, died before the war ended.

My father-in-law, Farish Donald Hemeon, who served with the Canadian Army, lived into his eighties in Massachusetts.

Four of them are alive as of this writing. Heli lives in Prague. She remarried after the war and adopted her husband's two sons. Lisl (Alisa) lives in Israel. She and Bruno (Ari) had two children. My brother Peter is married and lives in Boston. He and his wife had three children. I was married during the Korean War while I was stationed in France. I have two children by that marriage. I live now with my second wife, Leslie, in Cumberland Foreside, Maine, and have two stepchildren.